URBAN STRESS

Experiments on Noise and Social Stressors

SOCIAL PSYCHOLOGY

A series of monographs, treatises, and texts

EDITORS

LEON FESTINGER AND STANLEY SCHACHTER

Jack W. Brehm, A Theory of Psychological Reactance. 1966

Ralph L. Rosnow and Edward J. Robinson (Eds.), Experiments in Persuasion. 1967

Jonathan L. Freedman and Anthony N. Doob,
Deviancy: The Psychology of Being Different. 1968

Paul G. Swingle (Ed.), Experiments in Social Psychology. 1968, 1969

E. Earl Baughman and W. Grant Dahlstrom, Negro and White Children:
A Psychological Study in the Rural South. 1968

Anthony G. Greenwald, Timothy C. Brock, and Thomas M. Ostrom (Eds.),
Psychological Foundations of Attitudes. 1968

Robert Rosenthal and Ralph Rosnow (Eds.), Artifact in Behavioral Research. 1969

R. A. Hoppe, E. C. Simmel, and G. A. Milton (Eds.), Early Experiences
and the Processes of Socialization. 1970

Richard Christie and Florence Geis, Studies in Machiavellianism. 1970

Paul G. Swingle (Ed.), The Structure of Conflict. 1970

Alvin Zander, Motives and Goals in Groups. 1971

Stanley Schachter, Emotion, Obesity, and Crime. 1971

Charles A. Kiesler, The Psychology of Commitment:
Experiments Linking Behavior to Belief. 1971

Jacobo A. Varela, Psychological Solutions to Social Problems:
An Introduction to Social Technology. 1971

David C. Glass and Jerome E. Singer, Urban Stress:
Experiments on Noise and Social Stressors. 1972

In Preparation

Ivan D. Steiner, Group Processes and Productivity

Shelley Duval and Robert A. Wicklund, A Theory of Objective Self Awareness

URBAN STRESS

Experiments on Noise and Social Stressors

DAVID C. GLASS / JEROME E. SINGER

New York University
and
Russell Sage Foundation
New York, New York

State University of
New York at Stony Brook
Stony Brook, New York

ACADEMIC PRESS New York and London 1972

ACADEMIC PRESS, INC.
111 Fifth Avenue, New York, New York 10003

United Kingdom Edition published by
ACADEMIC PRESS, INC. (LONDON) LTD.
24/28 Oval Road, London NW1 7DD

LIBRARY OF CONGRESS CATALOG CARD NUMBER: 78-182640

PRINTED IN THE UNITED STATES OF AMERICA

To Polly, Linda, Palmer, Judith, and Kate

Contents

Preface   xi

1   **Introduction and Overview**

Plan of the Book   3

2   **Environmental Stress and the Adaptive Process**

Psychological Stress   5
Adaptation   7
Costs of Stress and Adaptation   9

Beneficial Aspects of Stress   12
Noise as a Stressor   14

3   Effects of Noise on Physiology and Task Performance

Physiological Response to Noise   25
Effects of Noise on Task Performance   36
Summary   44

4   Behavioral Aftereffects of Unpredictable Noise

Aftereffects of Periodic and Aperiodic Noise   47
Aftereffects of Signaled and Unsignaled Noise   55
Conclusions   58

5   Perceived Control and Behavioral Aftereffects
    of Unpredictable Noise

Effects of Perceived Control   61
Perceived Control: Variations on a Theme   69
Perceived Control: Avoidable and Unavoidable Noise   78
Proposed Explanation for the Effects of Perceived Control   86

6   Other Cognitive Factors and Behavioral Aftereffects
    of Unpredictable Noise

Relative Deprivation   92
Expectation   98
Necessity and Choice   102
Conclusions   107

7   Behavioral Aftereffects of Unpredictable and Uncontrollable
    Electric Shock

Experimental Procedure   110
Results   113
Discussion and Conclusions   118

8   Behavioral Aftereffects of Social Stressors

Bureaucracy   122
Discrimination   130
Discussion and Conclusions   136

9 Psychic Costs of Stress: Exposure or Adaptation

Differential Adaptation I   141
Differential Adaptation II   147

10 Summary and Implications

Social Implications of the Noise Research   162

References   167

Author Index   175
Subject Index   179

Preface

This book is a collaborative effort of two experimental social psychologists. Our concerns and methods reflect those of the field in general. In recent years, we have shared in the discipline's concern with effects of cognitive processes on social phenomena as well as individual behavior and physiology. Scholars have long been able to document these cognitive influences, but no really adequate conceptual mechanisms have been offered. Our work is no exception. We have demonstrated regularities in the influence of cognitive variables on stressors and their physiological and behavioral consequences. We are still trying to understand how these occur. We can rule out some explanations, but we cannot specify a coherent and comprehensive theory relating cognition to physiology and behavior. This is hardly a confession of weakness or incompleteness. We are, after all, working on one of the fundamental problems in psychology. We have now arrived at a logical place to take stock, summarize, and consolidate our work. This book is less than a final accounting, but more than a progress report.

The plan of the book is outlined in the first chapter. It is clear that most of our two dozen or so studies center around noise; yet we have never considered this a "noise" book. The use of noise stimuli in our research was simply a convenient device for studying antecedents and consequences of analogues of urban stressors. The analytically inclined may be disappointed to learn that the genesis of our research was not sleepness nights, jet overflights, or active two-year olds. Our general strategy arose from a more mundane interest in social psychophysiology, and empathy with contemporary research atmospheres relating cognitions to behavior. Admittedly, the dearth of a city relevant social psychology provided the catalyst for this mixture of interests, so that in addition to noise, we are concerned with other physical stressors and with social stressors such as bureaucratic harassment and arbitrary discrimination. We are confident that the model and procedures used in our research apply equally well to all of these domains of study.

Three concepts are central to this monograph: direct effects of stress, adaptation to stress, and adverse aftereffects of stress. Direct effects refer to the influence of an imposed stressor on task performance and autonomic reactivity. Adaptation refers to a series of measures, both autonomic and behavioral, intended to assess the degree to which the stress habituated and its direct effects were minimized. Aftereffects are almost self-explanatory: they refer to the subsequent consequences of stress exposure. Delineation of the complexities of relationship between these three factors occupies a major portion of the book. We attempt to show that while people adapt to stress, adverse aftereffects remain which are detectable in behavior.

It is unlikely that anyone will subject this volume to computer analysis to determine which author wrote what part—it is hardly the Federalist papers. For those interested in such tabulation, the description of each experiment contains its performance site; the ideas and procedures were freely exchanged over a four year period to the point where even the authors cannot make unequivocal attributions of paternity.

The studies reported in this book were conducted at the Rockefeller University, the Research Center for Human Relations of New York University, and the State University of New York at Stony Brook under grants from the National Science Foundation (GS-2405 and GS-2412) and Russell Sage Foundation. Our gratitude goes to both organizations for their generous support. We would particularly like to thank Orville G. Brim, Jr., President of Russell Sage, for his continued encouragement and support of our work. We also extend our warmest thanks to Leon Festinger who read earlier versions of the manuscript and made important criticisms and suggestions which enabled us to improve it substantially. We owe him a great debt of gratitude.

Our thanks also go to several of our graduate students who made substantial contributions to the design and actual conduct of the various studies. Bruce Reim, Lucy N. Friedman, Halleck Cummings, T. Edward Hannah, Patricia Mayhew, Joan Gruzen, Nataša Bauerova, Janet Shaban, Larry Shapiro, Ilene Staff, and Gail Welling will all find their ideas in the following pages. Sheldon Cohen and Karen Fagen have also shared with us their insights about people's reactions to aversive events. Bruce Reim and Halleck Cummings deserve special acknowledgment for their excellent work in carrying out many of the experiments described in this book. Reuben Silver and Felix Scherer provided outstanding technical assistance required in many of the experiments. We thank them both for their careful attention to detail. Finally, our appreciation goes to Joan Sahaida and Mary Hanthorn who typed innumerable drafts of the manuscript, and managed to meet often impossible deadlines. We thank them both for their forbearance, loyalty, and competence.

Introduction and Overview

This book is entitled *Urban Stress,* yet it is primarily about noise and behavior. Although noise is certainly a commonly noted characteristic of the city, it is hardly the most salient or even the most important one. And, as a social problem, despite the existence of task forces and public commissions to combat it, it hardly ranks with litter, drugs, schools, welfare, and crime in its need for immediate attention. We are neither so naive nor so myopic as to believe that noise is either the most important or the most pressing urban problem. Rather, we have been struck by the discrepancy between repeatedly stated condemnations of the quality of life in the city and the fact that many people not only survive in these circumstances, but actually thrive in and enjoy them. We speculated on the reasons for this disparate state of affairs, for we could see both factors at work in ourselves. Many things bothered us; few seriously disrupted our work. This intellectual paradox piqued our curiosity and we were soon able to suggest several possible theories and hypotheses about the nature and effects of urban stress.

The content of our conjectures was not tied to any one stress. We were concerned, rather, with general reactions and general effects. And, being trained as experimental social psychologists, we turned to the laboratory out of both inclination and habit. Our aims were to set up conditions analogous to those in the larger world, and, in our controlled experimental environment, to tease out and to manipulate independently those factors we regarded as most important. Now, since any research program must start somewhere, we selected noise as our first stressor. The choice was made for pragmatic reasons, since our original notions did not clearly differentiate between stressors. Noise provided as good a test as crowding, garbage, or interpersonal abrasiveness, and it had the advantage of technical specificity and easy production in the laboratory. As social psychologists, however, we have a particular perspective on the study of noise. Unlike sociologists and epidemiologists, we are not concerned with the incidence of hearing disorders in different segments of the population. Unlike human engineers and experimental psychologists, our major concern is not with task performance during acoustic stimulation. And, unlike otolaryngologists and other physicians, we have little interest in the physiological mechanisms of hearing loss. Instead, we are principally concerned with behavioral and psycho-physiological consequences of noise, as mediated by the setting in which this stress occurs.

Having initiated studies with noise, we found ourselves faced with a strategic choice at the conclusion of the first experiment. We could attempt to generalize our findings by repeating the initial study with other stressors, or we could extend our noise experimentation in an effort to answer those questions raised by the first study. In practice, we did both. We explored the ways in which predictability, perceived control, and other cognitive factors affected the aversive qualities of noise, and we engaged in parallel studies of the relationship of these cognitive factors to the stresses produced by electric shock, bureaucratic routine, and discrimination. We were particularly interested in behavioral aftereffects of these aversive events. The possibility that exposure to noise, for example, might produce subsequent impairment of performance has received virtually no attention in the technical literature. Our principal studies, by contrast, were specifically designed to examine the consequences of adaptation to unpredictable and uncontrollable high-intensity noise. Tolerance for frustra-tion, quality of task performance, and ability to resolve cognitive conflict were all impaired following exposure to unpredictable noise. Even though physiological adaptation occurred to an equivalent degree under predictable and unpredictable noise, the magnitude of the aftereffects was greater following the latter type of stimulation. Subsequent experimentation suggested that unpredictable noise has these effects because the individual believes he cannot determine the onset and/or offset of the stressor. The perception of potential control and the nonveridical perception of actual control over unpredicatble noise were manipulated in our research, with the result that frustration tolerance and postnoise task performance were appreciably improved. We concluded on the basis of these findings that cognitive factors, not simply physical parameters of noise, are the principal determinants of adverse aftereffects of noise exposure. Further evidence was adduced suggesting possible mechanisms underlying the ameliorative effects of perceived control, but the major thrust of our results is that while man adapts to unpredictable noise, behavioral residues occur inimical to his subsequent functioning. The findings of our research with non-noise stressors parallel those obtained with noise. There is a psychic cost for exposure to unpredictable and uncontrollable aversive stimuli, in spite of the fact that individuals seem able to adapt to a variety of such stressors.

The organization of the book follows neither the order of our experimentation nor the order of the development of our thought. It follows what seems to us the most sensible exposition. The book is tightly written, and the mystery story enthusiast who turns to the last chapter in hopes of verifying that the social psychological butler did it will be disappointed and deservedly so. We are, by intention, writing a research monograph and not a popularized narrative. We do, however, wish to reassure the serious reader, whether specialist or not, that technical detail and specifics are essential to our argument, though they are not an end in themselves. We see the forest as well as the trees, or more appropriately, we hear the orchestra as well as the instruments. We will often refer to the cycle of stress, adaptation, and aversive aftereffects by the term *psychic cost*. And it is precisely because we want this term to be more than a glib metaphor that we are being meticulous in our documentation. This reassurance is not provided as a warning but as a courtesy. It would ill behoove us to stress the reader with an unpredictable and uncontrollable aversive narrative.

Plan of the Book

We have arranged the experiments into chapters that permit an organized development of successive tests of our major propositions. The next chapter outlines the basic problem and discusses it in the context of one stressor—noise. Chapter 3 presents evidence of physiological adaptation to noise and data on the effects of noise on mental and motor performance. These findings, drawn from most of the studies reported in this volume, tend to confirm previous research in the area. Noise, *per se,* does not impair simple task performance probably because of the adaptation of stress responses. However, the introduction of cognitive factors, for example, aperiodicity or uncontrollability of the noise schedule, results in appreciable failures on complex tasks. Chapters 4 and 5 examine behavioral aftereffects of exposure to noise as a function of these same cognitive factors. These two chapters represent the main focus of the book. Chapter 6 examines the impact of several other cognitive factors on noise aftereffects, and Chapter 7 generalizes these phenomena to another physical stressor, namely, electric shock. Chapter 8 reports a pair of studies demonstrating the influence of social stressors (i.e., bureaucratic routine and discrimination) on some of the same dependent measures used in the noise research. Chapter 9 addresses itself to the main theoretical question of the book: whether behavioral aftereffects of exposure to stressors are the result of the effort entailed in the adaptive process, or if they occur in spite of the fact that the individual adapts to stressful stimuli. A final chapter summarizes the results of all of our research, explicates some theoretical implications, and then extends the results to current social problems.

Environmental Stress and
the Adaptive Process

Psychological Stress

Life in the city is an endless round of obstacles, conflicts, inconveniences, and bureaucratic routine. The urban dweller is confronted daily with noise, litter, air pollution, and overcrowding. Some of these conditions are pervasive. Others occur only at home, or at work, or in transit. Their incidence is profoundly disturbing, and many commentators on modern urban life allege that such conditions produce behavioral and physiological consequences inimical to the health and well-being of man. The study of these consequences may be subsumed under the category of *stress*, which has been generally defined as the affective, behavioral, and physiological response to aversive stimuli (Appley & Trumbull, 1967). A great variety of environmental events are capable of producing a stress response, but it is also recognized that the induction of stress depends on the mediation of cognitive factors. As we go up the phylogentic scale, stress reactions become less dependent on the direct impact of stimuli and more contingent on associated cues that signify the implications and consequences of these stimuli. For this reason, many investigators of human behavior prefer to speak of *psychological* stress, that is, the threat or anticipation of future harm (e.g., Lazarus, 1966). We have adopted this convention throughout the book.

Very little is actually known about the detailed effects of cognitive factors on the production of stress response, and we have equally imprecise notions about how man adapts to different stressors in different cognitive and social contexts. Yet, observation of urban life cannot but lead to the conclusion that despite the unpleasantness of stressful conditions, life goes on. Families are raised, jobs are accomplished, and even social graces and amenities are preserved in some quarters. Either the stressors are not as potent as popularly believed or else man has the capacity to adapt to or even shrug off the stress. Therein lie the makings of a seeming paradox: increasing amounts of stress with no signs of increasing consequences. The resolution of this contradiction rests with detailed studies of amplifying and attenuating effects of social and cognitive factors upon the stressors' impact.

A number of theorists have emphasized the importance of contextual variables in stress arousal and reduction (e.g., Janis, 1958; Zimbardo, 1969), and Lazarus (1966), in particular, has proposed that the distinguishing feature of psychological stress is the evaluation of threat cues accomplished through a process of cognitive appraisal that mediates the stressor's direct action. This process is presumed to depend on two classes of antecedent conditions: the psychological structure of the individual and cognitive features of the stimulus situation. The individual's psychological structure includes his intellectual resources, knowledge, and motive strength, while the cognitive features consist of degree of control over the threatening event, its predictability of occurrence, and its imminence. Both sets of factors determine whether a particular event will be judged as threatening or benign. Once it is appraised as threatening, subsequent coping processes, whose aim is to reduce or eliminate the anticipated harm, are presumably activated. The same cognitive and individual-difference factors that determine the initial appraisal of the stimulus also determine which strategy of coping is adopted by the individual. In Lazarus' words, "The end results [of this process] observed in behavior (for example, affective experiences, motor manifestations, alterations in adaptive functioning, and physiological reactions) are understood in terms of these intervening coping processes. Each pattern of reaction—for example, actions aimed at strengthening the individual's resources against anticipated harm, attack with or without anger, anger without attack, avoidance with fear, fear without avoidance, and defense—is determined by a particular kind of appraisal" (Lazarus, 1966, p. 26). For example, a New York City subway car during rush hour would probably be extremely threatening to an out-of-towner on his first subway ride, but hardly noticed by a grizzled veteran of everyday Bronx to Manhattan commuting. Two shoppers, competing for a bargain in a special basement sale in a department store, may appraise each other as equally threatening, yet one will respond by a cool and calculated elbow to the ribs on the way to the counter, whereas the other will stop trying for the merchandise and start yelling at the first.

Adaptation

Efforts to reduce stress through a process of cognitive appraisal may be considered a form of adaptation to aversive events: repeated presentation of a reappraised stressor will cease to yield an adverse reaction. Martin (1964) and Lazarus (1968) have provided excellent discussions of the diverse meanings of adaptation, and in so doing, they draw a number of important distinctions that help give precise definition to the term. To begin, adaptation refers to a response or structural change in an organism brought about by disturbances to an internal or organism—environment equilibrium.[1] Adaptive responses or changes have been subdivided into those that are relevant to evolution and survival of the species, and those that aid the individual organism to survive and function in his particular environment. Still another distinction is between adaptive responses that maintain internal equilibria, and those that maintain organism—environment relationships. In both cases, adaptation may be achieved through automatic physiological mechanisms (e.g., the restoration of bodily temperature by the evaporation of perspiration), or through cognitive and behavioral mechanisms (e.g., turning on air conditioning to aid in temperature regulation). Since the focus of this book is on the behavioral effects of exposure to environmental stressors, we are primarily concerned with cognitive and behavioral responses that maintain an organism—environment relationship. Following Lazarus' (1966; 1968) description of coping processes, these responses may involve mobilization of actions against the threatening stimulus, and/or the realistic or defensive

[1] When a species or an individual responds to an environmental stressor, it is possible to make a value judgment that the change helps or hinders the organism's or the species' survival. Some writers use the term adaptive to refer to helpful changes, and call harmful changes by some other term, for example, maladaptive. We will not at any time adopt this convention.

reevaluation of the stimulus as benign. In either case, the subsequent occurrence of the stimulus will elicit a seriously diminished stress response. An index of adaptation, then, is the organism's decreased response sensitivity following repeated exposure to aversive stimulation.

In adopting this definition, we are treating the term adaptation as synonymous with the term habituation. In the most comprehensive review of earlier literature on habituation, Harris (1943) defines the phenomenon as "response decrement as a result of repeated stimulation." Later theorists have proposed similar definitions, for example, the "decrease in an innate response as a result of the repetition of the stimulus" (Mackworth, 1969). Thompson and Spencer (1966) have presented the most up-to-date account of the general laws of habituation, and in so doing have asserted that habituation refers to the same phenomenon as does adaptation. Both adhere to a set of widely accepted principles; for example, habituation is faster if the stimuli are presented at a faster rate, or if their temporal occurrence is periodic rather than aperiodic. We follow Thompson and Spencer in using the terms habituation and adaptation interchangeably.

There may be general agreement on the definition of adaptation, but theorists differ in their explanation of the phenomenon. Some emphasize a neurophysiological approach (Thompson & Spencer, 1966; Groves & Thompson, 1970), whereas others adopt a cognitive point of view (Lazarus, 1968). The latter theorist offers the following description of the processes underlying adaptation to stressful events.

> Consider a stimulus which, because it is appraised as threatening ... results in a negatively toned emotional state. If this stimulus, on repetition, gradually loses its capacity to arouse an emotional response, this must mean theoretically that it has been reappraised as less harmful and, hence, less demanding of coping action. The organism has presumably 'discovered' through repeated presentation of the emotional stimulus that there is less danger than previously assumed (1968, p. 219).

Stated somewhat differently, the organism is at first threatened by the stimulus, and he responds to it with alertness and vigilance. With repeated presentations and without harm occurring, the individual discovers that the stimulus is actually benign, or if it is indeed harmful, that he can somehow cope with it. In either case, the magnitude of the initial stress response diminishes. Lazarus (1968) proposes, and we agree, that adaptation to stressful events is analogous to the process whereby the "orienting response" adapts (Sokolov, 1958). The orienting reaction occurs because the organism is uncertain about the adaptive significance of a neutral stimulus, and he responds with attention and alertness. The reaction fades upon successive presentations because uncertainty is reduced and the stimulus no longer requires attention. In the case of stressful stimuli, initial reactivity diminishes on successive presentations because the threat is reduced through cognitive reappraisals or active coping responses.

Standing in sharp contrast to the cognitive interpretation of adaptation is the neurophysiological view represented in the work of Thompson and Spencer (1966). These authors argue that adaptation of the hind limb flexion reflex involves the same neural processes as more complex adaptations in the intact organism. They use the fact of adaptation in decorticate animals as evidence for their position, and note that this fact raises serious difficulties for the role of the cortex in adaptation. However, they also point out that adaptations may occur at almost any level in the central nervous system, including the frontal cortex, in which case cognitive processes may well be implicated. It is likely "that as one moves from lower level examples of habituation [or adaptation] . . . to complex emotional habituation, or from habituation in the spinal . . . animal, to the intact and phylogenetically high-level animal, cognitive processes ought to assume greater importance" (Lazarus, 1968, p. 221). In this respect, we are in complete agreement with the cognitive approach. We differ only in preferring to use one term—adaptation—to describe the decrement in response sensitivity to repeatedly presented aversive stimuli. We maintain this preference with full knowledge that not all forms of adaptation or habituation necessarily involve the same basic processes. For the present, however, the single term is more parsimonious and less confusing.

The fine grain of the adaptive process is presented here because we regard adaptation as the key to understanding modern life—at least those aspects of it involving man—environment interactions. The most remarkable feature of current urban existence is not how stressful the city has become, but how unaffected day-to-day functioning of the city dweller is despite the indignities heaped upon him. The effects of stress are not only neurophysiological. It is not merely as if the ear were becoming less sensitive to sound, or pressure receptors were losing their ability to report the jostlings and bumpings of a busy street. What also happens is that complex events, for example, hurried meals, hectic traffic, brusque and even hostile interpersonal exchanges, also lose their apparent power to disrupt. It is this fascinating loss of reactivity to stimuli generally regarded as aversive that makes the general issue of adaptation not only pertinent to our studies but a *sine qua non* for understanding urban stressors.

Costs of Stress and Adaptation

We have implied that all forms of life experience stress at one time or another, and it can also be asserted that adaptation to stressful stimuli is a universal attribute distinguishing life from inanimate matter (Dubos, 1965).

Living organisms, as we suggested earlier, simply do not submit to environmental pressures, but attempt to respond in ways that promote their biological and psychological survival. From amoeba to mollusk, from insects to vertebrates, and from rats to monkeys to man, it is truly remarkable how readily adjustments are made to a wide range of threatening situations, some of which are inconsistent with life itself. But it is seemingly man alone who relies on cognitive processes to achieve these adjustments, and for this reason, he shows an almost limitless variety of adaptive mechanisms, which he brings to bear on the external environment in order to protect himself and satisfy his needs and desires. Experiences growing out of several world wars and a number of lesser conflicts have documented this ability. There are numerous accounts of individuals who managed to survive and function under appalling circumstances in combat, in concentration camps, and in the squalor and devastation of bombed-out cities.

But man's adaptability is continually put to test in far less extreme circumstances. Doctoral students are forced to take the preliminary examination; young men inducted into the Army must endure basic training; most people experience the anxiety and pain involved in treating dental cavities; urban man is subject to excessive noise and crowding; and the Sherpa tribesman is often forced to live at hypoxic elevations in the Himalayan plateau. However, most of these people manage to survive without immediate psychological and organic breakdown. They adjust to the stressful aspects of their environment and become accustomed to them. But this ability to survive the inevitable stresses and strains of life is only part of the story. More important, perhaps, are the less immediate consequences of threats from the environment. Responses to a stressful event may become adapted to it, yet the adaptation may take its toll. Important aftereffects may remain in the form of physical and mental disease, psychosomatic disorders, performance and learning deficits, and general social-emotional maladjustments.

The fact that adaptation occurs during the stress period suggests that reactivity is being minimized and that the individual is learning to work in spite of stress. However, continued exposure to the stressor may produce cumulative effects that appear only after stimulation is terminated. It is as though the organism does not experience maximal stress until he is no longer required to cope with the stressor. It is only then that behavioral consequences of the event become evident. Alternatively, constant vigilance and coping may in and of themselves be stressful if forced to become ceaseless processes. As long as it is punctuated by the occurrence of novel or aversive events, the activation produced by coping may sustain the organism's functioning. When activation is terminated, however, a double dose of reaction sets in, not only to the stressor but also to the strain of coping. Again, behavioral consequences would surface only after the stressful situation has passed. Stressor effects have in fact been reported relatively soon after termination of an aversive event, as in the case of increased anxiety among Army personnel in the period immediately following their graduation from airborne training school (Basowitz *et al.*, 1955). On the other hand, adverse consequences may not become evident for several decades. Milgram (1970) has suggested that a kind of cognitive overload typifies modern city life which forces urban dwellers to develop adaptive styles that reduce the overload. Thus, for example, less time is devoted to each stimulus input, with the result that social responsibility is reduced, everyday civilities are relatively absent, and there is little willingness to assist strangers. These behaviors can be viewed as long-term consequences of adaptation to the overload inherent in urban life; that is, the coping process of not attending to stimuli produces a sustained lack of reaction to the environment: our definition of adaptation.

In terms of both long-term and short-term aftereffects, it would thus seem important to question the validity of the simplistic idea that adaptation is unqualifiably beneficial to man. In spite of adaptation, a stressor may leave its imprint on behaviors occurring after stimulation has ceased. It is also possible that these adverse consequences derive from the very adaptive processes that enable the individual to function effectively in the presence of noxious stimulation. We have said that adaptation to stressful events can best be understood from a cognitive point of view, which means that the adaptive process involves some form of reevaluation of the aversive stimulus, or the development of more direct action strategies for coping with a truly threatening stimulus. The process of adaptation, so defined, obviously entails cognitive work, though we need make no assumptions about the individual being aware of his adaptive strategies in either prospect or retrospect. Such adaptive effort may leave the individual less able to cope with subsequent environmental demands and frustrations, and this reduction in coping ability can be described as the psychic cost of adaptation to stressful events.

The notion that adaptation is costly to the organism derives from several sources. Selye's (1956) theory of stress response has enunciated the principle for biological processes, and Basowitz *et al.* (1955), Dubos (1965), and Wohlwill (1966; 1970) have all taken similar positions with respect to behavioral responses to stressor stimuli. Selye, for example, states that "people can get used to a number of things (cold, heavy work, worries), which at first had a very alarming effect; yet, upon prolonged exposure, sooner or later all resistance breaks down and exhaustion sets in. It is as though something were lost, or used up, during the work of adaptation . . ." (Selye, 1956, p. 66). Dubos has made essentially the same point in his discussion of man's response to the environment: "Although man is highly adaptable and can therefore achieve adjustments to extremely undesirable conditions, such adjustments often have . . . indirect effects that are deleterious. . ." (1968, p. 39). This concept of "psychic cost" implies a related notion of "energy depletion"—both admittedly vague concepts. We recognize that ascribing properties of physical energy to behavior can result in serious confusion (Martin, 1964), but we also believe the concept is useful as an intervening variable. For one could postulate an exercise effect instead of a depletion one, and it still remains an empirical question whether differences in adaptive effort leave the organism more or less able to cope with subsequent environmental demands.

Beneficial Aspects of Stress

We wish to make clear that we do not regard stress and adaptation to stress as having unequivocably adverse consequences. In an era when anything annoying is tagged with an unfavorable epithet—noise pollution, odor pollution, "people" pollution—it is necessary to separate out the systematic effects of stress from the evaluation of its consequences. On the species level, the existence of powerful stressors may serve a vital function in maintaining adaptiveness in the face of a changing environment. Even to a nonbiologist, it is possible to see how selective factors in response to stress can maintain those traits which enable a population to survive. Wynne-Edwards (1968) gives a detailed picture of how the stress of food deprivation coupled with pressures of territorial scarcity differentially enables those ruffled grouse to survive who are best equipped to handle their environment. In any event, it is difficult to see how a species can avoid stress in the best of circumstances. Given its ecological niche, each species is either stressed by predators and disease or, in their absence, overreproduces to be stressed by a shortage of food. Stress, like food ingestion and reproduction, is a part of life, and short of Eden, it would be difficult to imagine how to remove the old stressors without engendering new ones.

In somewhat similar manner, it can be argued that stress is an unavoidable, even routine, component of each individual's existence. This assumption has been a dominant theme underlying the construct of motivation in twentieth-century American physiology and psychology. For motivation has most often been cast in a homeostatic framework (cf. Cofer & Apply, 1964), and this position in its various forms postulates that an individual, or one of his subsystems, has a quiescent equilibrium state. The disturbance of this equilibrium causes a need and associated drive, thereby impelling the organism to attempt to resist moving from the homeostatic state, or if he has already moved, to restore the equilibrium. Thus, in language parallel to that used earlier, the force or stimuli disrupting the homeostatic equilibrium is a stressor, the need or drive is a stress, and the return to equilbrium is adaptation. It is worthwhile to note that in these formulations the stressor, or the stress for that matter, is not regarded as a villain. Quite the contrary, it is regarded as a necessary component of the behavioral systems that the organism needs in order to function and survive. For example, the stressor, food deprivation, leads to the (anthropomorphically defined) stress of hunger, which in turn leads to the adaptation of activity. At very extreme chronic levels of a stressor (e.g., prolonged food deprivation), maladaptive reactions occur (e.g., death or starvation); nevertheless, at normal acute levels, the stressor and associated stress are regarded as beneficial. Of late, homeostatic theories have come under attack for their attempts to explain all of behavior; but that is not the point at issue, for even models of learning that reject the equilibrium notion of motivation (e.g., operant conditioning) utilize the stressor of food deprivation in order to study normal behavioral processes.

The case can be stated in more positive terms by looking at some situations in which stress is specifically beneficial. Two examples may be illustrative. First, there is a large body of literature, mostly dealing with infrahuman organisms but which can be extrapolated to humans, showing that early childhood handling results in a more competent adult (for a review, cf. Dennenberg, 1967). For the species usually studied, rats and mice, handling in childhood (more accurately puphood) is conceptualized as a stressor. And the usual indices of stress, for example, open field tests and corticosteroid levels, show handling to be stressful. Although particular studies vary in their details, when adult animals who have been handled in puphood are contrasted with nonhandled littermate controls, they are better able to cope with novel situations and function under conditions of aversive stimulation. Even more cogent are the parallel studies (e.g., Lindzey, Lykken, & Winston, 1960) in which animals directly stressed in puphood by electric shock or toe pinching, for example, are more competent as adults than nonstressed controls in precisely the same way as handled rats or mice outperform their littermates. Thus, for these studies, the presence of stress in childhood turns out to be a facilitating experience for adult animals.

A second example of the beneficial effects of stress concerns the absence of stress, which can itself be harmful. Many theoretical approaches assert that stress results from the onset or continued application of aversive stimuli. Without a stimulus, it would seem there is no stress. But this definition cannot be applied to stimuli that are needed to maintain an ongoing process, such as food, oxygen, and water, and even for most sensory stimuli, their absence may be as noxious as the presence of large amounts of stimulation. This is true whether the absence of sensory stimulation is considered developmentally with infant cats, chicks, or monkeys (Riesen, 1966), or acutely in human adults, as in the case of sensory deprivation studies (e.g., Bexton, Heron, & Scott, 1954). In the former case, receptors do not develop normally; in the latter, the absence of stimuli becomes a severe stressor. Stress, then, is a stimulus that is impinging on the organism at some optimum value, the optimum being a composite function of the nature of the stimulus, the tolerance of the organism, the conditions under which the stimulation takes place, and the organism's satisfaction–deprivation state at that moment (cf. Welch, 1964).

In brief, stress may be coterminous with a wide gamut of stimulation; then again, it may not. It may have deleterious consequences; then again it may produce effects that have significant survival value for the organism and his species. Our interest in stress and the concomitant adaptation phenomenon stems from their universality, not from any belief in reaching a Utopian situation of life without stress.

Noise as a Stressor

We suggested earlier that the effort entailed in adapting to aversive events may be achieved at some expense to the individual's behavioral functioning. Alternatively, deleterious aftereffects may be the direct result of a cumulative experience of stress, despite the fact that the individual has adapted to repeated occurrences of the aversive event. In either case, we might expect task degradations and other impairments of behavior following termination of the stressor. Any number of stimuli could have been used to test for these effects, including such familiar procedures as electric shock, the cold-pressor test, sudden noise, attacks on the self-esteem of subjects, and routinized performance of frustrating tasks. Unfortunately, there is no set of rules about why this variety of stimulus conditions produces the reactions typically identified as stress. Indeed, there is evidence suggesting that different stressors produce different consequences (Appley & Trumbull, 1967; Parsons, 1966), in which case it would be unwise to treat various stressor stimuli as equivalent.

We were faced, therefore, with the necessity of selecting a single aversive event that would enable us to test our basic hypothesis about behavioral aftereffects of stress and adaptation. As we noted in the previous chapter, high-intensity broad-band noise was selected as the principal source of stress. We chose noise for three reasons: (1) it is easier to manipulate in the laboratory than many other stressors; (2) people more frequently encounter it than they do stressors such as electric shock and hypoxic atmospheres; (3) it is alleged to be an increasingly important hazard to public health in modern cities. The latter point had a particular attraction for us, since there is a growing concern in psychology (e.g., Miller, 1969), with which we agree, to engage in research having relevance to pressing social problems. The public policy implications of the effects of noise satisfy requirements of relevance.

There are many ways in which noise can be defined, some technical, others popular. It can be considered as "random fluctuations . . . which distort [ed] all observations" (Freeman, 1958); as a broad-band energy without periodicity (Burns, 1968); or as any unwanted sound (Rodda, 1967; Berrien, 1946). The latter definition implies that noise is any sound that is physiologically arousing and harmful, subjectively annoying, or disruptive of performance (Anatasi, 1964). We follow this definition throughout the monograph.

But do we have any evidence that noise is in fact a stressor and that measurable consequences result from its repeated application? There have been dozens of newspaper accounts and magazine stories (e.g., Blum, 1967; Mecklin, 1969; Bailey, 1969) that suggest an affirmative answer. The mere fact that many cities have created task forces on noise control (e.g., Anderson, 1970) affirms that noise is one of "the most impertinent of all interruptions." However, psychoacousticians are not all convinced that noise has deleterious consequences for man.[2] Comprehensive reviews of systematic research on noise (Kryter, 1950; 1970; Broadbent, 1957) conclude that there is no compelling evidence of adverse effects of noise, *per se,* on mental and psychomotor performance, providing the tasks do not involve auditory communication. A typical explanation of the null effect is that man adapts to the noise and any initial task deficits soon disappear. Positive effects of noise have even been noted, as where it masks distracting sounds (Rodda, 1967), stimulates the individual to remain alert on an otherwise boring task (McGrath & Hatcher, 1961), or arouses a sleep-deprived subject to perform better than under quiet conditions (Wilkinson, 1969). A recent summary of conclusions drawn from research on noise and human task performance is contained in the following excerpt from Kryter.

> . . .[O] ther than as a damaging agent to the ear and as a masker of auditory information noise will not harm the organism or interfere with mental or motor performance. Man should be able, according to this concept, to adapt physiologically to his noise environment, with only transitory interference effects of physiological and mental and motor behavior activities during this period of adaptation (1970, p. 587).

[2] They are not, of course, referring to hearing loss due to repeated exposure to high-intensity noise. There is a sizable literature on temporary and permanent threshold shifts (e.g., Glorig, 1958; Kryter, 1970) which shows that loud noise can damage the peripheral mechanisms of hearing, and the development of damage-risk criteria for exposure to sound has been increasingly occupying the energies of large numbers of psychoacousticians (e.g., Kryter, Ward, Miller, & Eldredge, 1966). More recently, we have seen studies of auditory fatigue and permanent hearing defects from rock-and-roll music. At least one controlled experiment (Dey, 1970) has demonstrated such effects.

Another body of systematic research, however, suggests that high-intensity noise does have negative effects on performance. A major contributor of this evidence is D. E. Broadbent (e.g., 1958). His experimental paradigm usually involves a vigilance task in which the subject is required to maintain long-term monitoring of various dials, any one of which may unexpectedly show a deflection. Signal detection on such tasks is adversely affected by high-intensity noise (Broadbent, 1954; Jerison & Wing, 1957). Other studies have shown that task degradations are most likely to occur on those complex tasks that exceed the individual's total information-processing capacity. Thus Boggs and Simon (1968) demonstrated that 92-dB noise produced significantly greater increments in auditory monitoring errors when the monitoring task was paired with a complex reaction-time task than with a simple reaction-time task. Several studies have demonstrated that the nature of the noise is critical to the demonstration of task impairments; that is, intermittent noise has a greater tendency to impair performance than does steady noise. Smith (1951) has shown that subjects exposed to 100-dB intermittent sound bursts 10 to 50 seconds in length tried more items on name and number checking tests, and scored more correctly and incorrectly than the control group. Corso (1952) and Woodhead (1959) have replicated these effects, and Sanders (1961) has shown that randomly varying noise intensities also produce greater impairment on mental tasks than does steady noise. Although not explicitly so done in these intermittent-noise studies, it is reasonable to describe the noise bursts as aperiodic or unpredictable, in which case we may conclude that unpredictable sound has a more aversive impact on performance than predictable sound. We will return to this point later in the section.

There is still another psychological factor that appears to affect the noise–performance relationship. Azrin (1958) reports that high-intensity sound can become an aversive stimulus and reduce performance quality if it becomes associated with incorrect behavior. He has also shown that noise can facilitate task performance if it is perceived as rewarding, or contains information relevant to the task. Kryter has suggested that experimental results showing noise-in-duced task degradations (e.g., vigilance task data) may be attributable to such "stimulus and response contingency interpretations of the meaning of the noise by the subjects" (1970, p. 556). For example, the task becomes disliked and is performed poorly because it is seen as contingent on the noise (stimulus contingency), or subjects view noise as punishment and are motivated to perform better if they believe their responses will reduce the noise. What Kryter seems to be saying here is that the context in which noise occurs is a principal determinant of its effects on task performance. As we noted earlier, one way of coping with urban stress is to pay less and less attention to each stimulus, lessening the impact of each (Milgram, 1970). But this strategy can only work if one is willing to forego the information contained in the stimulus. Little is gained if, after asking a passerby in the city for directions to your destination, you ignore his answer. When noise is actually, or is perceived to be, part of a necessary task, it is less easily ignored and consequently shows greater task-related effects.

Stressful effects of noise can be assessed not only by performance deficits, but also by subjective reports of annoyance. That noise is considered a nuisance by most people would hardly seem to require documentation, yet there is considerable literature on the problem indicating that persons exposed to noise object to it (Broadbent, 1957; McKennell & Hunt, 1966). Among the factors affecting degree of annoyance are such properties of the sound as intensity, frequency, aperiodicity, and unexpectedness (Kryter, 1970). Even more important, perhaps, in determining degree of annoyance are various psychological and sociological factors. Thus, for example, the extent to which people take actions to control environmental noise reduces the annoyance caused by the noise. A survey by Irle and Rohrmann (1968) of several hundred men and women living near the Hamburg airport showed that those who did not attempt to escape from aircraft noise reported being more sensitive to and annoyed by noise than those who said they had taken a variety of direct actions, such as insulating their walls, attending protest meetings, and so forth. Aside from the factor of control, other studies have shown that individual differences play an important role in noise tolerance. Thus, anxiety neurotics suffer more under noise than do nonneurotic subjects (Jansen, 1969), and even sociocultural backgrounds have been found to contribute to differences in complaints about noise (Jonsson, Kajland, Paccaguella, & Sorensen, 1969). Studies by Kryter (1968) indicate that the specific noise levels found unacceptable also depend on the activity in which the individual is engaged; that is, variations in work and living requirements result in different sound-level tolerabilities. In addition, Broadbent (1957) has noted that the source of noise may affect degree of annoyance. Special meanings associated with given sources require different tolerable limits for different noises; for example, the sound of a neighbor slamming a door is more annoying than the sound of a truck delivering a parcel to the neighbor. At times, even the same noise may receive different interpretations. Our secretary's typewriter is less annoying than that of a colleague's secretary.

If noise causes annoyance, it is entirely possible that mental disorders are correlated with prolonged exposure to noise. Clinical experience suggests that there is such a relationship. For example, Tomkins (in Blum, 1967) asserts that "since a high level of noise arouses in us either distress or anger . . . we're paying a very high price for the noise that surrounds us . . . we are all much more ready to cry or become angry than we need to be." This tendency to "fly off the handle" at the least provocation has received much anecdotal documentation (e.g., New York Times, March 2, 1970; New York Post, April 16, 1968). Consider the latter newspaper account. Four boys were playing in a Bronx residential neighborhood. They were shouting and running in and out of an apartment building. Suddenly, there was a pistol shot from a second-floor window and one of the boys fell dead on the pavement. The killer eventually confessed to police that he was a nightworker, and that he lost control of himself because the noise was interfering with his sleep (Mecklin, 1969). An extreme example, perhaps, but it does lend support to the allegation of disturbed emotional consequences stemming from noise exposure.

Systematic evidence for this relationship is, however, far from conclusive. Rodda (1967) cites data from a survey of aircraft carrier crews which showed no evidence of a higher incidence of mental disorders among this group as compared with military personnel who were not exposed to intense noise. On the other hand, Jansen (1961) found that steelworkers in the noisiest work environments had a higher frequency of social conflict at home and in the plant. Weybrew (1967) also notes that under conditions of prolonged noise exposure, most people show symptoms of irritability and aggression. However, all of these and related studies are subject to criticism on one or more methodological grounds. It is therefore premature to conclude that there is or is not a relationship between noise exposure and emotional disturbance.

A third way of assessing the stressful impact of noise is through measurements of physiological functioning. The former Surgeon General of the United States, William H. Stewart, has stated that noise produces physiological changes such as "cardiovascular, glandular, and respiratory effects reflective of a generalized stress reaction" (1969, p. 9), and Rosen has given the following summary of nonauditory reactions to loud noise: "The [peripheral] blood vessels constrict, the skin pales, the pupils dilate, the eyes close, one winces, holds the breath, and the voluntary and involuntary muscles tense. Gastric secretion diminishes and the diastolic pressure increases. Adrenaline is suddenly injected into the blood stream . . ." (Rosen, 1970, p. 57). To this list might be added GSR increments, and certain chemical changes in the blood and urine from glandular stimulation. There is experimental evidence to support these statements (cf. reviews by Kryter, 1950; 1970; Broadbent, 1957; Plutchik, 1959), and the work of Davis (e.g., Davis, Buchwald, & Frankmann, 1959) and Jansen (e.g., 1969) has been particularly important in demonstrating autonomic responses to high-intensity sound. Davis notes that these responses cannot necessarily be called "fear" or "startle," for some of them are associated with emotion-arousing stimulation whereas others are related to emotion-suppressing activities of the autonomic nervous system. There is usually a change in heart rate from startle that is not found in the arousal caused by noise. It has been alleged, and there is some support for the allegation (e.g., Teichner, Arees,

& Reilley, 1963) that autonomic arousal, not S—R or cognitive linkages, is responsible for the noise-associated task impairments described above. This notion is consistent with the assumption that noise produces stress arousal and concomitant behavioral consequences.

More important, perhaps, than physiological response to noise is the pervasive phenomenon of adaptation to sound. All laboratory tests show that autonomic adaptation or habituation invariably occurs with repeated presentations of noise (Kryter, 1970). This does not mean, however, that people experience the noise as acceptable. Data on annoyance reactions cited above are a case in point, for people continue to complain about intense sound even though they show physiological adaptation. There is also some evidence that autonomic reactions do not always wane with repeated noise presentations. Jansen (1969) reports that subject continued to show constriction of the peripheral blood vessels when exposed to noise for the successive times they returned to the laboratory. Other studies have found similar effects. Rosen cites research indicating that "while after 5 minutes of noise, constriction of the blood vessels begins to disappear, the reaction may persist for as much as 25 minutes before disappearing completely" (Rosen, 1970, p. 57). Still other data show that if the noise occurs in a particular cognitive context, physiological adaptation may not occur. For example, Davis and Berry (1964) found that subjects who could avoid a loud tone by pushing a switch at the correct time exhibited greater gastrointestinal motility during the tone (i.e., when they failed to press the switch) than did subjects who had no means of avoiding the same tone. The noise became a more aversive stimulus because it signified incorrect behavior (see the Azrin study cited earlier in this section).

There is also evidence of harmful physiological effects because of long-term exposure to noise. Data from industrial settings suggest greater circulatory, heart, and equilibrium problems in workers from more intense noise environments than from less intense environments (e.g., Jansen, 1961). However, Kryter (1970) correctly points out that other important factors in these industrial situations (e.g., poor ventilation, anxiety over job security, danger from accidents) may be responsible for the presumably noise-induced health problems. In short, there is really little evidence to connect noise with identifiable physical disease (Burns, 1968; Kryter, 1970), but the possibility cannot be completely dismissed at this time. Even if intense noise does not produce measurable effects on health, it does induce stress under certain conditions, with a resultant increase in autonomic reactions, irritability, and social conflicts at work and at home (Cohen, 1969).

To sum up, there are three ways in which noise-produced stress may be exhibited: by disruption of ongoing tasks or behaviors; by subjective displeasure or annoyance as indexed by complaints; and by reaction of autonomic, cardiovascular and neuromuscular systems. We may relate these three types of measures by stating that aside from reactions of annoyance, high-intensity noise does not have adverse effects on performance probably because of the adaptation of disruptive physiological and behavioral responses. There are, however, data that seem to disagree with this conclusion. First, there is evidence that autonomic reactivity does not always habituate with repeated noise presentations, and that even when it does, initial physiological responses to noise have been shown to correlate with initial impairments of task performance. Second, task degradations that do not disappear with habituation are noted when: (a) the performance entails long-term vigilance; (b) the task is otherwise complex; (c) the noise itself is intermittent; and (d) the noise occurs in a context in which the individual associates it with certain stimulus and response contingencies.

There is one general consistency in these exceptions to the conclusion that noise, *per se*, does not have adverse effects on behavior. All four cases appear to reflect the operation, not of noise alone, but of noise mediated by cognitive processes. The first two are presumably situations in which the organism becomes overloaded; that is, task inputs are so numerous as to inhibit adequate information processing, and the noise becomes still another input for the organism to monitor (Weitz, 1970). The noise continually overloads the subject and in such a situation produces performance deficits that do not wane with repeated exposure. The deleterious effects of intermittent noise probably reflect the fact that such noise is often aperiodic, and unpredictable stressors have a more aversive impact on behavior than predictable stressors (e.g., Broadbent, 1957; Berlyne, 1960). Indeed, it has been suggested that where sound is aperiodic or unexpected, the absence of precise knowledge about when to anticipate the stimulus serves to increase its unpleasant effects (Broadbent, 1957). We may suppose, therefore, that unpredictable noise has consequences equal to those of a higher-intensity predictable noise, and to the extent that intensity relates to performance, the individual should have greater difficulty in performing under unpredictable than predictable noise stimulation. The fourth case, stimulus and response contingencies, also reflects the impact of cognitive processes, for such contingencies really refer to the information or signal value of the sound. If the subject associates noise with punishment, task performance is impaired. If he associates it with reward, or if the noise contains task-relevant information, performance is facilitated, or at least remains unimpaired.

That the effects of noise should depend on cognitive factors is nicely consistent with our earlier discussion of the role of cognition in stress arousal and reduction. It would appear that high-intensity noise becomes a stressor contingent on the cognitive and social context in which stimulation occurs. But it is also true that physiological and behavioral adaptation to noise eventually occurs even in these special contexts. To return to our original question, are these adaptations achieved at some cost to the individual such that deleterious behavioral aftereffects are observed? And do such consequences vary with the meanings attributed to the noise as it originally occurred? Unfortunately, there is a virtual absence of systematic research demonstrating postnoise effects, and there is certainly no evidence linking performance impairments after noise exposure with the adaptive process itself. This monograph is designed to fill these gaps in our knowledge.

Effects of Noise on Physiology
and Task Performance

In the preceding chapter, we asserted that noise, *per se*, has minimally deleterious effects on mental and motor performance; that noticed effects are probably due to cognitive factors surrounding noise exposure; and that while high-intensity noise may produce initial autonomic reactivity, responses generally wane with repeated stimulation. These conclusions were based on a review of available research in the area, and, as we will see in this chapter, data from our own laboratories provide unequivocal confirmation. Let us be as clear as possible about what we intend to show. We are obviously not saying that noise has no effects on behavior. There would hardly be a point to the monograph were that our conclusion. What we will document is that all of the possible effects that might be attributed to noise simply do not occur. In particular, most task activities under conditions of gratuitous noise show no performance degrada- tion—quite the contrary. In more familiar terms, consider again a typical urban office worker who performs a variety of clerical functions during the workday. Common sense might suggest that if the office were disturbingly noisy, errors, such as mistakes in filing, might increase over the day as the cumulative effects of noise took their toll. Laboratory analogues of this situation show no such effect. People adapt to noise and their task performances improve rather than suffer. We can demonstrate that this conclusion holds irrespective of the intensity of noise, but it can be modified by cognitive variables that set the context of the noise.

These variables are unpredictability of noise stimulation (e.g., randomly intermittent noise bursts) and perceived lack of control over noise offset (e.g., the perception that one cannot escape from noise). Each produced per- formance deteriorations on complex mental and psychomotor tasks, whereas predictable noise and/or perceived control over noise defined conditions that did not lead to such effects. On the other hand, quality of performance on simple tasks often improved over the course of noise exposure, and this adaptation effect occurred whether the noise was predictable or unpredictable, controllable or uncontrollable. A major purpose of this chapter is to present the results on which these generalizations are based. In so doing, we will show that noise affects human task performance only under specific psychological conditions; that otherwise, it has no appreciable deleterious effects. It should be empha- sized, however, that this conclusion refers only to the direct effects of noise on performance. As we noted in Chapter 2, task degradations and related behavioral impairments may not appear until after noise exposure. Indeed, this is precisely the evidence amassed in our research and we will be describing noise aftereffect phenomena in detail in subsequent chapters.

A second purpose of the present chapter is to describe results showing autonomic reactivity to noise and the inevitable adaptation of such arousal. Previous research, as we mentioned above, indicates that high-intensity noise produces physiological stress reactions that usually habituate with continued exposure. The absence of adverse effects on simple task performance has been attributed, in part, to this decline in arousal. Data from our own research indicate that physiological reactions to noise do indeed adapt, and there is a corresponding tendency for task errors to decline as the individual achieves adaptation. It is, perhaps, an oversimplified approach to the matter to treat noise adaptation as primarily a reduction of autonomic response to repeated acoustic stimulation. Adaptation is, in our view, a cognitive process in which the individual effects actual or perceived changes in the stimulus conditions impinging upon him. Threat reappraisal and active coping strategies, such as "filtering" aspects of the unwanted stimulus, are among the mechanisms employed to render an aversive event benign. We have little evidence from our research concerning the precise mechanisms used by subjects to adapt to noise; indeed we made no special effort to collect these kinds of data. Our strategy simply assumed the existence of a variety of adaptive mechanisms, and then demonstrated the occurrence of adaptation by examining an invariant indicator of the phenomenon, namely, the decline of autonomic reactions to repeated stimulation. We begin this chapter with a discussion of these physiological data and return to the task performance results in a subsequent section.

Physiological Response to Noise

It is generally agreed that physiological arousal will not occur to noises much below 60 to 65 dBA[1] (Kryter, 1970). Beyond that level, there are definite arousal effects, and at levels exceeding 130 dBA, we begin to observe pain and cutaneous stimulation of the ear. In our own research, we generally used 108-dBA[2] broad-band noise consisting of a specially prepared tape recording of the following sounds superimposed upon one another: (a) two people speaking Spanish; (b) one person speaking Armenian; (c) a mimeograph machine; (d) a desk calculator; and (e) a typewriter. We selected this particular concatenation of sounds as an analogue of the spectrum of complex noises often present in the urban environment. A sound-spectrographic analysis of the noise recording showed that energy did indeed occur over a broad range from 150 to 7000 cycles per second (Hz), with the mode at about 700 Hz. Free-field stimulation was used throughout the research, with the noise delivered over a horn speaker mounted on the wall directly behind the subject and approximately 6 feet over his head.

Two basic types of noise tapes were used: (a) fixed intermittent, in which noise bursts approximately 9 seconds in duration were presented at the same place every minute over either a 23-, 24-, or 25-minute period, depending on the particular study being conducted; (b) random intermittent, in which the intervals between noise bursts were random, as were the lengths of the bursts themselves. Randomization was achieved by dividing each minute of the total noise period into quarter parts, and then randomly assigning a burst to a

[1] The abbreviation dBA refers to the decibel measurement made on the A-scale of a noise level meter, where higher frequencies are weighted more heavily because they are more annoying to the human ear.

[2] A sound of 108 dBA is about what one would hear if he were operating a riveting machine. The ambient noise level in the experimental chambers varied from week to week, but on the average, it was 40 dBA in the studies reported in this book.

different part in each 1-minute segment. The length of these noise bursts was also varied in random fashion, ranging from 3 seconds to 15 seconds in the 23- and 24-burst tapes, and from 3 to 21 seconds in the 25-burst tape. The total amount of noise was always identical on the two types of tapes: 3 minutes and 33 seconds in the 23-minute tape; 3 minutes and 36 seconds in the 24-minute tape; and 5 minutes in the 25-minute tape. Each began with approximately 1 minute of silence.[3]

Autonomic reactivity to noise was measured by phasic skin conductance (GSR), finger vasoconstriction, and muscle action potentials from the neck or forearm.[4] Table 3.1 presents GSR data from the first of the unpredictable-noise experiments reported in Chapter 4. The designation "Loud Unpredictable" means that subjects were exposed to the 23-minute random-intermittent noise tape at 108 dBA; "Soft Unpredictable" means the same tape played at 56 dBA; "Loud Predictable" is the fixed-intermittent tape played at 108 dBA; and "Soft Predictable" is the same fixed-intermittent noise at 56 dBA. Scoring and analysis of electrodermal responses to these tapes involved taking sample readings of the minimum skin resistance (i.e., maximum conductance) within each of the noise-presentation intervals, as well as of the resistance level just prior to the onset of each noise burst (base-level resistance). A noise-presentation interval was defined by the onset and offset of the noise burst plus 3 seconds of record beyond offset. These readings were translated into ohms resistance using

---

[3] We altered this particular randomization procedure in creating tapes used in two or three of the experiments reported in subsequent chapters. However, the departure was very slight and could in no way have influenced the results.

[4] Palmar skin resistance was usually recorded with a Beckman Type R Dynograph and a Type 9892A GSR coupler with special battery-box attachment. A current density of approximately 15 microamperes/cm² was maintained at the site of the active electrode. Beckman silver—silver chloride biopotential electrodes were placed on the volar surface of the proximal phalanges of the first and third fingers of the subject's nonpreferred hand. A ground electrode was placed on the wrist of the same hand. The subject's hand was attached with an EKG strap to a movable arm rest fitted to the arm of the chair in which he was seated.

Vasoconstriction of blood vessels in the finger tip was also measured with the Dynograph and a Type 9874 Photo Cell coupler operating in the direct current (dc) mode. A Beckman photocell pickup was attached to the volar surface of the distal phalanx of the second finger of the subject's nonpreferred hand by means of a black Velcro ribbon, which also shielded the pickup from room light. The lights were always dimmed as much as possible when vasoconstriction was being measured.

Electromyographic measurements were made with a Beckman Type RB Dynograph and a Type 9852 EMG Integrator coupler. Two Beckman electrodes were placed on the side of the neck directly below the mastoid process. A ground electrode was attached to the inner surface of the nonpreferred arm between bicep and elbow. In cases where a subject's hairline prevented placement of the electrodes on the neck, the alternative site was the inner part of the forearm (cf. Lippold, 1967, p. 290).

calibration constants and then into log conductance units. Change scores were computed between the log conductance measure during each noise interval and the log conductance measure for the immediately preceding base-level period. Lader (1964) and Montagu and Coles (1966) have emphasized the significance of expressing GSRs to repeatedly presented auditory stimuli in terms of these "changes in log conductance." Difference scores for the No Noise Control group were computed by taking as the base-level score the log conductance of the first second of every minute during the entire period of task performance. The highest log conductance value during the subsequent 9-second period was then subtracted from each basal score.

The changes in log conductance scores were grouped for each subject into four blocks, and the scores then averaged for each block. It is the final conditions-means of the averages that are presented in Table 3.1. A repeated-measures analysis of variance of these data indicated that reactivity declined significantly over the four blocks ($F = 17.84$, $3/129\ df$, $p < .01$). In addition, there was a reliable Loud versus Soft effect ($F = 4.48$, $4/43\ df$, $p < .01$), and an interaction between this variable and the blocks factor ($F = 7.46$, $12/129\ df$, $p < .01$). As expected, there were no differences between the five scores in the fourth block ($F = 2.21$, $4/43\ df$). It is not surprising that GSRs to initial noise bursts were virtually identical in the predictable and unpredictable conditions. The aperiodicity of noise is not fully experienced until after some exposure, and by that time subjects in both conditions are adapting to the noise. Differences in initial GSRs between loudness conditions were also to be expected, in view of research cited earlier indicating autonomic differences as a function of noise intensity (cf. Kryter, 1970). In summary, Table 3.1 shows that noise of high intensity produced more autonomic reaction than low-inten-

TABLE 3.1

Mean Changes in Log Conductance

Experimental condition	Blocks of noise bursts			
	1 5 scores	2 6 scores	3 6 scores	4 6 scores
Loud unpredictable[a]	.078	.028	.021	.020
Soft unpredictable[b]	.022	.015	.014	.014
Loud predictable[a]	.078	.038	.034	.026
Soft predictable[b]	.016	.011	.013	.008
No noise control[b]	.012	.008	.011	.014

[a] $n = 9$.

[b] $n = 10$.

TABLE 3.2

Mean Changes in Log Conductance: Replication 1

| Experimental condition | Blocks of noise bursts | | | |
	1 6 scores	2 6 scores	3 6 scores	4 6 scores
Loud unpredictable[a]	.052	.035	.024	.020
Loud predictable[b]	.066	.034	.019	.013
No noise control[a]	.013	.012	.011	.010

[a] $n = 9$.
[b] $n = 10$.

sity noise. However, after 23 minutes of exposure to about 9 seconds of noise per minute, adaptation is so thorough that subjects in neither the high- nor the low-intensity groups differ in reactivity from subjects serving in a No Noise Control group.

To further document this point, comparable GSR scores from two subsequent replications are presented in Tables 3.2 and 3.3. We see again that reactivity waned over the course of the noise session, and the only significant differences among the first blocks of scores were between control groups and the noise conditions. Electrodermal data from all three studies, then, indicate that experimental subjects were more aroused by loud than soft noise; were equally aroused by predictable and unpredictable noise; and regardless of intensity or unpredictability, adapted to about the same extent following repeated exposure to the noise bursts.

These findings accord very nicely with physiological results reported by other investigators (see above). We also have a fair degree of confidence in their generality in view of the range of subjects used in our studies. Data in the first two tables come from college-age females, whereas the results presented in Table 3.3 are based on men and women between the ages of 35 and 65. Further evidence of autonomic reaction and adaptation to noise comes from vasoconstriction data (i.e., constriction of peripheral blood vessels in the finger) collected in this second replication. These responses, primarily monophasic in character, were measured by comparing the maximum deflection of the vasoconstriction wave within a noise-burst interval with the point immediately preceding the onset of the burst. All comparisons were made in millimeters from the bottom points on the pulse amplitude waves. The difference between the two points constituted our measure of vascular reactivity to noise.[5] The

---

[5] Vasodilation responses were scored as zero deflection. Such responses were relatively infrequent and tended to occur toward the beginning of the sequence of noise bursts.

TABLE 3.3

Mean Changes in Log Conductance: Replication 2

Experimental condition[a]	Blocks of noise bursts				
	1 5 scores	2 5 scores	3 5 scores	4 5 scores	5 5 scores
Loud predictable	.081	.052	.032	.027	.022
Loud unpredictable	.065	.026	.025	.018	.018
Loud unpredictable-perceived control[b]	.072	.036	.025	.025	.020
No noise control	.013	.006	.017	.015	.017

[a] There are 10 cases in each condition.

[b] Subjects in this condition were told that noise would be terminated if they pressed a button attached to their chair. The significance of this condition is deferred until our discussion of autonomic response to uncontrollable and controllable noise.

resulting 25 scores were grouped into 5 blocks and the conditions-means for these groupings are given in Table 3.4. There is a significant blocks effect in these data ($F = 6.24$, $4/144$ *df*, $p < .01$), despite increments from third to fourth blocks in the Loud Predictable and Loud Unpredictable conditions. The overall decline in vasoconstriction in each condition corresponds to the adaptation results obtained with phasic skin conductance. There is also a corresponding effect due to experimental conditions ($F = 2.56$, $3/36$ *df*, $p = .08$), but the interaction term failed to reach statistical significance ($F = 1.22$, $12/144$ *df*). Reliable differences within Block 1 are between control and experimental conditions (*ps* $< .05$), and between Loud Unpredictable—Perceived Control and

TABLE 3.4

Mean Vasoconstriction Scores: Replication 2[a]

Experimental condition[b]	Blocks of noise bursts				
	1 5 scores	2 5 scores	3 5 scores	4 5 scores	5 5 scores
Loud predictable	6.51	3.58	2.64	3.31	3.32
Loud unpredictable	7.11	4.40	4.11	5.49	4.10
Loud unpredictable-perceived control	4.73	3.53	3.44	3.15	1.77
No noise control	3.55	2.94	2.83	3.09	3.95

[a] Scores are given in millimeters.

[b] There are 10 cases in each condition.

the other two noise conditions. Within Block 5, the only differences are between Loud Unpredictable–Perceived Control and each of the other conditions ($ps < .05$).

A capsule summary of the vasoconstriction data reads like a reiteration of the skin conductance findings. Loud noise has an initial autonomic effect that wanes over time. By the end of the experimental session, subjects exposed to noise bursts show no more vasoconstriction than subjects in a No Noise Control group. The Loud Unpredictable–Perceived Control condition produced lower vasoconstriction scores than the other conditions, probably because of the impact of controllability on reactions to noise. We defer discussion of this issue until after we present electrodermal effects of controllable and uncontrollable noise.

In presenting the physiological results, we have used the word "unpredict-ability" advisedly, for the term refers not only to aperiodicity of noise stimuli, but also to situations in which such stimuli are unexpected. A frequently used definition states that a stimulus is unpredictable if its occurrence, or nonoccur-rence, is not predicted by a prior warning signal (Seligman, Maier, & Solomon, 1971), and much of the research on this variable has relied on signaled and unsignaled aversive stimulation (e.g., D'Amato & Gumenik, 1960; Lovibond, 1968).[6] Instead of limiting the term predictable to situations where noise occurrence was regular over time, analogous to a clock striking quarter hours, it seemed desirable to conduct a further experiment using aperiodic noise bursts that were and were not forewarned by a signal (see Chapter 4). Prior warning of the noise burst by a signal light constituted our manipulation of predictability, whereas unpredictability was aperiodic stimulation with no signal or with a signal that came on at random times so that it was uncorrelated with noise. Adaptation occurred in all three conditions, as can be seen in Table 3.5.[7] The monotonic decrement from first to fourth block was highly significant ($p < .01$), and there were no between-conditions differences within the first block of scores and within the fourth block of scores.

Similar analyses were carried out on electromyographic responses to each noise burst. The relevant means are presented in Table 3.6, and they clearly support the adaptation effect obtained with skin conductance and vasoconstric-tion (F (Blocks) = 11.41, 3/117 df, $p < .01$). There were no reliable differences within the first block or fourth block of scores.

[6] We will return to a discussion of this research in the next chapter.

[7] Computation of these GSR scores used somewhat different procedures than before (cf. Geer, 1968). Minimum skin resistance readings were taken from the onset of each noise burst to offset plus 5 seconds. These scores were converted to micromhos of conductance (times $10^6 + 1.0$) and subtracted from similar conductance-converted readings taken at the points of noise onset. The log values of these difference scores were grouped into successive blocks, and the means of each block were used in testing for adaptation effects.

TABLE 3.5

Means of the Logs of Conductance Change Scores

Experimental condition[a]	Blocks of noise bursts			
	1 6 scores	2 6 scores	3 6 scores	4 6 scores
Aperiodic noise with correlated signal	.187	.141	.141	.132
Aperiodic noise with uncorrelated signal	.279	.209	.177	.130
Aperiodic noise with no signal	.227	.175	.192	.161

[a] There are 14 cases in each condition.

Decreased responsiveness to successive noise bursts, then, characterizes subjects on all three autonomic channels, and the muscular-contraction results also suggest that initial "startle" responses wane with repeated acoustic stimulation.

Controllable and uncontrollable noise. An unpredictable stressor is one over which the individual has no control. He is unable to escape its onset and he is even powerless to prepare for its occurrence. Aside from making a stressor predictable, as we did in the research described above, an obvious way of inducing control is to provide the individual with actual means of escape or avoidance—manipulanda that terminate or prevent the occurrence of the unpredictable stressor. A number of studies have shown that an aversive event

TABLE 3.6

Mean Muscular Contractions[a]

Experimental condition	Blocks of noise bursts			
	1 6 scores	2 6 scores	3 6 scores	4 6 scores
Aperiodic noise with correlated signal	4.02	2.17	1.37	1.73
Aperiodic noise with uncorrelated signal	4.71	1.41	1.09	1.01
Aperiodic noise with no signal	3.67	2.15	1.59	.96

[a] Scores are given in millimeters of chart deflection.

produces lower autonomic stress responses if the organism can control its onset and offset (e.g., Haggard, 1946), and it has even been suggested that the mere perception of control is sufficient to reduce the physiological impact of a threatening event (Stotland & Blumenthal, 1964). We have also conducted research on the effects of perceived control, where the variable was defined as the belief that one could press a button, if he wished, that would terminate unpredictable noise. The experiments are reported in detail in Chapter 5, the discussion here being confined to autonomic data produced in this research. While we have demonstrated that, in general, autonomic reactions to noise dissipate with repeated exposure, there is still the possibility that people cannot so easily adapt to noise that, in particular, is embedded in a context of unpredictability or uncontrollability. Even a casual rereading of the previous tables will show that the unpredictability of noise poses not the slightest barrier to its adaptation; this is true regardless of whether unpredictability is produced by aperiodicity or by an uncorrelated signal.

A similar examination of the effects of controllability upon autonomic activation can be made by grouping data from studies varying control. These studies show unequivocal physiological adaptation in both Perceived Control and No Perceived Control conditions. Table 3.7 presents the relevant change in log conductance scores. Experimental procedures were virtually identical to those used in the unpredictable-noise experiments. Indeed, the No Perceived Control condition in the first two studies was an exact duplication of the Loud Unpredictable treatment discussed earlier. The results for No Perceived Control in the second replication are the average of three experimental conditions, each inducing perceived uncontrollability somewhat differently (see Chapter 5). Since the level and pattern of GSR scores was essentially the same in all three conditions, we combined them for purposes of the present discussion.

Table 3.7 shows that a significant decline in GSR reactivity occurred in all studies ($ps < .001$), though the overall level of response was somewhat lower in both treatments of the first replication. This difference probably reflects nothing more than variations in samples and experimenters. More important is the fact of approximately equivalent GSR adaptation for each condition in each study. There were no reliable differences between scores for the last block within any of the experiments. Further evidence of these effects can be found in Tables 3.3 and 3.4, which included a Perceived Control condition. Those results also show unequivocal adaptation for GSR and vasoconstriction. Similar findings were obtained in other controllable-stressor studies reported in this book. There is little need to present these data, for the effects were essentially the same as reported here. Subjects habituate to acoustic stimulation, irrespective of its unpredictability and perceived uncontrollability.

TABLE 3.7

Mean Changes in Log Conductance

Experimental condition	Blocks of noise bursts			
	1	2	3	4
Perceived control: First study[a]	.070	.035	.022	.023
No perceived control: First study[a]	.074	.037	.026	.025
Perceived control: Replication 1[b]	.024	.016	.011	.010
No perceived control: Replication 1[c]	.050	.034	.023	.016
Perceived control: Replication 2[d]	.068	.034	.023	.016
No perceived control: Replication 2[e]	.075	.046	.039	.033

[a] $n = 9$.

[b] $n = 16$.

[c] $n = 12$.

[d] $n = 11$.

[e] $n = 36$.

There is, however, one set of data that deserves special comment. It comes from a study in which perceived control was manipulated by informing subjects that noise occurrence (108-dBA sounds) was contingent on task performance. Good performance (defined as solving graphic puzzles) was supposed to prevent the next scheduled noise burst, whereas poor performance would inevitably bring on the next burst. In actual fact, both groups of subjects received the same amount and schedule of noise (see Chapter 5). Perceived Control in this study was thus defined in terms of perceived avoidance, not in terms of potential escape, as we did in the studies described above. The relevant adaptation results are shown in Table 3.8. It is quite evident that habituation occurred over the course of noise exposure in both experimental conditions ($p < .001$). We therefore conclude from these and preceding data that perceived uncontrollability, whether defined as escape or avoidance, has no appreciable effects on physiological adaptation to unpredictable noise.

But this conclusion is only part of the story. We have yet to consider differences in magnitude of autonomic response as a function of degree of

TABLE 3.8

Mean Changes in Log Conductance

Experimental condition	Blocks of noise bursts		
	1 6 scores	2 6 scores	3 6 scores
Perceived control: Avoidance[a]	.075	.028	.022
No perceived control: Avoidance[a]	.062	.026	.015
No noise 1[b]	.015	.014	.021
No noise 2[b]	.007	.009	.011

[a] $n = 10$.

[b] $n = 11$.

perceived controllability. Adaptation is documented by showing minimal reactivity at the end of noise sessions with no controllability differences. But the control factor may also affect reactivity by ameliorating the initial impact of noise so as to diminish its effective autonomic stress. This potential difference can best be detected by focusing on the first block of noise bursts—before reactivity levels in Control and No Control conditions begin to converge. Examination of each study reveals that with two exceptions, Tables 3.3 and 3.8, autonomic reactivity was lower in the Perceived Control treatment than in the No Perceived Control treatment. Since noise stimuli were always identical in the two conditions, we may attribute the differences to the control manipulation. However, statistical tests revealed that with two exceptions, Table 3.4 and the first replication in Table 3.7, the observed effects were not significant. The GSR results, then, are equivocal with respect to inferring a decrement in magnitude of initial stress as a function of perceived control.

Previous experimentation, however, has documented a significant reduction in electrodermal response where the subject (1) actually controls onset and offset of stressor stimuli (Haggard, 1946; Champion, 1950; Corah & Boffa, 1970); (2) simply believes that he has potential control (Stotland & Blumenthal, 1964; Corah & Boffa, 1970); (3) believes he has terminated or otherwise reduced the impact of the stressor through instrumental responding (Geer, Davison, & Gatchel, 1970). At first glance, these findings appear inconsistent with our own results, yet closer examination reveals that all of the studies, with one exception, used electric shock as the stressor stimulus. Autonomic arousal responses to sound are not necessarily the same as to other aversive events (Davis, Buchwald, & Frankmann, 1959), hence, we might expect the effects of control to differ with the particular stressor being administered. An even more important difference between previous research and our own controllability studies has to do with the way in which the control variable was manipulated. We were exclusively concerned with the *perception* of *potential* control, whereas three of the studies (Haggard, 1946; Champion, 1950; Corah & Boffa, 1970) dealt with *actual* control over the stressor. The Corah–Boffa design did include a pair of conditions that could be interpreted as simply giving the subject a sense of control or no control, but the way in which the variable was induced may have artifactually maximized GSR amplitude; that is, No Control subjects were given a button that could presumably terminate shock and were told not to press it. It is entirely possible that bringing up the issue of controllability in the No Perceived Control condition heightened the subject's subsequent frustration at being unable to escape from shock, hence increasing the magnitude of autonomic response. In our own research, the possibility of controlling noise offset was never mentioned in the No Perceived Control treatment.

The Geer *et al.* research also examined the perception of control, but again the manipulation was substantially different from that used in our studies; that is, subjects were led to believe that instrumental responding had resulted in a decrement in duration of shock. Since the decrement did in fact occur, it may be that lowered GSR amplitudes were a joint function of the perception of control and of actual reinforcement. Geer's subjects learned that their control was effective, whereas our subjects only had the perception of potential control.

The Stotland–Blumenthal experiment also studied the perception of potential control, but the stressor was a threat implicit in taking a series of tests measuring important abilities, and control consisted of believing one could determine the order in which the tests would be taken. Electrodermal response (i.e., palmar sweat) was measured during a waiting period after delivery of the control instructions and prior to test administration. No effort was made to determine autonomic reactions to the tests themselves. The obvious differences in procedure and measurement between this study and our own research are sufficiently great to raise doubts about the meaningfulness of comparing the two sets of findings. In short, the discrepancy may be more apparent than real.

To sum up, prior research has shown that controllability, actual and perceived, has reliable stress-reducing effects as measured by electrodermal responses. In general, our research has not supported these findings, but procedural differences may well account for the disparity. Moreover, we did find relevant GSR differences in the first replication reported in Table 3.7, and the presence of the control button substantially reduced vascular reactions to unpredictable noise bursts (see Table 3.4). The latter result has received confirmation in a subsequent study conducted in our laboratory, as can be seen in Table 3.9. Aside from the usual adaptation effects, the Block 1 score for Perceived Control is significantly lower than the corresponding score for No Perceived Control ($p < .05$). We tentatively conclude, therefore, that perceived

TABLE 3.9

Mean Vasoconstriction Scores[a]

Experimental condition	Blocks of noise bursts				
	1 5 scores	2 5 scores	3 5 scores	4 5 scores	5 5 scores
Perceived control [b]	5.19^d	3.87^d	4.58^d	3.88^d	4.66^d
No perceived control [c]	7.65^e	4.55^e	4.07^e	3.71^e	4.29^c

[a] Scores are given in millimeters.

[b] $n = 20$.

[c] $n = 30$.

[d] These values represent the average of two conditions in which perceived control was manipulated using slightly different procedures (see Chapter 5).

[e] These values represent the average of three similar conditions.

control can affect autonomic responding, even if the control is not exercised or is incorrectly perceived. More important, however, is the adaptation of such responses to successive acoustic stimulation. And physiological adaptation invariably occurred in our studies, regardless of the intensity of the noise, its unpredictability, or the subject's belief that he had control over its termination. In short, virtually nothing we did by way of manipulating noise presentation had any substantial effect on physiological adaptation. Yet, as we will see in later chapters, almost anything we did to manipulate the context in which noise occurred had major effects on postnoise behavior.

Effects of Noise on Task Performance

The preceding section provided unequivocal demonstration that physiological responses to noise adapt with repeated stimulation. We examined these responses for a variety of reasons; we reasoned that if repeated exposure to noise proved progressively debilitating, this deficit would appear in both autonomic and behavioral indices. Conversely, given our findings of autonomic adaptation and our belief in the loose coupling of physiological reactivity to behavior, it follows that physiological adaptation should be accompanied by minimal impairment of task performance—or at least an improvement in performance as autonomic responding declines. We are speaking here only of simple tasks. Research described in Chapter 2 indicated that high-intensity noise does impair performance on complex tasks in spite of physiological adaptation. Let us begin with a consideration of the effects of predictable and unpredictable noise on performance of simple mental tasks.

The most frequently used tasks in our studies were three standardized tests of cognitive performance, each divided into two parts of equivalent difficulty (French, Ekstrom, & Price, 1963). They were (a) Number Comparison, in which the subject inspected pairs of multidigit numbers and indicated whether the numbers in each set of the pair were the same or different; (b) Addition, in which the subject added columns of three 1- and 2-digit numbers; and (c) Finding A's, in which the task was to check the 5 words in each column of 41 words having the letter "a" in them. The Number Comparison test consisted of two sets of 48 comparisons each; the Addition test had two sets of 60 additions each; and Finding A's had two parts, each consisting of twenty-five 41-word columns.

During the first half of the noise session, subjects worked on the first part of each of the three tests. They were then told to stop even if they had not completed all of the test items. After a brief pause, they began work on the second half of the tests and continued for the remaining noise bursts. In this way, we were able to calculate differences in errors made on the two halves of each test and use these scores (relative to No Noise baseline changes) to assess whether performance improved with physiological adaptation. The order of presentation of the tests was the same in every experiment in which they were used: Number Comparison, Addition, and Finding A's.

Quality of performance on these tasks is presented in Table 3.10 for the first three unpredictable noise studies described in Chapter 4. The table shows the mean number of errors on Number Comparison and Addition during the first half of the noise session.[8] It is immediately evident that these means are no greater than in the No Noise Control group, irrespective of intensity and/or unpredictability of the noise ($ps > .10$). Despite initial physiological stress responses reported in the previous section, quality of performance on simple mental tasks was not impaired by exposure to noise. These findings are obviously in accord with the conclusions reached by previous investigators. High-intensity noise has minimal effects on simple task performance, to which we may now add that even unpredictable loud noise does not produce task degradations.

Errors in the noise conditions and in the No Noise Control were not significantly different, but there was in fact a tendency toward greater task impairment in the former conditions (see Table 3.10). It is therefore interesting to note the general decline in these errors from the first to the second halves of the testing session. These data can be seen in Table 3.11, which presents mean decrements in errors for both tests. The Number Comparison change scores in the first study were significantly different from zero in each experimental

[8] We do not present results on the Finding A's test, for there were virtually no errors on either part, presumably because its difficulty level was too low for most of our subjects.

TABLE 3.10

Average Number of Errors on Part 1 for the Number Comparison and Addition Tests

	Loud unpredictable		Loud unpredictable-perceived control		Soft unpredictable		Loud predictable		Soft predictable		No noise control	
	NC	A	NC	A	NC	A	NC	A	NC	A	NC	A
First study	2.44	6.67	—[a]	—	3.00	3.90	4.13	5.78	3.60	5.80	2.80	2.20
Replication 1	2.00	6.44	—	—	—	—	3.40	6.80	—	—	1.56	5.44
Replication 2	5.10	7.56	3.00	6.89	—	—	5.60	10.34	—	—	3.10	3.52

[a] A dash indicates that the condition was not included in the study.

TABLE 3.11

Average Decrement in Errors from First to Second Parts of Noise Exposure for the Number Comparison and Addition Tests

	Loud unpredictable		Loud unpredictable-perceived control		Soft unpredictable		Loud predictable		Soft predictable		No noise control	
	NC	A	NC	A	NC	A	NC	A	NC	A	NC	A
First study	−1.58	−.34	—[a]	—	−.56	−.73	−2.13	−1.50	−2.40	−2.07	−.20	−.08
Replication 1	−.89	−.22	—	—	—	—	−2.00	−.40	—	—	−.33	−1.89
Replication 2	−.90	+2.77	−.60	−.37	—	—	−1.70	+.32	—	—	−1.00	+5.80

[a] A dash indicates that the condition was not included in the study.

condition (ps $<$ .05), except Soft Unpredictable, where the decrement did not approach significance. The decrease in errors for the No Noise Control group was clearly nonsignificant. By contrast, the results for the first replication revealed that only the error-change score for Loud Predictable was reliably different from zero ($p < .01$), and in the second replication none of the Number Comparison change scores showed significant declines. There was also no evidence of reliable reductions in Addition errors in all three studies; indeed the Loud Unpredictable, Loud Predictable, and Control conditions in the second replication actually showed increments in errors. Only the means for Loud Unpredictable and the Control group were statistically significant from zero ($p < .05$).

Despite inexplicable deviations from a consistent pattern of data, the results indicate that noise does not produce substantial task degradations, and the few errors that do occur tend to wane with physiological adaptation. Further support for this conclusion comes from the signaled-noise experiment described in the previous section. In that study, subjects were required to press one of two buttons labeled "dot" and "dash" in order to reproduce patterns of 10 dots and dashes being projected on a screen throughout the noise session. Matching errors were recorded for each quarter of the noise session, as well as for noise onset and burst duration. Analysis of these data did not reveal significant differences between predictable and unpredictable conditions, although there was a general tendency for errors to decline with repeated stimulation. In sum, we conclude that high-intensity sound, even when unpredictable, does not have adverse effects on the performance of simple mental tasks.

In Chapter 2, we proposed that one of the necessary conditions for noise-induced task impairment was overloading the organism; that is, task inputs become so numerous as to inhibit adequate information processing. We further suggested that aperiodic (unpredictable) noise would produce more deleterious effects on performance than periodic (predictable) noise, and although we did not demonstrate this to be the case in our own research with simple tasks, we might still expect unpredictable noise intrusions to show their aversive effects on complex tasks. Performance impairments should be greatest where the subject works on a complex task during aperiodic noise stimulation, for the overload of the task will interact with the presumed greater aversiveness of unpredictable sound. In order to test this proposition the following experiment was conducted.

Effects of Aperiodic Noise on Complex Task Performance

This experiment (Finkelman & Glass, 1970) measured noise effects by means of a subsidiary task technique that derives from information theory (Boggs & Simon, 1968; Zeitlin & Finkelman, 1969; 1970). The individual is treated as a communication channel capable of processing a finite quantity of information. Cognitive overload is inferred by noting degradation of performance on a subsidiary task as the individual attempts to maintain a constant level of primary task performance. The primary task can be performed virtually without errors as long as its demands, in conjunction with psychological stress, are within the individual's total information-handling capacity. Increasing the demands imposed upon the individual by introducing an environmental stressor, such as unpredictable noise, is expected to result in impairment of subsidiary task performance. Our major prediction, therefore, was that more errors will occur on a subsidiary task under unpredictable noise conditions than under predictable noise conditions.

Experimental procedure. Subjects were 23 male volunteers enrolled in an undergraduate psychology course at the City University of New York, where the study was conducted. Noise stimuli consisted of white-noise bursts of 80 dBA delivered to the right ear of each subject over a headphone. The Predictable Noise condition consisted of 9-second bursts of noise interpolated with 3-second intervals of silence. The Unpredictable Noise condition consisted of noise bursts of random duration varying in ten 1-second steps between 1 and 9 seconds. The interpolated intervals of silence were likewise random, varying in three 1-second steps between 1 and 3 seconds. The total duration and ratio of sound and silence was identical for predictable and unpredictable conditions; only their distribution throughout a trial was varied.

The *primary* task on which subjects worked during noise was a vehicular steering simulator. It required tracking of a vertical stimulus input line displayed on an oscilloscope mounted atop a sports car steering wheel. In tracking the line, the subject had to center it on the midline of the display, as indicated by an arrow. Time on Target was the principal measure of performance. The *subsidiary* task required the subject to repeat a previously announced digit upon presentation of the subsequent digit. Each trial consisted of a different set of 60 random digits, one being presented every 2 seconds while the subject was working on the primary task. An error score was determined by counting the number of times a subject failed to repeat correctly the previously announced digit.

The study consisted of nine conditions with each subject serving as his own control. He engaged in the primary task alone, the subsidiary task alone, or both tasks together. He did this under conditions of No Noise, Predictable Noise, and Unpredictable Noise. Only two of these conditions are relevant to a test of our major hypothesis: (a) Predictable Noise, in which subjects worked on primary and subsidiary tasks in conjunction with predictable noise; and (b) Unpredictable Noise, in which performance on the primary and subsidiary tasks occurred with unpredictable noise. Of the remaining conditions, three provided data for independent verification of the subsidiary task technique, and four examined the effects of noise on the primary task alone or on the subsidiary task alone. In view of our previous data on simple task performance, there was no reason to expect degradations in these circumstances, and the results supported expectations.

The trials in the Predictable Noise and Unpredictable Noise conditions were counterbalanced in randomly assigned ABBA and BAAB orders. Each of the nine conditions was presented twice, although no single condition was repeated until all others had been presented once. A given trial was 2 minutes in duration with a 1-minute interpolated rest period.

Results and discussion. The mean number of errors on the subsidiary task was 4.0 in the Predictable Noise condition and 8.0 in the Unpredictable Noise condition. A t test of these means was significant at the .05 level ($t = 2.37$). The average Time-on-Target scores for the primary task were 44.6 seconds in the Predictable Noise treatment and 42.5 seconds in the Unpredictable Noise treatment. A t test of these scores was clearly nonsignificant ($t < 1$).

These results provide support for the hypothesized increment in errors on the subsidiary task associated with the occurrence of unpredictable noise in contrast to predictable noise. Degradations in performance appeared on the subsidiary task only in the unpredictable condition. Such a result is consistent with initial expectations. There is no effect of noise on a primary, simple task. However aversive the stimulation may be, subjects were able to adapt to it and to perform accurately. But, when a secondary task was added that placed heavy demands on the subjects' resources—they were at the limits of their abilities in handling both tasks simultaneously—the deleterious effects of the noise appeared. Furthermore, unpredictable noise produced a significantly greater number of secondary task errors than predictable noise. Earlier findings of no performance degradation under noise are not surprising: noise only affects performance when the subject is working at maximum capacity, and even then, the noise must be especially aversive, in our case, unpredictable, to degrade complex task performance.

Effects of Controllable and Uncontrollable Noise on Task Performance

We have suggested that perceived lack of control over noise termination might be expected to produce noise-induced task degradations. The physiological results did, after all, indicate a tendency for uncontrollable noise to produce greater stress reactions than controllable noise. In point of fact, however, the task results from our uncontrollable-noise research look very much like those reported for the unpredictable-noise experiments. Performance of simple mental tasks such as Number Comparison are just not affected by

TABLE 3.12

*Average Number of Errors on Part 1 of
the Number Comparison and Addition Tests*

	Experimental condition			
	Perceived control		No perceived control	
	NC	A	NC	A
First experiment	4.44	5.84	3.33	7.24
Replication	1.87	6.20	2.42	8.83

high-intensity noise, whether perceived as controllable or uncontrollable. We need not present all of these data, but an illustrative table or two might be appropriate. The Perceived Control columns in Tables 3.10 and 3.11 showed some of these results, and Tables 3.12 and 3.13 provide additional data. The noise consisted of the usual 108-dBA randomly intermittent bursts. It is immediately apparent from Tables 3.10 and 3.12 that there is a general tendency for fewer errors to occur in perceived-control conditions, but the differences are not statistically significant in any of the three studies. Perception of control over noise offset does not reduce Number Comparison and Addition errors during the first part of the noise session. Examination of Tables 3.11 and 3.13 reveals the expected reduction in mean number of errors over the course of noise exposure, although most of the change scores were not reliably different from zero. Exceptions were the Addition mean (+ 2.77) in Table 3.11, which reflects a significant *increment* in errors in the No Perceived Control condition (i.e., Loud Unpredictable), and the Number Comparison mean (− .87) in the replication in Table 3.13, which reflects a significant decline in errors in the Perceived Control condition.

These results are essentially the same as those obtained by comparing unpredictable and predictable noise (see Tables 3.10 and 3.11). Cognitive factors

TABLE 3.13

*Average Decrement in Errors on the
Number Comparison and Addition Tests*

	Experimental condition			
	Perceived control		No perceived control	
	NC	A	NC	A
First experiment	−2.22	−1.27	−.44	−2.99
Replication	− .87	−2.87	−.42	−3.17

TABLE 3.14

*Average Changes in Tracking
Errors on the Pursuit Rotor*

	Uncontrollable noise conditions			Controllable noise conditions	
	1	2	3	1	2
Changes in errors from 1st to 2nd 12.5 minutes	+ 4.42[a, b]	+ 1.69	+ 1.99	− 4.10	− 3.57

[a] A plus sign means an increment in errors; a minus sign a decrement in errors.
[b] $F = 2.05, 4/37\ df, p < .10$.

such as aperiodicity of stimulation and perceived lack of control do not produce failures of performance on simple tasks. We did demonstrate, however, that unpredictable noise impairs performance of complex tasks, and while we do not have data to show a comparable effect for uncontrollable versus controllable noise, we do have evidence that perceived lack of control interacts with another kind of complexity to reduce quality of performance. The task of interest is a pursuit rotor (revolving at 68 rpm) used in one of the experiments reported in Chapter 5. Accuracy of tracking performance deteriorated over the course of the noise session in uncontrollable–unpredictable noise treatments, whereas improvement occurred in controllable treatments. Table 3.14 presents average changes in tracking errors from the first 12.5 minutes to the second 12.5 minutes of the total testing session.[9] The increment in errors in the uncontrollable conditions, like subsidiary task performance, probably reflects the interaction of cognitive overload with unpredictable and uncontrollable stress. It was noted earlier that such overload also occurs on tasks of vigilance, and while difficulty with the pursuit rotor is caused simply by failure to maintain a repetitive series of hand motions, it does demand considerable attention for accurate tracking. It seems reasonable to expect, therefore, that when a task requires more than routinized execution of simple operations, performance deterioration will appear during exposure to uncontrollable noise. Mere physical intensity of noise is not sufficient to produce these effects. Previous research has already shown that even long-term exposure to high-intensity sound does not impair pursuit rotor performance (Kryter, 1950).

[9] Apparatus failure reduced the usable number of cases from 10 to 8 in the second uncontrollable noise condition and in the two controllable noise conditions. Similar apparatus difficulties forced us to eliminate one of the 10 cases from the first uncontrollable noise treatment. The third uncontrollable noise condition had 10 cases.

Summary

At this point, it would be perfectly understandable if the reader were puzzled. The intent of the monograph is to document the effects of stressors such as noise, yet this chapter has gone to great pains and some length to document the following conclusions.

1. In most cases, noise does not affect task performance or psychophysiological reaction.

2. Even when the noise is made especially aversive by presenting it unpredictably or in circumstances where the subject has no control over it, the noise does not prevent either behavioral or autonomic adaptation.

3. The only occasions when noise produces task decrements are those in which the individual is working on a highly complex task or is engaged in a vigilance-type task; even then, only unpredictable or uncontrollable noise will disrupt performance.

It would be all too easy at this point to assume that aversive effects of noise are overrated and that it is, at best, only a second-class stressor. But granting that the individual adapts to aversive sound, and task degradations appear only under special conditions of cognitive overload, one may still ask to what extent exposure to unpredictable and uncontrollable noise produces aftereffects detectable in behavior? As we have already noted, deleterious effects of noise appeared in our studies after termination of the stressor when adaptive coping was, presumably, no longer required. And the magnitude of these aftereffects varied with the assumed greater aversiveness of unpredictable and/or uncontrollable noise. The following chapters present a series of experiments from which these generalizations are derived. The results show that noise can indeed be a stressor with demonstrable effects on behavior, but detection of these effects requires that we look at postnoise and postadaptation behavior. We pay a price for the noise that surrounds us, though it may not be immediately evident during the aversive stimulation.

Behavioral Aftereffects
of Unpredictable Noise

It has long been acknowledged that the same physical stressor produces different effects depending on whether its occurrence is or is not anticipated. Unsignaled electric shocks are more stressful than signaled shocks, as indicated by higher levels of autonomic arousal, subjective reports of painfulness, and preference for signaled over unsignaled stimulation (D'Amato & Gumenik, 1960; Pervin, 1963; Lanzetta & Driscoll, 1966; Weiss, 1970). In a nonlaboratory context, Janis (1958) has demonstrated that the expectation of postoperative pain among surgical patients lowered their level of postoperative anxiety, whereas those who did not expect pain suffered greater anxiety. In the second chapter, we reviewed evidence showing that high-intensity aperiodic noise produces effects similar to those resulting from unsignaled aversive stimulation. For example, subjective reports of annoyance are greater where noise is intermittent and irregular rather than steady (Broadbent, 1957; Kryter, 1970), and aperiodic noise affects task performance more than does steady noise (Smith, 1951; Sanders, 1961). Our own research has not provided unequivocal support for these generalizations. Data reported in Chapter 3 showed that, in contrast to predictable noise, unpredictable noise had more deleterious effects on human task performance only under certain conditions. If the task involved relatively simple mental operations, there was no difference in performance quality under the two types of noise. On the other hand, if the task was complex and overloaded the organism, performance failures were greater with unpredictable than predictable noise. Failure to find differences in performance of simple tasks does not rule out the possibility that other types of differences may exist that are directly attributable to noise scheduling.

If an individual, engaged in some mental task, is confronted by randomly occurring noise bursts, he may adapt to these sounds by, for example, learning to ignore them or in some other way maintaining his level of performance in spite of the noise. However, this adaptation does not mean the sounds have become acceptable or even nondisturbing. Prior research has, after all, shown that loud intermittent noise can be more arousing than equally loud predictable noise. Adaptation unquestionably occurs in both instances, but it is conceivable that negative effects of unpredictable noise do not become evident until after sound has terminated. The individual manages to contain his affective reactions to noise until it is no longer necessary to maintain effective performance levels. At this point, where coping and defensive tactics cease to be necessary because noise is terminated, the effects of differential stress arousal become apparent. We do not prejudge whether these effects are the result of stress exposure in spite of noise adaptation, or whether they may be attributed to the effort entailed in the adaptive process itself. We defer this consideration to Chapter 9. In either event, we do suggest that the end result of exposure to unpredictable noise is aftereffects that are more deleterious than those resulting from exposure to predictable noise. More specifically, we expect a greater decrement in the individual's tolerance for postnoise frustrations and a greater deterioration of his subsequent performance on tasks requiring care and attention. We have restricted our investigations to aftereffects occurring within about an hour following noise cessation. In order to test the predictions, the next experiment was conducted (see Glass, Singer, & Friedman, Experiment I, 1969).

Aftereffects of Periodic and Aperiodic Noise

Design

The effects of two stimulus factors were examined simultaneously in this study: the intensity of the noise and the aperiodicity of its occurrence. The noise itself consisted of the specially prepared tape recording described in the previous chapter. Both the fixed-intermittent (predictable) and the random-intermittent (unpredictable) tapes were used, each consisting of 23 bursts played at 108 dBA or 56 dBA. The resulting design consisted of these treatments: (a) Loud Unpredictable, (b) Loud Predictable, (c) Soft Unpredictable, and (d) Soft Predictable. Subjects were randomly assigned to one of these conditions, or to a No Noise Control group.

Procedure

Subjects were tested individually. After being seated in the experimental chamber, the experimenter said,[1] "The purpose of today's experiment is to study the effects of different noise levels on your performance of some simple verbal and numerical tasks. While you are working, you will hear loud noises over that speaker from time to time. We are interested in how this noise affects the quality and speed of your work. In addition to our interest in noise and performance, we will be looking at your physiological responses as you work on the tasks. In order to measure these responses, we monitor your skin conductance with leads which are connected to electronic recording equipment in the next room. Incidentally, there is no danger at all in this procedure; you won't feel a thing—no shock or anything like that." (At this point, the electrodes are attached.) "Now, please relax for a few minutes in order to give the jelly a chance to make good contact with your skin."

In the No Noise Control condition, the foregoing instructions were modified to read: "The purpose of today's experiment is to study physiological correlates of your performance of some simple verbal and numerical tasks. While you are working, we will monitor your physiological responses with these leads." From this point, the instructions were about the same as in the noise conditions.

Following attachment of the electrodes, the experimenter left the chamber for a 15-minute hydration period. When he returned, he instructed the subject

[1] Actual phraseology varied somewhat from study to study, but the basic instructions in all of our research are as described here.

on how to do the tasks to be worked on during the noise. In the present experiment, these consisted of the three standardized tests of cognitive performance described in Chapter 3; that is, Number Comparison, Addition, and Finding A's. Following these instructions, the experimenter left the chamber and the noise session commenced.[2]

After the last noise burst, the experimenter returned and introduced the postnoise tasks by saying: "O.K. We are finished with the first part of the study—no more noise. However, there are several additional tasks I would like you to work on." At this point, the subject was told about the postnoise measures (described in the next section). Following completion of these tasks, the subject responded to a short questionnaire asking for his reactions to the noise. The final step in the procedure consisted of an interview and debriefing.

Tolerance for frustration. The postnoise task measuring frustration tolerance was adapted from one used by Feather (1961), and consisted of four line diagrams printed on 5 X 7-inch cards arranged in four piles in front of the subject (see Figure 4.1). Each pile was about 1 inch high and contained only one kind of puzzle. Cards were face down, so a subject was unable to see the puzzle until he began work on that particular pile of cards. The task was to trace over all of the lines of a diagram without tracing any line twice and without lifting the pencil from the figure. He was informed that he could take as many trials at a given item as he wished. However, he was also told that there was a time limit on how long he could work on a given trial, and the experimenter would inform him when his time was up over a loudspeaker. It was emphasized that such notification did not mean he had to go on to the next pile. That was his decision. It simply meant that he must decide whether to take another card from the same pile or move on to the next item. If the subject wanted another trial, he discarded his unsuccessful card into a bin and took another copy of the same item. If he went on to the next pile, however, he could not go back to the previously unsolved item. The subject immediately went on to the next pile following a successful solution.

Two of the line diagrams were mathematically insoluble but sufficiently complex so that subjects were unable to see this. (Postexperimental interviews revealed that most subjects believed the insoluble puzzles were potentially soluble.) The puzzles were arranged in front of the subject so that the first pile always consisted of the same insoluble puzzle, the second the same soluble puzzle, the third the same insoluble puzzle, and the fourth the same soluble

---

[2] We described the measurement of physiological adaptation and the effects of noise on task performance in the preceding chapter. We will not repeat any part of that presentation here, but remember that those data were collected in studies being discussed in this and the succeeding chapter.

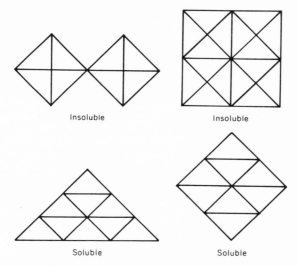

Insoluble   Insoluble

Soluble   Soluble

Figure 4.1 *Insoluble and soluble puzzles.*

puzzle (see Figure 4.1). The items were done in prescribed order from the subject's left to his right.

Insoluble puzzles were presumed to lead to failure and frustration. Indeed, we repeatedly observed outward signs of exasperation as subjects attempted over and over again to solve the insoluble. While this was going on in the experimental chamber, the experimenter was in the control room observing and recording the number of trials taken by a subject on each of the four puzzles. These data provided us with a measure of his persistence on the insoluble puzzles; namely, the fewer the number of trials, the less the persistence and, by interpretation, the lower the subject's tolerance for an inherently frustrating task.

Quality of performance. Subjects were given a proofreading task immediately following completion of the graphic puzzles. They were asked to correct errors in a passage seven pages in length taken from *The Death and Life of Great American Cities* by Jane Jacobs (1961).[3] They were told that each page should be read carefully, the errors detected and underlined, but not actually corrected, and check marks placed in the margin at the level of the errors. The errors had been deliberately introduced by the typist and consisted of misspellings, grammatical mistakes, incorrect punctuation, transpositions, and typographical

[3] The actual passage with the uncorrected errors has been deposited with the National Auxiliary Publications Service. Order Document No. NAPS-01418 from CCM Information Corporation, NAPS, 866 Third Avenue, New York, New York 10022. Remit in advance $5.00 for photocopies or $2.00 for microfilm and make checks payable to CCMI-NAPS.

errors. Each subject was given 15 minutes on this task (although nothing was actually said about time), and the final instruction stated: "Please work as quickly and as accurately as possible. I will let you know when to stop." Quality of performance was measured as a percentage of "errors not found" of the total number of errors that could have been detected at the point the subject was told to stop work (i.e., after 15 minutes).

Subjects

Subjects were 48 undergraduate women recuited from Hunter College, who were paid $3.50 each for their 2 hours of participation. They ranged in age from 17 to 24, and all grew up in New York City or its immediate environs. Fifty-six subjects were actually used in the experiment, but eight cases had to be eliminated for the following reasons: (a) two because of failure of the apparatus used to deliver the noise; (b) two because of failure of the physiological recording apparatus; (c) three because they failed to show evidence of adaptation to the noise; and (d) one because she misunderstood the directions for doing the frustration-tolerance task. Inclusion of these subjects would not have substantially changed the results.[4]

Replications

It seemed desirable to replicate significant aspects of the study with different experimenters and different samples of subjects. Accordingly, we conducted two additional studies using only the Loud Unpredictable, Loud Predictable, and No Noise Control conditions from the original design. All other features of experimental procedure and measurement were identical, except 24 bursts of noise were used instead of 23 in the first replication. Twenty-eight paid college women constituted the sample in this study.[5] The second replication (Reim, Glass, & Singer, 1971) used 32 women and 8 men between the ages of 34 and 65. All of these people lived in New York City for at least 20 years and had grown up in an urban or nearby suburban setting. The noise stimuli in this study were increased from 24 to 25 bursts. Postnoise effects observed in all three experiments are presented in the next section. They are identified as Original Study, Replication 1, and Replication 2.

[4] Elimination of the three cases that did not adapt was justified on the grounds that virtually all subjects used in experiments conducted in our laboratories adapted to the noise. That a very small percentage, less than 1%, did not adapt suggests that this group may be different in a variety of unknown ways from the bulk of cases sampled in our research.

[5] Thirty-five cases were actually used, but 7 had to be eliminated because (a) 2 began to cry after the first few noise bursts; (b) 1 removed the skin electrodes and left the experimental chamber; (c) 2 produced unreadable GSR records; and (d) 2 misunderstood the instructions for doing the insoluble puzzles.

Results

As described earlier, subjects completed a series of graphic puzzles following termination of the noise. Two of these puzzles were insoluble, and persistence (i.e., total number of trials taken) in trying to solve them was used as a measure of tolerance for frustration. Tables 4.1 and 4.2 show the average number of trials on these puzzles.[6] A 2 × 2 analysis of variance of data in the first row of Table 4.1 showed a significant main effect due to fixed versus random scheduling of the noise ($F = 25.64$, $1/34 df$, $p < .01$). Subsequent individual comparisons revealed that Loud Unpredictable was significantly different from Soft Unpredictable at the .08 level, and from Loud Predictable and Soft Predictable at the .01 level. Soft Unpredictable was also significantly different from Loud Predictable and Soft Predictable at the .02 level. Dunnett's *t* statistic (Winer, 1962) was used to compare each experimental mean with the mean for the No Noise Control group. The results indicated that Loud Unpredictable was reliably different from the Control ($p < .01$), and Soft Unpredictable showed a comparable trend at the .08 level. The Loud Predictable and Soft Predictable means did not differ from the Control group. Analysis of comparable results in the first row of Table 4.2 (Replication 1) revealed that the Loud Unpredictable condition differed from Loud Predictable and the Control at less than the .05 level, whereas the latter two conditions were virtually identical in amount of persistence on the first insoluble puzzle. Thus, postnoise frustration tolerance is less dependent on the physical intensity of noise than on its aperiodicity, although loudness certainly exerted an effect.

The results for the second insoluble puzzle in both tables support this conclusion. In Table 4.1, the main effect for random versus fixed noise was significant at beyond the .01 level ($F = 25.69$, $1/34 df$). Individual comparisons showed that Loud Unpredictable was significantly different from Soft Unpre-

TABLE 4.1

Average Number of Trials on the First and Second Insoluble Puzzles
(Original Study)

Puzzle	Experimental condition				
	Loud unpredictable[a]	Soft unpredictable[b]	Loud predictable[a]	Soft predictable[b]	No noise control[b]
1st insoluble	3.67	9.60	18.55	19.90	16.90
2nd insoluble	6.33	12.00	26.78	25.80	24.30

[a] $n = 9$.

[b] $n = 10$.

[6] The puzzles task was not included in the second replication.

TABLE 4.2

Average Number of Trials on the First and Second Insoluble Puzzles (Replication 1)

| | Experimental condition | | |
Puzzle	Loud unpredictable[a]	Loud predictable[b]	No noise control[a]
1st insoluble	8.56	22.20	19.00
2nd insoluble	11.33	26.50	19.67

[a] $n = 9$.

[b] $n = 10$.

dictable, Soft Predictable, and Loud Predictable at less than the .01 level. Soft Unpredictable was also reliably different from Loud Predictable and Soft Predictable ($p < .02$), whereas comparisons of the Control group with Loud Predictable and Soft Predictable did not reach statistical significance. In Table 4.2, we also see that Loud Unpredictable is reliably different from Loud Predictable and the No Noise Control ($p = .08$), whereas the latter two conditions do not differ from each other.

We must be cautious in interpreting the results for the second insoluble puzzle. There is always the possibility that these data were contaminated by sequence effects; that is, subjects worked on the second insoluble task only after successfully solving the first *soluble* puzzle. In this connection, it should be noted that almost every subject in both studies solved the soluble puzzles, and there were no significant between-conditions differences. In the original study, for example, the average number of trials to solution for the first soluble puzzle was 1.89 in Loud Unpredictable, 2.30 in Soft Unpredictable, 3.11 in Loud Predictable, 1.40 in Soft Predictable, and 1.90 in the Control condition. For the second soluble puzzle, the respective means were 3.44, 3.70, 2.89, 3.40, and 2.88.

Quality of performance. It was also predicted that noise exposure would impair quality of subsequent task performance, and the specially prepared proofreading task was used to test this prediction. In all three studies, there were no significant between-conditions differences in the number of lines read by the subjects ($Fs < 1$), but Table 4.3 reveals sizable differences in mean percentage of errors missed in the completed part of the task. It is gratifying to note the similarity in parametric values (within the limits of error variance) in the three experiments. Analysis of the first column of data yielded a significant effect due to random versus fixed noise scheduling ($F = 7.05$, $1/34\ df$, $p < .05$). Subsequent comparisons showed that Loud Unpredictable was reliably greater than Soft Predictable ($p < .02$), but only marginally greater than Loud Predictable

TABLE 4.3

Mean Percentage of Errors Missed in the Proofreading Task

Experimental condition	Original study	Replication 1	Replication 2 [a]
Loud unpredictable	40.11	41.82	48.35
Loud unpredictable– Loud unpredictable– perceived control [b]	–[c]	–	32.09
Soft unpredictable	36.70	–	–
Loud predictable	31.78	29.24	30.79
Soft predictable	27.40	–	–
No noise control	26.40	29.60	27.37

[a] There are 10 cases in each condition in this study.

[b] The significance of this condition is discussed in Chapter 5.

[c] A dash indicates that the condition was not included in the study.

($ps < .10$). The comparison of Loud Unpredictable with the No Noise Control group was significant at the .02 level. Unlike the frustration-tolerance measure, the comparison between Loud Unpredictable and Soft Unpredictable failed to reach statistical significance, although Soft Unpredictable was different from both Soft Predictable ($p < .05$) and the No Noise Control ($p = .08$). Comparable analyses for each of the other columns in Table 4.3 showed that the primary source of the significant main effects was the difference between Loud Unpredictable and the remaining conditions ($ps < .05$). Again, this time for proofreading, noise intensity had less of an effect on postnoise performance than unpredictability.

Evaluation of the noise. The behavioral results stand in sharp contrast to the ratings made of the noise at the end of the three experiments. Subjects in noise conditions were asked to respond to the following items: (a) "The noise I heard while working on the verbal and numerical tasks was": 1 = "extremely relaxing" and 9 = "extremely irritating," and 1 = "extremely pleasant" and 9 = "extremely unpleasant"; (b) "To what extent was the noise you heard distracting?" where 1 = "the noise made it extremely easy to concentrate" and 9 = "the noise made it extremely difficult to concentrate." Table 4.4 presents the mean ratings to these items for the original study. Analysis of the results showed uniformly significant main effects due to the energy level of the noise ($ps < .05$). There were no reliable differences between similar ratings made in the first replication, and the second replication included only one of the three items (i.e., distraction); it too failed to show experimental effects.

TABLE 4.4

Mean Ratings of the Noise
(Original Study)

	Experimental condition			
Item	Loud unpre-dictable	Soft unpre-dictable	Loud pre-dictable	Soft pre-dictable
Irritating	8.11 [a]	5.85	8.00	5.60
Distracting	6.67	5.20	7.00	6.20
Unpleasant	8.11	5.40	7.89	5.70

[a] A high score means the noise was rated as more aversive.

It would appear that subjective ratings of noise correlated more strongly with its intensity than with its predictability or unpredictability. This result is not only inconsistent with the behavioral effects reported above, but also with prior experiments showing that aperiodic noise can be more annoying than equally loud periodic noise. It is difficult to account for this discrepancy, but it may simply reflect a culturally based belief that one complains about loud noise and not about soft noise, irrespective of its randomness. This belief was un-doubtedly reinforced by the fact that all subjects knew we were studying the effects of noise levels on performance.

Summary and Discussion

Taken together, the results of these experiments demonstrate substantial impairments of task performance and decrements in frustration tolerance immediately following termination of noise. However, physical intensity was not a sufficient condition for these negative aftereffects, for performance showed greater deficits following exposure to soft aperiodic noise than loud periodic noise. It appears that postnoise behavior is influenced by cognitive features of the stimulus situation much as performance occurring during noise was affected by similar contextual variables (see Chapter 3). The difference between the two sets of findings is that unpredictable noise exerts its more aversive impact on postnoise behavior presumably in the absence of task overload, whereas the latter condition was essential for the occurrence of task degradations during exposure to noise. In other words, we obtained a predictable–unpredictable difference on postnoise performance even though the tasks subjects worked on during and after noise exposure were relatively simple.

The results of the second replication require special comment. They also show that adverse aftereffects appear only where the noise has been unpredictable. However, the effects appeared to be more severe among these older urban subjects; that is, the differences in proofreading scores between Loud Predictable and Loud Unpredictable conditions were greater in this study than in the first two experiments (see Table 4.3). It is difficult to evaluate this finding since the younger subjects worked on the frustration-tolerance measure before proofreading, and the negative effects of aperiodic noise could have been dissipated by this previous test. Even if we conclude that there are no major differences between younger and older subjects, this does not necessarily mean there is a corresponding absence of differential tolerance for noise. Noise tolerance may develop during an early "critical period" following chronic exposure to acoustic stimulation. Since both types of subjects lived in an urban (or at least suburban) setting during childhood, there may be no reason to expect differences in their ability to tolerate noise. We do not have evidence for a critical period in the development of noise tolerance, but its existence is certainly a possibility.

The term unpredictability, as we noted before, refers to both aperiodicity of stimulation and the extent to which the occurrence of stimuli is signaled. Indeed, the latter definition has been more frequently used in classical autonomic conditioning experiments, such as some of those cited at the beginning of this chapter. We also conducted a study of signaled and unsignaled noise to see if postnoise behavior is affected in the same way as was observed following exposure to aperiodic and periodic noise. Physiological and task performance data from this study were described in Chapter 3. We now turn to a presentation of the aftereffect results.

Aftereffects of Signaled and Unsignaled Noise

Design and Procedure

There were three conditions in this experiment:[7] (a) Signal Light, in which a light bulb mounted in front of the subject was automatically activated 3 seconds before each of 24 aperiodic noise bursts; (b) Uncorrelated Light, in which 24 light flashes were randomly interspersed among the 24 noise bursts, with at least 15 seconds of separation from a noise burst; and (c) No Light, in which the noise was delivered over the speaker without signal lights. Noise intensity was identical at 108 dBA in all three condtions, and the duration of each light flash was about 3 seconds. Subjects were 42 female college students who received $4.00 for their participation in the experiment. They were randomly assigned to one of the three treatments.

[7] Conducted by Halleck Cummings and T. Edward Hannah at the State University of New York at Stony Brook.

Subjects in the Signal Light treatment were told that "the lights will come on just before the sounds . . . serving as a signal . . .," whereas nothing was said about the significance of the light in the Uncorrelated Light treatment. In most other respects, the experimental instructions were similar to those used in the aperiodic-noise experiments. However, a different task was used during noise exposure, namely, the matching task described in Chapter 3. This task, it will be recalled, required the subject to press two buttons on the side of her chair in an effort to reproduce patterns of dots and dashes being projected on a screen in front of her. Adaptation was measured by decrements in phasic skin conductance and by changes in muscular contractions in the neck. These data were also described in the preceding chapter. Postnoise measures were frustration tolerance and proofreading. Administration of the proofreading task was the same as in the other studies, but the puzzles were given to the subject with an experimenter in the room throughout the task.

Results

The results for the insoluble puzzles show again that individuals are less able to tolerate frustration following exposure to unpredictable noise than to predictable noise. Table 4.5 presents the means for each insoluble puzzle. Both rows of data were statistically significant at the .05 level or beyond ($F = 4.17$, $2/38\ df$; $F = 7.23$, $2/39\ df$).

Unlike previous experiments, the predictability of the noise bursts made little difference in proofreading accuracy ($F < 1$). The parametric values for Uncorrelated Light and No Light conditions, shown in Table 4.6, are similar to the Loud Unpredictable error scores reported in Table 4.3. However, the use of signaled noise did not result in the significant reduction of errors that was observed in the periodic-noise studies, though the smaller percentage of errors in the Signal Light condition was in the predicted direction.

TABLE 4.5

Average Number of Trials on the First and Second Insoluble Puzzles

Puzzle	Signal light	Uncorrelated light	No light
1st insoluble[a]	12.08	5.85	4.00
2nd insoluble[b]	11.00	6.15	5.53

[a]One extreme case was eliminated from each condition.
[b]One extreme case was eliminated from the Uncorrelated Light and No Light conditions.

TABLE 4.6

*Mean Percentage of Errors Missed in
the Proofreading Task*

Signal light	Uncorrelated light	No light
39.08	40.08	42.53

Postexperimental Ratings

A postexperimental questionnaire asked all subjects to evaluate the aversiveness of the noise and the tasks on which they had worked. There were no differences between experimental conditions on any of the items. Indeed, the only item in the questionnaire to show an effect was designed to check on the subject's perception of the significance of the signal light. It asked, "In predicting when the noise was going to come on, the signal was" where 0 = "Not at all consistent" and 8 = "Very consistent." The mean rating for the Signal Light condition was 5.64 and for the Uncorrelated Light condition 2.43 ($F = 14.12$, $1/26\ df$, $p < .01$).[8]

Summary and Discussion

The main finding of this study is that frustration tolerance is significantly lower following unsignaled noise than signaled noise. Proofreading performance did not show a comparable effect, although the treatment means corresponded closely to those obtained in other studies. One result of the aperiodic noise experiments is thus replicated and another is not. However, in view of the overall consistency of results reported in this chapter, we are relatively confident in concluding that exposure to unpredictable noise, whether defined in terms of aperiodicity or unsignaled stimulation, produces more adverse aftereffects in behavior than exposure to predictable noise.

Just why proofreading errors were not reduced by signaled noise stimulation is unclear. It is, of course, true that the aperiodic- and unsignaled-noise studies differed in a number of ways, but there is no particular reason to expect that relatively minor procedural differences would produce a null effect on the proofreading task. The only major difference was the way in which predict-

[8] We also tried to assess differential perceptions of aperiodic and periodic noise, but found it extremely difficult to phrase the rating scales properly. Our general impression was that subjects could not report whether noise bursts had occurred in a fixed or random sequence. They tended to rate the noise schedule as falling somewhere between these extremes. An exception occurred in one of the experiments reported in Chapter 9, where subjects rated aperiodic noise as significantly more "irregular" than periodic noise.

ability was manipulated, and this difference in no way alters theoretical expectations regarding the effects of noise adaptation on quality of postnoise performance.

One possible explanation for the discrepancy in results is that the particular signal-light manipulation was not an effective way of varying predictability. Perhaps the 3-second interval between light and noise was either too short or too long. It is interesting to note, in this connection, that neither muscle tension nor GSR habituated to the light flashes. Indeed, skin conductance responses to the light in the Signal Light condition increased over time. This trend may reflect nothing more than a classical conditioning effect, but it might also be interpreted as evidence that light adaptation was inhibited while noise adaptation was achieved. Since the light stimulus was relatively neutral, it cannot be argued that this failure to adapt increased overall psychological tension. On the other hand, subjects had to attend to the light flashes in the Signal Light condition since they signaled onset of the distracting noise. Having to attend to the lights could itself have interfered with task performance, and the resultant frustration might have impaired subsequent work on the proofreading task. Just why a similar effect did not occur on the puzzles task is unclear, unless frustration interacts differently with the two measures. For example, it may facilitate persistence on insoluble puzzles but interfere with the care and attention needed for successful proofreading (cf. Amsel, 1958).

Still another explanation is that there may be severe limitations on the ameliorative influence of being able to anticipate an aversive stimulus. Recent experiments by Furedy and Doob (1971) suggest that, contrary to previous evidence, signaling electric shocks does not always reduce rated aversiveness of and increase preference for the shocks. If these investigators are correct about the limited generalizability of signaled-shock effects, there may be every reason to expect similar limitations on poststressor effects. Again, of course, we cannot explain why signaling exerted a positive influence on frustration tolerance and not on proofreading. In short, each of the explanations offered here has a certain cogency, but for the moment we are really left without a compelling explanation for the anomalous proofreading result.

Conclusions

We have seen that exposure to unpredictable noise is associated with behavioral deficits after noise termination. The case for the existence of this phenomenon is strengthened by the range of conditions over which postnoise deficits occurred, including different: (a) ways of manipulating unpredictability; (b) levels of physical noise intensity; (c) subject populations; (d) laboratory settings (i.e., New York University, Rockefeller University, State University of

New York at Stony Brook). The studies establishing aftereffect phenomena do not, however, provide a precise theoretical understanding of why they occur. It is not enough to assume, as we have, that unpredictable noise is more aversive than equally intense predictable noise. For we still need to specify why it is more aversive and why the negative effects appear only after noise termination. A possible answer to the first question is based on the notion that exposure to unpredictable stressors induces feelings in the individual that he cannot control his environment—or at least certain stressful aspects of it. Under these conditions, we might well expect lowered frustration tolerance and impaired proof-reading accuracy. The individual has experienced not only the aversiveness of the noise, but also the anxiety of being unable to do anything about it. On the other hand, providing him with information about when to expect the noise affords a measure of cognitive control over the situation that reduces the adverse effects of unpredictability. The validity of this general line of reasoning was tested in a series of experiments described in the next chapter.

Perceived Control and Behavioral
Aftereffects of Unpredictable Noise

Effects of Perceived Control

The behavioral aftereffects of predictable and unpredictable noise were interpreted in terms of the notion of *informational control* (cf. Furedy & Doob, 1971), that is knowing when to expect sound was assumed to provide a measure of cognitive control over stimulation that reduced its adverse effects. Prediction reduced aftereffects because it functioned as a means of control, and as we noted in a previous chapter, an aversive event appears to be less painful if an organism can terminate or avoid it than if he has no control over it. A more direct way of testing this explanation is to induce control by providing individuals with actual means of escape or avoidance, for example, a button that terminates or prevents the noise. One early study demonstrated this effect by showing that the eating behavior of rats trained to turn off electric shock was less inhibited than the eating behavior of no-control rats receiving the same amount and duration of shock (Mowrer & Viek, 1948). Another study (Haggard, 1946) measured phasic skin resistance responses (GSR) to intense electric shock in a sample of 18 college men. Subjects who administered the shocks to themselves, upon being signaled to do so, showed weaker GSR deflections than subjects who had the shocks administered by the experimenter.

These results have been replicated using self-reports of preference for controlled versus uncontrolled shocks as the principal dependent measure (Pervin, 1963). Subjects could determine who administered electric shocks on particular trials by pressing one of two levers. Depression of one lever meant direct delivery of shock; depression of the other lever signaled the experimenter to administer the shock. The results showed that subjects preferred the situation in which they had direct control of shock administration. They also reported somewhat less anxiety when they delivered the shocks themselves than when the experimenter had control. More recently, LePanto, Moroney, and Zenhausern (1965) showed that a preference for control over stimulus onset is reflected in an actual reduction of pain sensitivity. The mean pain threshold for radiant heat was lower when the experimenter had control of the pain source than when the subject was in control.

In each of these studies, except the Mowrer–Viek experiment, subjects could in no way avoid or escape shock, nor could they reduce its intensity. All they were able to do was control the agent of punishment. Two other experiments with humans have shown that the exercise of and/or perception of escape also reduces aversiveness of shock. Champion (1950) found that GSR recovery responses were greater among subjects who believed that clenching their hand would terminate shock than among subjects who were uninformed of such a contingency. More recently, Corah and Boffa (1970) have shown that providing subjects with a button that terminates aversive sound leads to reductions in GSR amplitude and ratings of discomfort. They also found that giving subjects a choice about escape, even on no-escape trials, produced a decrement on both dependent measures. (Only two subjects actually exercised the option, and they were eliminated from analysis.) In other words, the mere perception of escape operated "to reduce the aversive quality of the stimulus and the resultant physiological arousal" (p. 4).

Further support for this conclusion comes from a study by Stotland and Blumenthal (1964). Subjects were told they would have to work on an I.Q. test consisting of several subtests. One group was told they could take the subtests in any order they wished, whereas the second group was told that they must take the tests in a prescribed sequence for "administrative reasons." Subjects with no choice over the order of the subtests increased in palmar sweating during this instruction period, whereas those who were given a choice did not appreciably change from the preinstruction period. It would appear that the cognition, "If I choose to order the tests, I have control over my environment," is sufficient to reduce the impact of a threatening event, even though there is no immediate confirmation of the belief. Recall, also, that our own research produced data indicating somewhat lower magnitudes of GSR and vasoconstriction in conditions where subjects perceived control over noise (see Chapter 3).

The preceding research demonstrates that if an organism controls the onset and/or offset of stressful stimuli, or if he simply expects to have such control, behavioral and autonomic indices of stress are reduced. In three experiments (Mowrer & Viek, 1948; Corah & Boffa, 1970; and Champion, 1950) an instrumental response (e.g., lever or button pressing) permitted escape from the stressor; in other studies (Haggard, 1946; Pervin, 1963; and LePanto et al., 1965) the stressor was inevitable, but the subject could determine some aspect of its occurrence, such as who would be directly responsible for onset; and in still other studies (Corah & Boffa, 1970, and Stotland & Blumenthal, 1964), there was only the perception of potential control over the stimulus. There are at least two other types of control requiring comment: (a) situations in which an instrumental response permits temporary avoidance or reduction of the aversive event; (b) situations in which there is a nonveridical perception of this effective control. Behavioral and physiological effects of these manipulations have received empirical documentation (e.g., Azrin, 1958; Seligman, Maier, & Solomon, 1971; Geer, Davison, & Gatchel, 1970). The results indicate that when nonoccurrence of a stressor is made contingent on the subject's response (e.g., pressing a lever or performing a task correctly), indices of stress arousal decrease. Moreover, the ameliorative effects extend to the case where the subject simply believes he has control over the stressor, even though there is no actual contingency between response and stimulation.

The foregoing set of results suggests that the aversive impact of an unpredictable stressor is partly attributable to the individual's inability to control the stressor, or even to perceive the possibility of escape or avoidance. Providing him with knowledge of when to expect the stressor affords a measure of control over the situation, though we do not propose that predictability is exactly the same as controllability. An individual can obviously have little control over the occurrence of a predictable stressor (e.g., the imminence of a hurricane), but this lack of control will result in weaker stress reactions than where the stressor is unpredictable. Conversely, one can have a good deal of control over an unpredictable stressor (e.g., a flat tire), but there will be more stress than where the aversive event is also predictable. We propose, therefore, that the joint effect of uncontrollable and unpredictable aversive events will be greater than the effect of either variable alone. Evidence for this hypothesis was presented in Chapter 3. Autonomic reactivity (e.g., vasoconstriction) to unpredictable and uncontrollable noise tended to be higher than to controllable or predictable noise. In this chapter, we turn from physiological effects occurring during the noise trials to behavioral differences following exposure to noise. More specifically, we present a series of experiments designed to test the following general hypothesis. If perceived lack of control is indeed responsible for the postnoise effects obtained in previous experiments, subjects who believe they have control over noise offset, in contrast to those who do not, will show higher frustration tolerance and better proofreading performance. The principal thrust of the research, then, is to demonstrate reduced postnoise deficits where subjects perceive they have potential (although unexercised) control over termination of unpredictable noise.

Experimental Procedure

The procedure described here was adapted from Experiment II of Glass, Singer, and Friedman (1969). Two groups of subjects listened to the 23-burst random-intermittent noise tape played at 108 dBA. One group (referred to as Perceived Control) was given control over termination of the noise, whereas the other group (No Perceived Control) did not receive this option. Immediately following the usual introductory instructions, Perceived Control subjects were shown a microswitch attached to the side of their chair and told, "Now this button affects the noise you will be hearing while you work on the tasks. You can terminate the noise by pressing the button; that is, pressing the button will end the noise for the remainder of today's session. Of course, whether or not you press it is up to you. Some people who come here do in fact press the button; others do not. We'd prefer that you do not, but that's entirely up to you." The latter part of these instructions was designed to induce forces against pressing the switch, while giving subjects the feeling that they could press it, if they wished. We decided upon this strategy after several pilot sessions in which the button was presented without the experimenter indicating his own preference. Five out of seven pilot subjects pressed the switch after the third or fourth noise burst. In the actual experiment, which included the "choice-type" instructions (cf. Brehm & Cohen, 1962), none of the subjects used the switch, although four cases did exercise the option in a subsequent replication.

All other details of procedure and measurement in this study were virtually identical to those used in the unpredictable-noise experiments. Indeed, the No Perceived Control treatment was an exact duplication of the Loud Unpredictable treatment described in the previous chapter. Subjects were 18 paid undergraduate women ranging in age from 17 to 22.

The entire experiment was replicated by Patricia Mayhew (in preparation) with a sample of 28 paid undergraduate women[1] using 24 rather than 23 random-intermittent noise bursts. Data from both studies are presented below.[2]

Results

In order to determine whether or not we were successful in inducing feelings of control, all subjects were asked to respond to the following rating scale in a postexperimental questionnaire, "To what extent did you feel that you really could have had the noise stopped during today's session?" where 1 = "No control at all" and 9 = "Complete control." The mean for the Perceived Control condition was 7.44 and for No Perceived Control, 3.00 (t = 4.64, 16 df, $p < .002$). This induction of Perceived Control was successfully replicated in the second experiment. Perceived Control subjects rated their degree of felt control as 6.09, whereas No Perceived Control subjects gave a rating of only 2.67 (t = 3.61, 26 df, $p < .01$).

Table 5.1 presents the average number of trials taken by subjects in each condition on the first and second insoluble puzzles. These tasks, it will be recalled, were administered immediately after noise exposure and following adaptation to noise. In the first study, it is clear that for both puzzles, feelings of

TABLE 5.1

*Average Number of Trials on the First
and Second Insoluble Puzzles*

	Puzzle	
Experimental condition	1	2
Perceived control: First study	22.11^a	19.56^b
No perceived control: First study	4.44^a	6.44^b
Perceived control: Replication	19.94^c	18.56^d
No perceived control: Replication	7.92^c	16.75^d

$^a t$ = 4.14, 16 df, $p < .002$.
$^b t$ = 4.54, 16 df, $p < .002$.
$^c t$ = 2.05, 26 df, $p = .05$.
$^d t < 1$.

[1] Thiry-five cases were actually recruited for the study, but four pressed the micro-switch after the first few noise bursts, and three in the No Perceived Control condition began to cry or show other signs of distress, causing the experiment to be terminated.

[2] Data on physiological adaptation and task performance during noise were presented in Chapter 3 (see Tables 3.7, 3.9, 3.12, and 3.13).

control induced by the presence of the microswitch had ameliorative effects on tolerance for frustration. The same result occurred in the replication, at least as measured by the first insoluble puzzle. On the second puzzle, subjects persisted equally in Perceived Control and No Perceived Control conditions. We are unable to explain this result at the present time.

Data from the proofreading task were more compelling. The mean percentage of errors missed by subjects in the Perceived Control condition of the first study was 28.22, whereas the No Perceived Control subjects produced a mean percentage of 42.44 ($t = 3.65$, 16 df, $p < .01$). The comparable results for the replication were 32.88 in the Perceived Control condition and 43.21 in the No Perceived Control condition ($t = 2.08$, 24 df, $p < .08$).

In the postexperimental questionnaire, subjects also rated how distracting, irritating, and unpleasant they felt the noise to be. The 9-point scales were identical to those used in the first aperiodic-noise experiment presented in Chapter 4. Table 5.2 shows the mean ratings on each item for both experiments. In the first study, Perceived Control subjects rated the noise as significantly less aversive than No Perceived Control subjects on only one of these items (i.e., irritating), although a marginally significant tendency in the same direction occurred for the distraction ratings. In the replication, there were no significant between-conditions differences on any item, although a tendency did emerge for unpleasantness ratings.

TABLE 5.2

Mean Ratings of the Noise

| | First study | | Replication | |
| | Perceived control | No perceived control | Perceived control | No perceived control |
Item				
Irritating	7.22[a]	8.61[a]	7.33	7.79
Distracting	6.11[b]	7.28[b]	6.53	6.54
Unpleasant	7.67	8.22	7.30[c]	8.00[c]

[a] $t = 2.95$, 16 df, $p < .01$.
[b] $t = 1.93$, 16 df, $p < .10$.
[c] $t = 1.93$, 25 df, $p < .10$.

Discussion

These two experiments replicated the postnoise phenomena observed in the unpredictability studies, and also showed that they can be reduced if the subject believes he has potential control over the noise. Providing the individual with control, or at least the perception of potential escape, reduces negative aftereffects of exposure to noise. This finding is consistent with some of the effects of perceived control occurring during noise exposure. Recall that autonomic responses were generally lower, and pursuit-rotor performance superior, in the controllable conditions than in the uncontrollable conditions (see Chapter 3). We tentatively conclude, therefore, that perceived uncontrollability and its exacerbation of stress are the mechanisms mediating between unpredictable noise and decrements in frustration tolerance and quality of postnoise task performance.

The exclusive use of aperiodic noise was an unfortunate limitation of the foregoing experiments. It means that the only possible comparison was between two unpredictable conditions: one where subjects believed they controlled noise offset and the other where they did not have this perception. It would be nice to have a direct comparison between predictable noise and controllable, unpredictable noise. We could do this by contrasting results from studies in this section with results from Loud Predictable conditions in the experiments reported in Chapter 4. Statistical evaluation of such findings would yield only suggestive conclusions. A preferred strategy is to include all conditions to be compared in the same experimental design. The experiment using older subjects, also reported in Chapter 4, fulfills these requirements. Aside from replicating the effects of Perceived Control on proofreading (see Table 4.3, Replication 2), this study also showed that mean scores on this task were about the same in Loud Predictable, Loud Unpredictable–Perceived Control, and No Noise Control conditions. Perceived Control appears to reduce the aftereffects of unpredictable noise to a point where they resemble performance following predictable noise, or no noise at all. This is indeed a fascinating result, for it supports the notion that uncontrollability is intimately involved in the process by which unpredictability has its adverse consequences.

The results of the experiments reported in this section form a pattern consistent with expectations. But, in truth, this consistency is surrounded by ambiguity. Though we interpreted the results in terms of the ameliorative effects of perceived controllability, there are at least three plausible alternatives. The first suggests that Perceived Control effects might occur because subjects formed a more favorable impression of the experimenter. He did, after all, show concern for their welfare by providing them with a "safety button." If such a perception did in fact occur, subjects may have found the noise more tolerable, and hence negative aftereffects were reduced. Alternatively, positive impressions of the experimenter may have motivated subjects to please him by trying to do their best on postnoise tasks. In either case, we would expect subjects to indicate greater liking for the experimenter in the Perceived Control condition than in the No Perceived Control condition. We did not check on this possibility in the experiments reported above, but fortunately, we did obtain "liking" ratings from subjects in a subsequent controllability study (i.e., the "relative deprivation" experiment described later in this chapter). At the end of the experiment, subjects were asked to complete an "anonymous" questionnaire for the psychology department, presumably for purposes of evaluating all research projects being conducted by members of the department. Included in the questionnaire was the key item: "In general, would you say you liked today's experimenter?" where 1 = "Very much" and 61 = "Not at all." The mean rating for Perceived Control conditions was 25.30, while the mean for No Perceived Control conditions was 34.93. The difference was not statistically significant ($t = 1.83$, 48 df). Subjects liked the experimenter to about the same extent, irrespective of whether he provided them with the escape button.

Two other explanations for the controllability effects are the theory of cognitive dissonance (Festinger, 1957; Brehm & Cohen, 1962), and Bem's "radical behaviorism" (e.g., Bandler, Madaras, & Bem, 1966). In terms of dissonance theory, Perceived Control subjects were given a choice about exposure to noise, whereas No Perceived Control subjects did not receive this option. Assuming dissonance arousal depends on prior choice in commitment, it can be argued that Perceived Control subjects experienced dissonance over the choice not to use the switch and attempted to reduce dissonance by reevaluating the noxious quality of the noise. Support for this hypothesis comes from the fact that Perceived Control subjects rated the unpredictable noise as less aversive than No Perceived Control subjects (see Table 5.2). Such reevaluation may have decreased stress during noise exposure and thereby reduced adverse aftereffects.

Closely related to the dissonance interpretation is Bem's radical-behavioristic approach. According to this theory, an individual's perception of the painfulness of a stimulus is an inference from his observations of his response to that stimulus. Thus, subjects in the Perceived Control condition might have inferred from their failure to press the switch that the noise was really not so noxious after all. These subjects would experience the noise as less aversive than No Perceived Control subjects and show less severe aftereffects. These predictions are essentially the same as those made from a dissonance model; the difference lies in the proposed explanatory mechanism.

There is at least one major difficulty with the foregoing explanations. Both require subjects in Perceived Control conditions to rate noise as less aversive than subjects in No Perceived Control conditions. However, differences between ratings in Perceived Control and No Perceived Control were at best suggestive; only one item in the first study actually produced a significant difference. Moreover, subsequent experiments in our laboratory (described later) have not replicated the rating effects. Without strong evidence of differential perceptions of noxiousness, it is difficult to maintain either a dissonance or a Bem-type explanation for the influence of perceived control. This argument does not, of course, rule out these interpretations. In the final analysis, they must await empirical test. We are thus left with the conclusion that perceived control somehow reduces the aversive impact of unpredictable noise and, in consequence, the negative aftereffects of exposure to such noise. Just why perceived control has these effects is discussed further in the last section of this chapter.

Perceived Control: Variations on a Theme

The discussion has so far dealt exclusively with the effects of direct control over noise termination, or at least the perception of such control. But in the natural environment outside the laboratory, one is not often in a position to control aversive events personally and directly. For example, there is very little one can effectively do (short of cathartic aggression) about sanitation men who throw around garbage cans at 5:00 a.m. We can, of course, complain to the appropriate officials at City Hall. It is questionable whether satisfaction would be obtained, but at least there is a belief in possible redress. In more general terms, we may ask whether the perception of access to a representative who has control over aversive events will actually result in the perception of control. We may also ask whether indirect control acts like direct personal control in reducing negative aftereffects of unpredictable noise. The experiment described below was designed to test whether unpredictable noise results in fewer subsequent performance deficits among individuals who feel they have access to others with control over the noise than among individuals who do not have this perception (see Glass, Reim, & Singer, 1971).

Experimental Procedure

Forty-seven[3] male undergraduate volunteers were exposed to the 24-burst random-intermittent noise tape used in previous studies. The design consisted of the following four condition: (a) Perceived Indirect Control, in which subjects believed they could signal another subject to press a button that would terminate noise; (b) No Perceived Indirect Control, in which the other subject had a control button, but no opportunity was given to communicate to him; (c) Together—No Perceived Control, in which neither subject could control the noise; and (d) Alone—No Perceived Control, in which the subject was exposed to noise without anyone else in the room and without explicit means of terminating

[3] Two subjects were eliminated from analysis because they failed to adapt to the noise. Retention of these cases would not have altered the final results (see Footnote 4, Chapter 4).

noise available to him. The postnoise measure was quality of performance on the proofreading task.[4]

Subjects were tested individually. When a subject arrived in the reception area of the laboratory, he was greeted by the experimenter and introduced to a second subject (actually a confederate of the experimenter). Both were taken into the laboratory and seated in chairs separated by a wooden partition. The general experimental instructions were identical to those used in the other experiments. After time was allowed for the GSR electrodes to hydrate, the confederate, in both Perceived Indirect Control and No Perceived Indirect Control, was given a switch box and told that depressing the button would terminate the noise he and the subject would be hearing later on. The experimenter emphasized that the confederate alone would have such control, and then added: "If you press the button, this will terminate the noise for the remainder of today's session. Whether you in fact press the button is entirely up to you."

In the Perceived Indirect Control condition, the naive subject was given an additional instruction which pointed out that although he did not have the control button, he did have the option of communicating *once* to the "other subject." He was told that this communication would mean he wanted the noise stopped. The subject was given a toggle switch and told he could contact the confederate only by pressing the switch, which would then activate a signal light on the confederate's side of the partition. The experimenter again stated that the subject could signal only once during the session. Turning to the confederate, the experimenter said: "When the light is activated, this means Mr. (name of subject) would like you to press the control button. And again, whether or not you press the button is up to you." The experimenter turned back to the subject and said: "Some people who come here activate the light; others do not. We'd prefer that you do not, but the decision is up to you."

In the No Perceived Indirect Control condition, the experimenter said nothing to the subject about signaling the confederate. Subjects in all conditions had been told that verbal and nonverbal communications were prohibited throughout the experiment. The Together—No Perceived Control treatment was identical to No Perceived Indirect Control, except that the confederate was not given a control button. The Alone—No Perceived Control treatment was, of course, a duplication of the No Perceived Control condition used in the other

---

[4] During noise exposure, subjects worked on the three cognitive tasks described in Chapter 3. Adaptation was measured by decrements in amplitude of phasic skin conductance responses to successive noise bursts. The results for both sets of measures were essentially the same as those reported for the other controllability studies in Chapter 3. Indeed, GSR data in Table 3.7 (Replication 2) were taken from the present experiment.

noise experiments. The remainder of the procedure was also identical to these previous studies.

Results

Manipulation checks. In order to determine whether we were successful in inducing differential perceptions of indirect control, all subjects were asked to respond to the following rating scales in a postexperimental questionnaire: (a) "To what extent did you feel you could have contacted the other partici- pant . . . ?" where 1 = "Definitely felt I could not make contact" and 9 = "Defi- nitely felt I could make contact"; (2) "To what extent did you feel that you could have stopped the noise during today's session?" where 1 = "Definitely could not have stopped the noise" and 9 = "Definitely could have stopped the noise." The first item was not relevant to Alone–No Perceived Control subjects and therefore was not included in the version of the questionnaire given to these subjects. Table 5.3 shows the mean responses to the two scales.

Analysis of responses to the first item revealed a significant effect due to experimental conditions ($F = 36.20$, $2/32\,df$, $p < .001$). Subsequent t tests showed reliable differences between Perceived Indirect Control, on the one hand, and No Perceived Indirect Control and Together–No Perceived Control on the other ($ps < .001$).

Responses to the second item asking specifically about control over noise were also subjected to analysis of variance. The results revealed a significant conditions effect ($F = 28.76$, $3/43\,df$, $p < .001$), and subsequent individual

TABLE 5.3

Mean Ratings of Perceived Contact with "Other Subject" and
Perceived Ability to Terminate the Noise

Experimental condition	Rating scale	
	Contact	Ability to terminate
Perceived indirect control ($n = 11$)	7.45	6.86
No perceived indirect control ($n = 11$)	1.82	1.27
Together-No perceived control ($n = 13$)	2.00	2.92
Alone-No perceived control ($n = 12$)	—[a]	2.67

[a] Subjects in this condition did not respond to the item.

TABLE 5.4

Mean Percentage of Errors Missed in the Proofreading Task

Perceived indirect control	No perceived indirect control	Together–No perceived control	Alone–No perceived control
31.00	49.91	41.08	37.92

comparisons yielded reliable differences between Perceived Indirect Control and each of the other conditions ($ps < .001$). The mean for No Perceived Indirect Control was also significantly lower than the means for Together–No Perceived Control and Alone–No Perceived Control at the .02 and .05 levels, respectively. Indeed, the variance in the No Perceived Indirect Control condition was reliably lower than in any of the other conditions ($ps < .01$), indicating that virtually all subjects in this treatment did not perceive even minimal control over the noise. On the basis of these results, we conclude that differential perceptions of control over noise offset were successfully induced.

Aftereffects of noise. Table 5.4 shows the average percentage of errors missed in the completed part of the proofreading task. Analysis of these data provided confirmation of our initial hypothesis about the effects of indirect control. Apart from a significant main effect ($F = 8.41$, $3/43\, df$, $p < .01$), individual comparisons indicated that the mean for No Perceived Indirect Control was significantly higher than the means for each of the other conditions at the .02 level or beyond. The Together–No Perceived Control and Alone–No Perceived Control conditions were also higher than Perceived Indirect Control at less than the .01 and .07 levels, respectively. As expected, the Together–No Perceived Control and Alone–No Perceived Control means were not reliably different from one another.

Previous studies induced perceptions of control by giving a single subject a button that could terminate noise. By contrast, the control manipulation was indirect in this experiment; that is, the subject was able to signal another person, who had control, that he wanted the noise stopped. It is therefore gratifying to note the replication of major results, and even more gratifying to obtain essentially the same parametric values in several experiments using controllable and uncontrollable noise. Table 5.5 presents these comparative data. It is obvious that the means for each type of condition are virtually identical ($ps > .20$).

Discussion

This experiment has shown again that exposure to uncontrollable, in contrast to controllable noise results in greater subsequent performance errors

TABLE 5.5

*Mean Percentage of Errors Missed in the Proofreading Task:
Data from Perceived Control Experiments*

Experiments	Type of experimental condition	
	Perceived control	Alone-No perceived control
A. First study	28.22	42.44
B. Replication	32.88	43.21
C. Perceived indirect control	31.00	37.92

on a proofreading task. We had demonstrated the reduction of these errors when a subject believes he has *direct* control over noise termination. It is not necessary that he actually exert control, but only that he perceive control is possible. The present experiment indicates that the perception of *indirect* control (through access to another who presumably has direct control) also reduces postnoise deficits. The important percept seems to be knowledge that one can contact the person in power, even if there is no guarantee that he will come to one's assistance. Having access to "the top" appears to be a sufficient condition for inducing the perception of control and easing the stressful consequences of uncontrollable noise.

It is, of course, possible that the proofreading effects had little to do with control over noise. Subjects in the Perceived Indirect Control condition may have been engaged in a contest with the confederate to see who can best resist saying "uncle." Since none of these subjects pressed the light switch, they obviously succeeded in their contest and it is safe to assume that they experienced feelings of successful achievement. It could be argued that these feelings counteracted the detrimental effects of unpredictable noise, thereby leading to better proofreading performance. This explanation fails to account for the high degree of congruence between proofreading results in the Perceived Control conditions in this and previous experiments. Table 5.5 showed that the mean scores from different studies were virtually identical, yet the other designs induced control in subjects run one at a time where there was no opportunity for competition with a confederate.

An unexpected finding in this study is that subjects in the No Perceived Indirect Control condition reported significantly less control over the noise than subjects in the other no control conditions (see Table 5.3). This particular result might be attributable to feelings of "relative deprivation" experienced by subjects in the No Perceived Indirect Control condition (see, e.g., Pettigrew, 1967). It was in this treatment, after all, that a seemingly arbitrary decision was made to give the control button only to the confederate. But, irrespective of the source of differential perceptions of control, the effects of uncontrollability are consistent with theoretical expectations. Given that subjects in No Perceived Indirect Control experienced less control than other No Control subjects, they would be expected to show greater deficits on proofreading. This is precisely what occurred. It would appear that perceived uncontrollability results in deleterious aftereffects, both as hypothesized and serendipitously.

The possibility that some subjects experienced relative deprivation is indeed intriguing. To be deprived relative to another is intuitively similar to perceived uncontrollability, for the deprived individual is also powerless to influence his environment. Therefore, if both psychological states are aroused simultaneously, we should expect maximal stress and heightened postnoise consequences. The present experiment appears to confirm this line of thought, but a number of controls were missing that make unequivocal conclusions impossible. In order to settle the issue of relative deprivation effects, the following experiment was conducted by Joan Gruzen and Larry Shapiro at New York University.

Experimental Procedure

Fifty undergraduate female volunteers[5] were exposed to the 25-burst random-intermittent noise tape at the customary 108 dBA. The design consisted of five conditions: (a) Relative Deprivation, in which a confederate was given the control button and the subject was not; (b) Absolute Deprivation, in which neither subject nor confederate received a button; (c) Equity, in which both subject and confederate had the button; (d) Alone–Perceived Control, in which the subject was exposed to noise without anyone else present and with a button available to him; (e) Alone–No Perceived Control, in which the subject was also tested alone but without a control button. Again, the postnoise measure was proofreading performance.[6]

Both general and specific experimental procedures used in this study were virtually the same as in the previous indirect control experiment. The only deviations were in the instructions designed to induce feelings of Relative Deprivation or Equity. The Absolute Deprivation and Alone–No Perceived Control conditions were the same as the Together–No Perceived Control and

---

[5] Fifty-two subjects were actually used, but 1 walked out of the session and 1 yielded an unusable physiological record. Both subjects had been randomly assigned to the Alone–No Perceived Control condition.

[6] During the noise, subjects worked on a pursuit rotor. Performance data for this task were presented in Chapter 3, as were the vasoconstriction results in Table 3.9 of the same chapter. The GSR adaptation effects in this study have not been presented, for they were essentially the same as in other perceived control experiments.

Alone—No Perceived Control treatments of the prior study; Alone—Perceived Control was identical to the Loud Unpredictable—Perceived Control treatment included in previous experiments.

For ease of matching conditions across experiments, the following table summarizes the condition names and the presence or absence of a confederate or microswitch as used in the experiments reported in this chapter.

Condition	Confederate	Noise-terminating microswitch
Alone-No perceived control	Absent	Absent
Alone-Perceived control	Absent	Present, under subject's control
Absolute deprivation (Together-No perceived control)	Present	Absent
No perceived indirect control (Relative deprivation)	Present	Present, under confederate's control with no communication possible
Perceived indirect control	Present	Present, under confederate's control with communication between subject and confederate possible
Equity	Present	Present in duplicate, one switch under subject's control, the other under confederate's control

Following the introductory remarks and usual hydration period, the experimenter explained the pursuit-rotor task to the subject. This was the drill for all five conditions. In Relative Deprivation, however, the experimenter hesitated a moment after concluding the task instructions, and then handed a switch box to the confederate saying, "This button affects the noise you and (subject's name) will be hearing while you work on the task. If the button is pressed, it will terminate the noise for the remainder of today's session. You and you alone, (confederate's name), can terminate the noise . . . ." There followed the usual button instructions, ending with a statement designed to heighten the subject's feelings of relative deprivation. Thus, the experimenter paused briefly after explaining the button to the confederate, turned to the subject and said: "And you (subject's name) do not have a control button."

In the Equity condition, subject and confederate were each given a microswitch. The standard Perceived Control instructions were delivered, but it was also emphasized that if either one pressed the button, the noise would be ended for both of them.

The noise session began almost immediately after the control manipulation. It was followed by administration of the proofreading task and two postexperimental questionnaires. The first of these included an item checking on the effectiveness of the Perceived Control induction, while the second was designed to check on whether differential feelings of relative deprivation had been induced. The latter questionnaire was presented as coming from the Department of Psychology, which was interested in evaluating research being conducted under its auspices. The subject was told that her responses would be anonymous, and to ensure this, she was to place the completed questionnaire in a sealed envelope, which would then be transmitted directly to the departmental chairman.

Results and Discussion

Manipulation checks. There are two experimental manipulations requiring assessment. The first is perceived control, which was checked by the rating scale: "To what extent did you feel that you could have had the noise stopped during today's session?" where 1 = "Felt I had no control at all over the noise" and 9 = "Felt I had complete control over the noise." Table 5.6 shows the mean ratings on this item, which yielded a significant main effect ($F = 14.95$, $4/45$ df, $p < .001$). A Duncan Multiple Range Test revealed that Relative Deprivation, Absolute Deprivation, and Alone—No Perceived Control were not reliably different from one another, but each was different from Equity and Alone—Perceived Control at the .01 level. The latter two conditions also differed at the .05 level, which is perfectly reasonable if one recalls that control over noise was presumably being shared by subject and confederate alike in the Equity condition.

The foregoing results indicate that the Perceived Control manipulation was successful. But what of the Relative Deprivation induction? Since comparison with a nondeprived referent is supposed to lead to feelings of unfairness and discrimination (e.g., Davis, 1959), we included the following two items in the "anonymous" questionnaire. (a) "If there was another participant with you in today's experiment, did you feel that he was somehow given preferential treatment by the experimenter?" where 1 = "Definitely not given preferential treatment" and 61 = "Definitely given preferential treatment"; (b) "Did you feel that the way in which today's experiment was conducted was fair or unfair?"

TABLE 5.6

Mean Ratings of Perceived Control

Relative deprivation[a]	Absolute deprivation	Equity	Alone-Perceived control	Alone-No perceived control
2.65	1.35	5.75	8.16	3.10

[a] There are 10 cases in each condition.

TABLE 5.7

*Mean Ratings on Items Checking on the Effectiveness of the
Relative Deprivation Induction*

Item	Experimental condition				
	Relative deprivation	Absolute deprivation	Equity	Alone-Perceived control	Alone-No perceived control
A. Preferential treatment	19.15	3.40	3.40	—[a]	—[a]
B. Fairness	19.95	4.90	7.00	11.00	20.40

[a]Subjects in these conditions were not asked this question, since it was obviously inap-appropriate to their experimental experience.

where 1 = "Extremely fair" and 61 = "Extremely unfair." Table 5.7 presents the mean ratings on these items, both of which yielded significant main effects with analysis of variance ($F = 6.16$, $2/27$ df, $p < .01$; $F = 3.08$, $4/45$ df, $p < .05$). A Duncan Multiple Range Test confirmed that Relative Deprivation subjects perceived preferential treatment of the confederate, while Equity and Absolute Deprivation subjects did not have this perception ($ps < .01$).

A similar effect was revealed for differential perceptions of fairness ($ps < .05$), although Alone–No Perceived Control subjects appear to have viewed the experiment as equally unfair as Relative Deprivation subjects. The latter result makes eminently good sense. Subjects in Alone–No Perceived Control probably saw the experimental situation as one in which they were mistreated. They did, after all, come to the laboratory because of a course requirement, and once there, they were subjected to an unpleasant experience over which they had little control. When asked later if the experiment was conducted unfairly, we can well understand their tendency to give an affirmative answer. Though Absolute Deprivation subjects were treated identically, they did have a peer (i.e., the confederate) with whom to share the unpleasant experience. Since he did not voice any complaints, the naive subjects probably inferred that the procedure was legitimate; and, assuredly, they had no grounds for an accusation of preferential treatment.

In general, then, the results indicate that our manipulations successfully induced differential feelings of relative deprivation, and we can now proceed to evidence of noise aftereffects.

Noise aftereffects. The proofreading results in Table 5.8 are unequivocal in revealing superior performance in the two controllable-noise conditions: Equity and Alone–Perceived Control. The three uncontrollable conditions show about

TABLE 5.8

Mean Percentage of Errors Missed in the Proofreading Task

Relative deprivation	Absolute deprivation	Equity	Alone-Perceived control	Alone-No perceived control
42.30	44.40	26.20	25.70	47.30

equal impairment, and the means are all significantly greater than the two means for the controllable conditions ($ps < .01$, by the Duncan Multiple Range Test). Once again, we have demonstrated the importance of perceived control in reducing deleterious postnoise effects. We have not, however, shown relative-deprivation effects; instead we have confirmed the notion that the consequences of noise exposure are greater in uncontrollable conditions.

Further support for this conclusion comes from a correlation between self-ratings of control and the proofreading scores. The product-moment coefficient was $-.26$ (49 *df*, $p < .05$), which agrees rather closely with a similarly obtained correlation ($-.34$) from the previous indirect control study. A correlation between proofreading and self-ratings of fairness in this experiment did not yield a reliable coefficient ($+.03$). It would therefore appear that perceived controllability, however induced, is a sufficient condition for ameliorating behavioral deficits following exposure to unpredictable and uncontrollable noise.

It is, of course, still unclear why the previous experiment produced particularly severe deficits in the No Perceived Indirect Control condition. In view of the present study, we can no longer be certain about attributing these results to feelings of relative deprivation. For some reason, perceived lack of control was maximal in the prior experiment, and it is probably because of this effect that proofreading degradations were magnified.

Perceived Control: Avoidable and Unavoidable Noise

The theme of this chapter has been the perception of potential escape from aversive noise and how this influences behavior following exposure to noise. Our main finding is that negative aftereffects of unpredictable noise are reduced by the perception of potential control. This effect is not confined to the laboratory. Knowledge that we can control events in our surroundings, or can at least escape from unpleasantness, clearly influences our daily lives. We know, for example, that if heat and humidity become unbearable, we can escape into an air-conditioned building; if congestion of city streets becomes intolerable, there is always the possibility of an extended weekend in the country; if the jangling telephone never seems to stop, we can, *in extremis*, remove the receiver; and the construction worker who operates the buzzsaw or compressed-air gun can turn it on or off at his convenience. The perception of escape eases adaptation to aversive events and generally makes life more pleasant. It is not necessary that we exercise control; in most cases, we need only believe that control is possible.

The perception of escape from aversive stimulation is only one type of environmental control. It often happens that stressful events do not occur, or at least are temporarily forestalled, if we take certain prior actions. The simple precaution of tripping the circuit breaker before repairing a faulty switch has protected many an amateur electrician from severe shock. That individuals can be conditioned to avoid aversive events has been a subject of behavioral research for a good many years (e.g., Azrin, 1958). More recently, there has been an upsurge of interest in how avoidable and unavoidable stressors influence stress responses (e.g., Seligman, Maier, & Solomon, 1971). We alluded to some of this literature at the beginning of the chapter when we suggested that being able to avoid an aversive event is similar in its effects to escape from this event. In either case, we are dealing with an instance of control over the environment and should therefore expect stress and its effects to be influenced in similar ways. For example, if an individual can avoid unpredictable aversive events by instrumental responding, we should anticipate a reduction in stress response. Support for this hypothesis comes primarily from experiments on infrahuman species (see Seligman, Maier, & Solomon, 1971). The concept of control in these studies has been operationalized almost exclusively in terms of the experimenter's arrangement of experimental events. There has been virtually no concern with the perception of avoidance—understandably, because the research has used animals as subjects. Recently, Geer, Davison, and Gatchel (1970) proposed that the stress-reducing effects of experimental avoidance paradigms may be attributed to the subject's belief that he can control the amount and/or occurrence of the stressor by instrumental responding. We referred to this study earlier in the chapter, and in the previous chapter on autonomic reactivity to aversive events. At this point, we describe the experiment in more detail.

College-student subjects were given 10 trials in which they had to press a reaction-time switch as they felt an electric shock. The shock lasted 6 seconds and was always preceded by a 10-second warning signal. In a second part of the study, half the subjects (Perceived Control) were told shock duration would be reduced to 3 seconds if their reaction times attained a certain speed. The other half of the subjects were told that shocks would be shortened, but nothing was said abouts its being contingent on speed of reaction time (No Perceived Control). Geer found that skin conductance responses to shock during the second part of the study were smaller among Perceived Control than No

Perceived Control subjects. He also found fewer spontaneous GSRs among Perceived Control subjects. In short, the perception of control through instrumental responding, even though not veridical, reduced autonomic reactivity. The perception of control as avoidance of the full impact of the stressor appears to have a similar effect to the perception of control as escape from the stressor.

The study by Geer *et al.* (1970) was not concerned with differential effects of perceived control following exposure to stress. It was exclusively concerned with the reduction of stress responses during the aversive trials themselves. It would therefore be interesting to examine poststressor consequences within a perceived avoidance paradigm similar to that developed by Geer. We have in fact conducted two such studies, one with noise and one with shock, but both designed and carried out prior to having seen the Geer design. Accordingly, our experiments are not exact duplicates of Geer's study; however, they do examine differential aftereffects of exposure to aversive events as a function of perceived avoidance. We report the noise study here and defer discussion of shock until Chapter 7. The general hypothesis of the noise study[7] was as follows: If an individual is led to believe that avoidance of unpredictable noise bursts is contingent on instrumental responding, postnoise task deficits will be less than where the individual does not have this perception.

Experimental Procedure

The stimuli consisted of 18 bursts of 108-dBA noise randomly spaced over a 20-minute period. The length of each burst was fixed at 9 seconds, but interburst intervals (in seconds) varied as follows: 23, 100, 40, 60, 55, 50, 60, 130, 35, 25, 175, 60, 110, 15, 25, 75, 30. These values were selected for reasons that will become apparent later. The nature of the noise and the way in which it was delivered were identical to our previous experiments.

The basic design consisted of two experimental conditions: (a) Perceived Avoidance, in which subjects, working on primarily soluble puzzles during noise exposure, were led to believe that successful solution of the puzzles would prevent some of the scheduled bursts; (b) No Perceived Avoidance, in which subjects, working on insoluble puzzles, were also led to believe that successful solutions would prevent noise. In short, both conditions induced initial perceptions of control, but only one positively reinforced this belief. In the other condition, subjects were ostensibly unable to avoid the noise because of their poor task performance. Both groups actually received the same number of noise bursts. Adaptation was again measured by decrements in phasic skin conduc-

[7] Conducted by Bruce Reim at New York University.

tance,[8] and the postnoise measures were proofreading and the Stroop Color Word Test (see the next section.) Subjects were 20 paid male undergraduates.

The general procedure and introductory instructions were essentially the same as in the other noise experiments. Following the hydration period, the experimenter introduced a modified version of the graphic puzzles task employed as a dependent measure in previous studies. Subjects were told they would work on the puzzles during the noise session and the experimenter explained how the puzzles were supposed to be solved (see Chapter 4). After these instructions, all subjects were told: "The noise bursts you will be hearing are of constant intensity—as predetermined by our apparatus. However, the number of bursts you hear is determined only by you. That is, if you succeed in correctly tracing over a figure, the next scheduled noise burst will not occur. In fact, after you solve a particular puzzle, you will notice a period of time during which there is no noise. Your successful performance on the puzzle prevented the next set of scheduled noise bursts. On the other hand, if you fail to successfully complete the puzzle, the delivery of noise is inevitable . . .."

In the Perceived Avoidance condition, subjects were presented with three soluble and two insoluble puzzles in the order depicted in Figure 5.1. In the No Perceived Avoidance condition, three insoluble puzzles were used in the order shown in Figure 5.2. The final (soluble) puzzle in each figure was actually administered after the last noise burst and constituted a dependent measure discussed later in this chapter. Providing only insoluble puzzles to No Avoidance subjects permitted them to infer that they were receiving noise bursts because of their inability to solve the problems. Providing mostly soluble puzzles to the Avoidance subjects permitted them to make precisely the opposite inference, particularly since almost all of them solved the solubles. We could not use exclusively soluble puzzles in this condition because it was necessary to have some failure to rationalize delivery of noise. The amount of time subjects devoted to each puzzle was determined by pilot testing. It was therefore possible to arrange the order of the puzzles to that occurrence of the schedule of noise

---

[8] Table 3.8 presented the GSR adaptation results for this study. Examination of the table also reveals that the Perceived Avoidance condition had a slightly higher mean GSR score (.075) to the first block of noise bursts than did the No Perceived Avoidance condition (.062). This nonsignificant difference is inconsistent with other autonomic results for initial noise bursts, and is also discrepant with the perceived control findings of Geer *et al.* (1970) discussed above. However, the discrepancy is understandable if we recall that both groups of subjects expected to avoid some of the noise bursts. The No Perceived Avoidance group probably became aware of their inability to do this only after the noise session was well under way, by which time they were adapted to the noise. In short, we did not expect, nor did we find, reliable GSR differences between the two avoidance conditions.

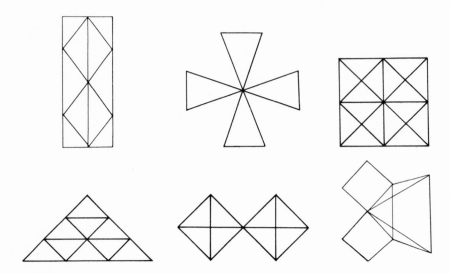

Figure 5.1 *Puzzles for the soluble sequence.*

bursts (see p. 80) would not be inconsistent with a perception that they had been avoided by successful task performance. On the assumption that perceived avoidance, whether veridical or not, is a form of perceived control, subjects in Perceived Avoidance should experience greater feelings of control than subjects in No Perceived Avoidance.

Postnoise Measures

Along with the proofreading task, a second postnoise measure was also used. The Stroop Color Work Test (cf. Jensen & Rohwer, 1966), was selected to complement our other dependent measures because it presumably requires an alert organism capable of resolving competition between opposing response tendencies. An individual who has been exposed to an uncontrollable stressor is not likely to fulfill these requirements, and we therefore expected him to have difficulty in naming the colors of the words, a difficulty that would be manifest in longer reading times.

The Color Word Test requires the subject to read aloud the names of four colors (green, red, orange, and blue), each of which is printed in incongruent color names. For example, if the word "red" is printed in blue ink, the subject is to read "blue." The four color words are repeated randomly for a total of 110 color names. Two other reading tasks precede the critical color-naming task, which we designate Part III. Part I consists of a single page of color names printed in black, and Part II is composed of a page of 86 sets of five colored

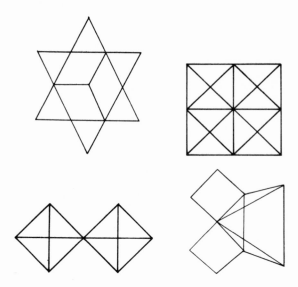

Figure 5.2 *Puzzles for the insoluble sequence.*

asterisks. Each set is printed in one of the same four colors used in Part III. The experimenter times the subject's performance on all three parts of the test. Our principal Stroop score was computed by subtracting the subject's speed of color work naming in Part I from his reading speed in Part III (see Houston & Jones, 1967; Jensen & Rohwer, 1966, for alternative scoring procedures).[9] Since subjects were told to correct themselves, errors were so infrequent as to make an error score meaningless.

Baseline Conditions

An obvious defect in this study is that significant effects could be attributed to the fact that a different set of puzzles was used in each experimental condition. It could be argued, for example, that impaired proofreading in No Perceived Avoidance is the result of greater failure and frustration following work on exclusively insoluble puzzles. Perceived Avoidance subjects, in contrast, work on soluble puzzles and therefore have greater success experiences leading to better proofreading performance. The solution to this dilemma is quite simple: the design needs two no-noise control conditions, one in which subjects

---

[9] A typical scoring formula for the Stroop is Part III minus Part II. We also computed Stroop time scores using this formula and, though mean values changed slightly, relative magnitudes remained essentially the same as those shown in Tables 5.10 and 7.3.

work on the same six puzzles as the Avoidance group, and the other in which subjects work on the same four puzzles as the No Avoidance group.

In the normal course of events, we would have included no-noise soluble and no-noise insoluble conditions in our basic design. However, the study was conducted immediately after the electric shock experiment reported in Chapter 7. Since experimental operations used in the two studies were similar, and since the shock experiment included two No Shock control groups—the very ones needed for the noise study—we decided to rely on these controls rather than duplicate them. This decision seemed reasonable in the interests of conserving time and energy, and we could see no serious objections to using control groups that were identical to what we would have designed for the present study. The only difference was that experimental subjects in the noise study were paid college men, whereas control subjects in the shock study were college men recruited from the subject pool at New York University.[10] In any event, the No Shock control subjects were included in the analyses reported below. We will hereafter refer to these groups as Soluble Control and Insoluble Control, remembering that they were exposed neither to shock nor to noise.

Results

Manipulation checks. If subjects in Perceived Avoidance believed they had really avoided some of the noise bursts, whereas subjects in No Perceived Avoidance did not have this perception, we should find differences between the two conditions on the following items from a postexperimental questionnaire: (a) "To what extent did you feel that your performance on the puzzles enabled you to prevent the occurrence of some of the noise bursts?" where 1 = "Did not at all enable me to prevent some of the noise bursts" and 9 = "Completely enabled me to prevent some of the noise bursts"; (b) "How many noise bursts did you receive?" where 1 = "Very few" and 9 = "Very many." The first two columns of Table 5.9 present mean responses to these items, and the differences are significant in the expected direction. Perceived Avoidance subjects felt they had been able to avoid noise to a greater extent than No Perceived Avoidance subjects; they also reported receiving fewer bursts.

Since avoidance is assumed to be a form of perceived control over noise, we expected similar differences between the two conditions on the item: "To what extent did you feel that you could have controlled the occurrence of the noise bursts in today's session?" where 1 = "Definitely could not have controlled

---

[10] Another minor difference was that the soluble puzzle in the second position (see Figure 5.1) was slightly different for the control groups.

TABLE 5.9

*Mean Ratings on Scales Checking on the Effectiveness of
Perceived Avoidance Manipulations*

Experimental condition	Rating scale		
	Prevented noise bursts	Number of bursts received	Perceived control of the noise
Perceived avoidance	6.60[a]	3.70[b]	6.80[c]
No perceived avoidance	2.70[a]	5.00[b]	2.20[c]

[a] $t = 9.11$, 18 df, $p < .001$.
[b] $t = 3.08$, 18 df, $p < .001$.
[c] $t = 9.48$, 18 df, $p < .001$.

noise" and 9 = "Definitely could have controlled noise." The third column of Table 5.9 shows the mean ratings on this item, which are clearly in the anticipated direction. Perceived Avoidance subjects reported greater feelings of control than No Perceived Avoidance subjects. We conclude, therefore, that the operations designed to induce differential perceptions of control were overwhelmingly successful.

Noise aftereffects. Performance deficits are clearly reduced by the perception of having avoided noise. Table 5.10 presents mean scores for the two postnoise measures, proofreading and the Stroop. The difference in Stroop reading time for experimental groups is statistically significant ($p < .01$ by the

TABLE 5.10

*Mean Performance Scores on the Proofreading Task
and the Stroop Color Word Test*

Experimental condition	Postnoise measure	
	Proofreading[a]	Stroop[b]
Perceived avoidance	36.50	63.80
No perceived avoidance	53.10	90.80
Soluble control	37.18	67.73
Insoluble control	29.64	72.82

[a] Mean percentage of errors not detected in the completed part of the proofreading task.
[b] Reading time (in seconds) for Part III minus reading time (in seconds) for Part I.

Duncan Multiple Range Test), whereas the difference between control groups does not even approach significance. As expected, the Perceived Avoidance mean is virtually identical to Soluble Control, and the mean for No Perceived Avoidance is reliably higher than its counterpart.

The proofreading results generally correspond to data from the Stroop. A Duncan Multiple Range Test indicates that Perceived Avoidance differs from No Perceived Avoidance ($p < .01$); the former treatment is the same as Soluble Control; and the latter treatment is significantly greater than Insoluble Control at the .01 level. Unexpectedly, the two control groups also differ from each other ($p < .05$). We have no immediate explanation for the difference, but it is, in any case, opposite of what one would expect if the soluble puzzles *per se*, and not perceived avoidance, were responsible for the decrement in proofreading errors. We are thus confident in attributing the results to the experimental variation.

Taken together, the proofreading and Stroop findings confirm previous conclusions about the impact of perceived controllability on aftereffects of noise exposure.[11] They do more than that, however; for the control variable in this study was based on subjects' perceptions of having avoided the noise. That they did not actually receive fewer bursts is irrelevant to the reduction of postnoise deficits. The mere belief that they avoided noise was sufficient to produce this effect.

Proposed Explanation for the Effects of Perceived Control

The perception of control, however induced, appears to reduce negative aftereffects of exposure to high-intensity unpredictable noise—but why? What specific stress-reducing mechanisms are aroused by the manipulation of perceived control? To help answer these questions, consider first what an organism experiences during inescapable or unavoidable stress. Nothing he can do will affect the occurrence of the stressor, for there are no available resources that will enable him to counter it. If the aversive event is also unpredictable, there cannot even be preparation for stimulation. The individual is at the mercy of his environment, in which case we may describe his psychological state as one of helplessness.

---

[11] An alternative explanation for both dependent variables is based on the assumption that subjects in the No Perceived Avoidance condition were repeatedly frustrated in their attempts to prevent stressful stimulation. It can be argued that this frustration led directly to behavioral deficits. However, this explanation has been refuted by data from one of the conditions in the electric shock experiment, and the reader is referred to Chapter 7, where these results are reported in detail.

The notion that uncontrollable stress results in a sense of helplessness has been developed in a number of earlier studies, including Grinker and Spiegel's (1945) analysis of battle neurosis among World War II flyers, and Janis' (1962) account of the effects of warnings of community disasters on the mechanisms by which the individual copes with such emergency situations. Lazarus has cited research on shipwrecked sailors showing that they appear to die after 3 days even though it is possible, from a medical point of view, to survive hunger and thirst for much longer periods of time. "It is often assumed that the marooned men 'give up'. . . . Those who succumb are overwhelmed by helplessness and believe their position is hopeless" (1966, p. 99). The theme of uncontrollability and helplessness is also evident in animal research. Writing about the behavior of dogs in a two-way shuttle-box following prior exposure to inescapable shock, Seligman states:

> At the onset of the first shock . . ., the dog howls, runs around, defecates and urinates—but only for a few seconds. It then settles down and takes the shock, whining and howling but making few escape movements . . .. On the second trial, the dog runs around a little, but soon stops; it again stands or sits, howling and whining. After a few more trials, the dog makes virtually no escape movements, and appears to have given up . . . (1969, p. 43).

All of these observations illustrate the role of helplessness in mediating the aversive impact of uncontrollable stressful stimuli. It follows that providing the individual with control over the stimulus, or at least giving him that impression, should reduce his sense of helplessness and decrease the magnitude of his stress response. This view is in line with a number of recent conceptions of the importance of controlling events in one's environment. Mandler (Mandler, 1964; Mandler & Watson, 1966) has stated that anxiety, that is, heightened autonomic and behavioral arousal, occurs when an organized response sequence is interrupted and there are no substitute sequences available. The inability to complete a sequence produces disorganization of behavior that results in feelings of helplessness and anxiety. On the other hand, if the individual has control over the interrupting stimuli, he is able to plan the sequence of events to occur. Any interruption becomes part of his overall plan for coping with the stimuli and reduces level of anxiety.

Lazarus (1966) has taken a similar position on the role of controllability in response to stressor stimuli. He speaks about the "relative balance of power" between the aversive stimulus and the resources of the individual and his environment to cope with the stimulus. When the balance favors the stimulus, stress responses are increased; when the balance favors the resources, stress responses are reduced. Lazarus is referring here to the individual's perception of control. In so doing, he is equating perceived lack of control with feelings of helplessness to cope with stressful stimuli. This view of environmental control also bears resemblance to White's (1959) idea of competence as a personality variable. A sense of competence is presumably aroused by the individual's perception that he has control over his environment. Feelings of incompetence may be described as the helplessness that develops when an individual is unable to cope with stressful events confronting him.

One other theory of control that should be mentioned is the idea of "learned helplessness" developed by Seligman and his colleagues (e.g., Seligman, Maier, & Solomon, 1971). The basic premises underlying this theory are (1) when aversive events are uncontrollable, the organism learns that his responses are independent of his outcomes; (2) the acquisition of this relationship interferes with the learning of a subsequent relationship in which the organism's responses would in fact control the aversive event. To explain what is essentially an instance of proactive interference, Seligman proposes the following mechanisms.

> ... S's *incentive* [italics ours] for initiating active instrumental responses during a[n electric] shock is assumed to be partially produced by its having learned that the probability of shock termination will be increased by these responses. When this expectation is absent the incentive for instrumental responding should be reduced . . ... The presence of shock in the escape/avoidance training situation should then arouse the same expectation that was previously acquired during exposure to inescapable shocks: shock is uncontrollable. Therefore, the incentive for initiating and maintaining active instrumental responses in the training situation should be low . . . (Seligman, Maier, & Solomon, 1971, p. 369).

It is the relationship between these expectations and incentives that Seligman has labeled "learned helplessness." In terms more appropriate to our previous statements about uncontrollability and helplessness, it is not the stressful event alone that causes interference, but rather the individual's lack of control over the event. This lack of control induces a state of helplessness in which there is an absence of incentives for initiating strategies designed to avoid or escape from the aversive stimulus. If, on the other hand, the individual has learned that he can control the stimulus, escape behaviors will be facilitated in subsequent exposures to the stressor. Seligman explicitly states that his definition of control is in terms of the experimenter's arrangement of experimental events, not in terms of the individual's perception of them. By contrast, our primary concern has been with perceived control, that is, the belief that control over aversive stimulation is possible even though the individual does not actually exert control. The difference in definition does not necessarily imply an inconsistency, and for our purposes, we may consider Seligman's theory a special case of a more general helplessness hypothesis that deals with a wide gamut of consequences resulting from uncontrollable stressful events.

The helplessness hypothesis provides a nice explanation for the relationship between unpredictable and uncontrollable noise and deleterious aftereffects. If the impact of a repeatedly presented aversive event is greatest when feelings of helplessness are maximal, it follows that adverse aftereffects will also be maximal. This is, of course, precisely the result obtained in the uncontrollability studies. For the time being, then, we conclude that unpredictable noise produces deleterious aftereffects because it is more aversive than predictable noise, its greater aversiveness being a function of the sense of helplessness induced in an individual who believes he is unable to control, or even predict, the onset and offset of the noise.

But what evidence do we have that helplessness actually mediates the effects of unpredictable and uncontrollable noise? We did not attempt to measure feelings of helplessness directly; our emphasis in most experiments was simply on the consequences of perceived uncontrollability. However, the unavoidable-noise experiment departed from this usual strategy by measuring a type of task performance that seems related to a state of helplessness. The No Perceived Avoidance subjects learned that there was little they could do to solve the puzzles and therefore nothing they could do to avoid the noise bursts. It may be assumed that incentives for avoidance declined over time, and by the end of the noise session, subjects had lost interest in trying to avoid the bursts through instrumental responses.

This process of incentive reduction following repeated disconfirmation of an expectancy is analogous to Seligman's notion of learned helplessness. While we hesitate to draw direct parallels between Seligman's dogs and our own subjects, the analogy is not so remote if we confine ourselves to suggesting that human organisms also behave in ways indicative of helplessness when they have just experienced unavoidable aversive stimulation. The dogs, it will be recalled, did not actively seek to avoid shock during a subsequent period when avoidance had become possible. In similar fashion, subjects in the No Perceived Avoidance condition may show reduced motivation to avoid noise. Having learned that their task performance is inadequate to prevent the bursts, we may expect a decline in active problem solving. If, for example, these subjects were given a soluble puzzle, their time to solution should be greater than for the subjects who presumably succeeded in avoiding noise.

In order to test for this consequence of helplessness, we included a soluble puzzle as the last problem in the series administered to both groups of subjects. This was the fourth problem in No Perceived Avoidance and the sixth problem in Perceived Avoidance. The line drawings were identical in the two conditions (see Figures 5.1 and 5.2). Noise was terminated immediately before subjects began work on this puzzle (though they were unaware of this fact), and the experimenter recorded the amount of time each subject took to reach a solution.

TABLE 5.11

Mean Time Spent Solving the Final Puzzle [a]

Perceived avoidance	No perceived avoidance	Soluble control	Insoluble control
95.40	209.80	185.82	124.55

[a] Time is given in seconds.

In the interests of conserving time, subjects were told to stop work if they had not solved the problem after 400 seconds. This happened in only one case (in No Perceived Avoidance), and elimination of his data would not have substantially changed the results. We therefore assigned him a score of 400 and included him in the analysis.

The average amounts of time spent in solving the final puzzle are presented in Table 5.11. It is obvious that mean time was greatest in the No Perceived Avoidance condition, and it is indeed significantly different from Perceived Avoidance ($p < .05$ by the Duncan Multiple Range Test). However, it is only marginally greater (at about the .10 level) than mean time for the Insoluble Control condition. The controls themselves do not differ from each other. These results indicate that active problem solving declines when subjects learn they cannot prevent the noise. In the light of our theoretical discussion, we interpret this effect as reflecting a state of helplessness. It is as if subjects gave up trying to master their environment and became temporarily resigned to aversive stimulation. The comparison of the Perceived Avoidance condition with the Soluble Control condition is also interesting, for the former group of subjects had an incentive—noise termination—that the latter group did not. Successful problem solving *per se* was not a sufficient motivating condition; only when the ability to solve was yoked to an instrumental utility was the success able to carry over to the final problem.

Other Cognitive Factors and Behavioral Aftereffects of Unpredictable Noise

The findings have thus far documented the pervasiveness and magnitude of the impact of perceived controllability upon the aftereffects of noise. Predictability and its effects were also studied, but they were interpreted as a special case of controllability. We now consider other cognitive factors that may be expected, on *a priori* grounds, to interact with noise. The presentation of experiments dealing with these factors can serve several useful purposes. It illustrates the extension of our cognitive approach while delimiting the scope of our effects; it is as important to know which cognitive variables do not affect noise as to know which do. The studies also raise ancillary questions that, although of importance, could not easily have been dealt with in previous discussions. Finally, since two of the studies reported in this chapter are somewhat less than completely successful, they bolster the previous material with a sort of probabilistic credibility. No experimenter bats 1.000 all of the time. Yet, an experienced investigator riding a hot streak in the laboratory may seem to have a special touch, turning every study into gold. Our selectively ordered presentations in Chapters 4 and 5 may leave the impression that, like apocryphal medieval alchemists, we have transmuted lead to gold. Not every time, perhaps, but at better than the .05 level. The present chapter will dispel that illusion.

There is one alternative explanation that may be raised which, though not dealing with stress itself, might explain away all of our findings. The charge may be leveled that we have been capitalizing on favorable experimenter bias (Rosenthal, 1966; Rosenthal & Rosnow, 1969). That is, a series of interested and committed investigators have, through subtle cues and body English, communicated their expectations to the subjects and induced them to behave in accord with the experimenters' hypotheses. Although it is impossible to refute such considerations in the abstract, it should be noted that we took concrete steps to preclude such an explanation. Specifically, for about half of the studies reported in this book, two experimenters were used. One administered general instructions and noise stimuli; the second, ignorant of the subjects' experimental conditions and, in some cases, of the hypothesis of the study, administered the aftereffect tests—problem solving, proofreading, and color-word naming. In these circumstances, consistent experimenter effects could not be postulated. There was indeed no systematic difference in the production of successful results between studies run by one experimenter and those run by two experimenters.

Relative Deprivation

Chapter 5 introduced the concept of relative deprivation and described a noise study addressed to that point. In that study, subjects were relatively deprived of access to control: the confederate had a noise-terminating switch, they did not. But both the advantaged confederate and the deprived subject were exposed to the same noise. There was no relative deprivation with respect to the stressor. A different, though equally intuitive, approach to relative deprivation would have a subject exposed to a greater amount of noise than a confederate, or even more to the point, the subject should perceive he is undergoing more noise when in fact both he and the confederate are undergoing the same degree of stimulation. In these circumstances, it is possible to derive the prediction of greater than normal adverse aftereffects for the deprived subject.

An individual exposed to a physical stressor such as noise will experience a certain amount of discomfort and incur a certain measure of after-the-fact liability. If that same individual is exposed to noise under identical physical conditions but with knowledge that someone similar is being exposed to less intense noise, the resultant feelings of relative deprivation should increase the aversiveness of the noise and consequent negative aftereffects. This prediction assumes that frustration stemming from relative deprivation generalizes to the stressful event itself and makes for a more generally aversive experience. In those instances where a subject finds himself better off relative to a comparison person, there should be arousal of relative satisfaction rather than relative deprivation. This satisfaction will lower the total aversiveness of the situation by a similar process of generalization and, therefore, we may expect less severe poststress effects. These predictions constitute the basis for the following experiment, conducted by Brett Silverstein and Ilene Staff at Stony Brook.

Experimental Procedure

Subjects were recruited by advertisements offering $3.00 for participation in research. Each volunteer was individually scheduled and, upon arrival at the experimental suite, was joined by a confederate posing as a second subject. The confederate was the same sex as the subject. The experimenter greeted both of them and proceeded with a general introduction to noise research. Three experimental conditions, one of Low Relative Deprivation (i.e., high relative satisfaction), a second of High Relative Deprivation, and a third of No Relative Deprivation, were created by the instructions given below. Ten subjects were randomly assigned to each condition.

In the Low Relative Deprivation condition, subjects were told: "In order for us to really tell something about how noise affects people, we are using two levels of noise. That is, some of our subjects will have as high a level of noise as we can give them without risk of physiological damage. Other subjects will receive only a moderate level of noise, so that we may compare the effects of two levels of noise. We use a high level of noise so that we can tell the maximum effect noise is likely to produce; we use a moderate level so that we can tell the usual effects. Each of you has been randomly assigned to a noise level condition." The confederate was then informed: "You have been assigned to a high level of noise, and will be taking the experiment in the other acoustic chamber; physically it is set up identically to this one. There, you will be subjected to the highest possible level of noise we are able to generate without causing physiological damage." By contrast, the subject was told: "You will be seated in this room and will receive a moderate level of noise."

To create High Relative Deprivation, subjects assigned to this condition were given these instructions: "In order for us to really tell something about how noise affects people, we are using two levels of noise. That is, some of our subjects will have as low a level of noise as we can give them and still qualify as technically audible sound. Other subjects will receive a moderate level of noise, so that we may compare the effects of two levels of noise. We use a very low level of noise so that we will be able to tell the minimum effect noise is likely to produce. We use a moderate level so we can tell the usual effects. Each of you has been randomly assigned to a noise level condition." The confederate was then told: "You have been assigned to the low level of noise, and will be taking the experiment in the other acoustic chamber; physically it is set up identically to this one. You will be subjected to the lowest possible level of noise we are able to generate and still technically call noise." The subject was told: "You will be seated in this room and will receive a moderate level of noise."

The No Relative Deprivation subjects received these instructions: "In order to tell how noise affects people, we are exposing each of our subjects to a moderate level of noise. We pick a moderate level so that we are able to tell the usual effects noise is likely to produce. The level we are using is roughly midway between being barely audible but still technically noise, and being physiologically damaging." The experimenter then said to the confederate: "You will be taking the experiment in the other acoustic chamber; physically it is set up identically to this one. There, you will receive a moderate amount of noise." The subject was given the alternate instruction: "You will be seated in this room and will also receive a moderate level of noise."

Following appropriate instructions, the confederate was led out of the room, ostensibly to go to the other experimental chamber. The subject was then exposed to the 24-burst, 108-dBA random noise tape, during which time he was asked to perform a spatial relations task. Slides of three-dimensional geometric figures were presented on a projection screen and the subject was asked to locate corresponding sides of folded and unfolded versions of these figures on a test sheet in front of him (cf. French, Ekstrom, & Price, 1963). After noise exposure, each subject was taken out of the experimental chamber to a separate room and given the proofreading task, a paper-and-pencil version of the Stroop Color Word Test,[1] and a postexperimental questionnaire.

---

[1] The version of the Stroop used in this study was a modification of the form published by the Educational Testing Service (Item No. 613400). It is a self-administered test in which the subject writes the letter of the appropriate color under the color names. There are four pages of these names, each one containing 176 items. Subjects were given 2 minutes to work on each page, and they were told to correct themselves if they made an error. As in the version used in the previous noise experiments, this task was preceded by Part II, naming colored asterisks, which was scored only for purposes of eliminating color-blind subjects. Unlike the other version, however, there was no Part I.

Results

Analysis of questionnaire data confirmed that the deprivation manipulation was successful. Subjects were asked to rate, on 7-point scales, the intensity of the noise to which they had been exposed and then to rate the intensity of the noise to which they believed the other subject (i.e., the confederate) had been exposed. As can be seen in Table 6.1, all subjects felt the noise was intense (mean = 5.2), and there were no differences in subjects' perceptions of what they had been told was moderate–intensity noise. However, there were large differences in subjects' perceptions of the noise to which the confederate had been exposed ($p < .01$), with High Relative Deprivation subjects reporting a significantly lower level for him than No Relative Deprivation or Low Relative Deprivation subjects. The difference between the latter two groups is reliable at the .05 level, although there is some indication of a ceiling effect for Low Relative Deprivation subjects. If their own noise was already at the 5.10 level of intensity, and the other subject's is presumably much more intense, the 7-point scale limits their ability to describe the other subject's noise. The difference column in Table 6.1 sums up the effects of the manipulation. Subjects in High Relative Deprivation felt they had received more intense noise than the confederate, subjects in Low Relative Deprivation felt they had received less intense noise, and No Relative Deprivation subjects perceived no difference.

Psychophysiological measures were not recorded during this study, but the typical pattern of adaptation to noise can be seen in the performance on the spatial relations task presented in Table 6.2. The task was divided into five parts and errors for each part were tabulated. There were no differences between these part performances under the three conditions. The only effect (significant at the .01 level) was a decrease in errors over time—an index of adaptation.

The proofreading task was administered immediately after the noise, followed by the Stroop test. The instructions and timing for these tasks were essentially the same as previously described, except for minor modifications to accommodate differences in task format between their use in this experiment and in others reported in this volume. Table 6.3 reports the results for both

TABLE 6.1

Ratings of Noise Intensity

Experimental condition	Own noise	Other subject's noise	Difference
High relative deprivation	5.70	2.95	-2.75
No relative deprivation	4.80	4.40	-.40
Low relative deprivation	5.10	6.56	+1.46

TABLE 6.2

Errors on the Spatial Relations Task

Experimental condition	Task parts				
	1st fifth	2nd fifth	3rd fifth	4th fifth	5th fifth
High relative deprivation	1.80	2.10	1.50	1.00	.40
No relative deprivation	2.00	.90	1.30	1.20	.40
Low relative deprivation	2.20	1.10	.90	.90	.20

aftereffect measures; as can be seen, they reflect the effects of the deprivation manipulation. Proofreading performance shows a deficit between the High Relative Deprivation condition and the other two ($ps < .02$). The measure reveals no differences in performance between No Relative Deprivation and Low Relative Deprivation conditions, but this apparent lack of difference may be attributable to a ceiling effect. If No Deprivation subjects are working at the limit of errorless proofreading, the presumably less stressed Low Deprivation subjects could hardly improve their performance. The Stroop Color Word Test does show an ordered effect. Administration consisted of timed trials on each of four different pages. Table 6.3 presents results for the first of these pages and for the four-page total as well. On the first test page, the overall difference was at the .01 level of significance, with differences between adjacent conditions being reliable at the .05 level. Over the entire series of test pages, performances of all three groups retained their relative separation with the same levels of significance (see the last column of Table 6.3).

TABLE 6.3

Performance on Aftereffect Tasks

Experimental condition	Proofreading: Percent errors missed[a]	Stroop task: Number of items completed[a]	
		1st page	Total
High relative deprivation	30.90	89.80	375.60
No relative deprivation	17.00	101.70	402.50
Low relative deprivation	17.30	108.90	423.00

[a] Parametric differences between these values and those reported in Chapters 4 and 5 are, in part, attributable to differences in task specifications.

Discussion

A summary of the results presents a clear picture. The No Relative Deprivation subjects (those who were presumably exposed to the same stress as the confederate) provide a bench mark for comparison purposes. They were told they would receive moderately intense noise—neither inaudible nor physiologically damaging—and this is what they did hear. Their performance on the spatial relations task during noise exposure, as well as on the proofreading and Stroop tests afterward, reflect the processes involved in coping with a noxious stressor in noninvidious circumstances. The High Relative Deprivation subjects underwent the same promised moderate level of noise, but were made aware that another subject would receive a less intense, barely audible set of stimuli. Although the High Deprivation subjects adapted behaviorally as indexed by performance improvements on the spatial relations task, they did less well on the proofreading and Stroop tasks than the No Deprivation subjects. In mirror image fashion, the Low Deprivation subjects also adapted during the noise, but the effect of knowing that another subject was undergoing a more aversive stress ameliorated the aftereffects. The Low Deprivation subjects did better on the Stroop than the No Deprivation subjects, and showed the same high level of performance on the proofreading task.

The process by which relative deprivation exerts its effects can be formulated in a manner somewhat similar to that which we used to explain the effects of perceived control. The basic assumption we make is that the noxiousness of a stress depends, in part, on the person's evaluation of the stressor in relation to his ability to cope with it. The more overwhelming it seems and the less likely his adaptive resources, the more threatening will be his appraisal. Perceived control would reduce the stressor's effects primarily by increasing the person's evaluation of his coping resources. The next assumption is that the more noxious or threatening the stressor is, the more effort the person will exert in functioning under its duress. Relative deprivation may exert its effects by providing the subject with additional information for assessing the magnitude of the stressor confronting him. The person who is not in a relative deprivation situation judges the stressor within the context of his immediate environment and his past experience. The person who is in a state of high relative deprivation has the additional knowledge that others are faced with a less threatening situation. This may cause him to reassess both the stressor's magnitude and the amount of energy required to cope with it. Alternatively, the person in a state of low relative deprivation has the cognition that there is an even more intense level of stress; this may enable him to revise his assessment as less threatening and cause him to allocate less coping energy for combatting the stressor.

Stated somewhat differently, the High Relative Deprivation subject expends more energy in working under stress and, in one way or another, he has less resources to use on the aftereffect measures—hence a performance deficit. The Low Relative Deprivation subject, in contrast, expends less energy in coping with the stress and has more left for effective performance on the aftereffect tasks. Consequently, the High Relative Deprivation subject does worse on aftertasks than No Deprivation and Low Relative Deprivation subjects.

It is instructive to compare this relative deprivation experiment with the one previously described in Chapter 5. At that time, we concluded that relative deprivation had little effect. And, given differences between the two studies, the statement is still appropriate. The experiment reported in Chapter 5 induced relative deprivation only with respect to access to control of the stressor, not in regard to level of the stressor itself. In the former case, there are little or no relative deprivation effects; in the latter case, the effects are well documented.

Expectation

We have suggested that cognitive factors influence reactions to stress by modifying both the assessment of the seriousness of the stress and the coping resources necessary to cope with it. This notion serves not only as an explanation for the impact of relative deprivation, but also leads to further speculation. A preeminent factor in shaping such assessments is the person's expectations about the magnitude of stress. For example, if a person is given a "set" that an impending stress will be severe, he may precommit a heavy battery of coping resources such that he will expend a larger-than-usual amount of energy in working under stress; in parallel fashion, the expectancy of a mild stress will lead a person to devote less energy to coping with the stress. In short, the expectancy of stress magnitude can influence the stressor's debilitating effects.

Unfortunately, this prediction is not unequivocal, for the opposite results can also be derived. The previous model would only be effectual if the magnitude of stress were concordant with the expectancy. That is, if you expect the stress to be severe, it must be harsh enough when it occurs to conform to that set. If it is not, the discrepancy between commitment of coping resources and the fraction of that commitment actually needed may, by contrast, cause the stressor to be evaluated as less severe than usual and mitigate its effects. And, without elaborating other possible outcomes, we can note that whenever a discrepancy arises between expectancy and outcome, dissonance and its attendant processes will be aroused. One conclusion is possible: expectancy is a likely candidate as a cognitive factor influencing reactions to noise, although the direction and magnitude of its effects are not specifiable in advance. In an attempt to explore some of these considerations, the following experiment was conducted by Nataša Bauerova at Stony Brook.

Experimental Procedure

Sixty-eight undergraduate subjects were recruited for an experiment on the effects of noise. They were individually scheduled and, upon their arrival, the experimenter gave each a version of the standard instructions previously described. Twelve subjects, those randomly assigned to a No Expectation condition, were not given further information. Twenty-eight subjects, those assigned to a High Expectation condition, were given the expectation that the noise would be intense. They were told that the noise would be "as intense as possible without causing physiological damage." A Low Expectation condition, consisting of 28 subjects, was informed that the noise would not be very intense: it would be "as mild as possible and still within the technical definition of noise."

Subjects were then given forms to complete, which in addition to serving as consent agreements and receipts for payment, contained questions measuring expectations of the impending noise. Next, each subject was seated in the experimental room and exposed to the 24-burst, 108-dBA random noise tape while performing the spatial relations task described earlier in the relative deprivation study. Upon completion of the noise, the subject was taken to another room where a second experimenter administered two aftereffect measures, the proofreading task and the Stroop Color Word Test. A postexperimental questionnaire was then administered. Finally, the second experimenter stepped out of his role, introduced himself as an undergraduate assistant, and asked the subject to volunteer time for an unrelated experiment he was conducting as part of a course requirement.

Results and Discussion

Performance of the subjects during noise exposure parallels the results of previous studies. Improvement occurred in all conditions. The details are presented in Table 6.4, and, as can be seen, there were no systematic differences between experimental groups. Overall, there was a significant diminuation of errors over time ($p < .05$), and for some unknown reason, the fourth part of the task yielded significantly fewer errors than any other period.

The three aftereffect measures yielded outcomes easy to summarize: no differences of any sort. The results are presented in Table 6.5. The proofreading scores are virtually identical. The Stroop Color Word Test scores are marginally significant ($p < .10$), with Low Noise Expectation subjects completing more than the other two groups. However, whatever trend these data may suggest is contraindicated by the Volunteer Request results where, at the .20 level, Low Noise Expectation subjects offer somewhat less time than do the other two groups.

TABLE 6.4

Errors on the Spatial Relations Task

Experimental condition	Task parts				
	1st fifth	2nd fifth	3rd fifth	4th fifth	5th fifth
High noise expectation[a]	1.28	1.60	1.22	.43	1.05
Low noise expectation[a]	2.04	1.72	1.18	.36	1.00
No expectation[b]	2.00	1.25	1.17	.50	.83

[a] $n = 28$.
[b] $n = 12$.

The experiment obviously did not produce the anticipated effects. Reasons for such failure are myriad. They range from inept experimentation to incorrect hypotheses to counteracting trends. Some additional data can be reviewed that may clarify the situation. The questions that verified the success of the manipulation were administered before the noise was presented. Subjects in the High Noise Expectation condition uniformly expected to receive intense noise, those in the Low Noise Expectation condition expected to receive mild noise, and those not given an expectation had a mean expectation roughly midway between the other two groups. The differences between groups are significant at the .01 level. On the basis of these data, the manipulation appeared to work. Subjects reported back the explanation they were given about the noise.

The question at issue is, however, whether expectations carried over and affected subjects' perceptions of the noise. Two items in the postexperimental questionnaire provide data addressed to this point. One asked subjects to report how the noise they received compared to what they had expected. Scores

TABLE 6.5

Performance on Aftereffect Tasks

Experimental condition	Proofreading: Percent errors missed	Stroop task: Number of items completed		Volunteer request: Minutes offered
		1st page	Total	
High noise expectation	44.10	99.64	393.64	42.86
Low noise expectation	44.22	104.56	408.04	36.79
No expectation	43.03	97.92	398.08	44.17

ranged from +1, maximally greater than expected, through 0, equal to expecta-tions, to −1, maximally less than expected. The other item, scored on a 9-point scale, asked subjects to report the intensity of the noise they actually received. The answers to both questions are tabulated in Table 6.6. The results for the first item show that the noise stimulus was loud and unambiguous, so much so that it appeared to overwhelm the effects of the expectation manipulation. The High Noise Expectation subjects received the noise they had expected, the No Noise Expectation subjects received somewhat more than expected, and the Low Noise Expectation subjects received much more than expected. The net result is shown in the second column of Table 6.6. Subjects in all conditions regarded the noise as equally intense. If this reappraisal determines the amount of resources the subject allocates to coping with the noise stress, then all three groups had equally aversive experiences and, not surprisingly, showed similarly adverse aftereffects.

These findings do not mean that expectations have no influence on performance; rather, they suggest that our experiment was not designed to allow them to manifest themselves. If the noise stimulus had been either less intense or more ambiguous, the intensity could have been assimilated into expectation and the effects of the stimulus moderated or exacerbated. Even with the 108-dBA stimuli used in the present study, there should have been expectation effects up to the point where they were eradicated by the impact of nonassimilable noise. If we had included pretask measures, that is, proofreading and Stroop-like tasks after the expectation induction but before noise, we might have detected performance differences. High Noise subjects, planning to expend coping energy on the impending stressor, would be expected to show deficits on the prenoise tasks. Low Noise subjects, led to believe the stressor would utilize little in the way of coping resources, would be expected to show facilitation on the prenoise tasks. In any event, the issue is moot pending acquisition of empirical evidence.

TABLE 6.6

Ratings of the Noise

Experimental condition	Items	
	How did it compare to expectations[a]	How intense was it[b]
High noise expectation	.07	6.64
Low noise expectation	.86	6.89
No expectation	.58	7.17

[a] A positive number means that the noise was more intense than expected.

[b] Higher numbers represent more intense noise.

Necessity and Choice

During World War II, while engaged in research on audition, Harvard psychologists produced intermittent bursts of high-energy noise across the Harvard Yard. Although many students were living and studying in the area, they received no complaints. When the researchers asked several students why they did not complain about the sound, the students replied that they knew the project was important to the war effort and therefore did not object to the attendant noise. On the surface, this incident suggests that necessary noise may not be as bothersome as gratuitous noise. However, closer analysis suggests more intriguing possibilities.

The level of complaint about unwanted noise is not solely an index of its annoyance value. The complaints also reflect the desirability and perceived possibility of producing change. Thus, if complaints by homeowners contiguous to airports decrease with time, this may reflect either adaptation to the noise or resignation about the ineffectiveness of their complaints. Similarly, if the Harvard experience were a controlled field experiment, it would still not be possible to tell whether the subjects were suppressing complaints because of the importance of the research, or whether the importance of the research was a factor in reducing the bothersomeness of the noise. And when a direct measure of noise bothersomeness or of noise aftereffects is substituted for complaint as a dependent variable, two contraposed hypotheses, stated below, are generated about the relationship of noise necessity to subsequent disturbance.

The necessity of a stressful event like noise may be another cognitive factor ameliorating its aversiveness. This rather straightforward hypothesis can be contrasted with the prediction that necessary noise may be regarded as more disturbing than an equal amount of nonnecessary noise. The latter hypothesis is an extension of dissonance theory, particularly those studies dealing with hunger and thirst motivation (Brehm, 1962). Thus, nonnecessary (in a sense, unjustified) noise may produce dissonance as well as discomfort, and the dissonance may be reduced by a reevaluation of the noise. Necessary (in a sense, justified) noise may not produce dissonance, hence may not be subject to cognitive reevaluation and diminution. This is the third time we have referred to dissonance as a cognitive process that may influence the effects of noise in Chapter 5, for example, a dissonance alternative was suggested as a mechanism by which perceived control might decrease adverse aftereffects of noise. In recent years, a number of investigators have established that dissonance exerts influence over a wide variety of motivational states (Zimbardo, 1969). While dissonance theory can be used to derive specific alternative explanations for some of our studies, its widely documented and pervasive effects deserve more direct test. In other words, can dissonance reduction processes mitigate the effects of noise?

Aside from manipulating justification for commitment to aversive stimulation, one of the more effective ways of arousing dissonance is to give a person a choice about whether or not to experience the stressful event. Perceived choice creates the cognition, "I freely chose to undergo this experience," which is dissonant with the cognition, "This event is unpleasant or painful." The resultant dissonance can be resolved by reevaluating the unpleasantness of the event—if the noise is not noxious, dissonance disappears. On the other hand, dissonance is only minimally aroused if the choice to undergo aversive stimulation is accompanied by substantial justification. A rationale for voluntary commitment to an unpleasant event introduces cognitions consistent with the commitment, thereby short-circuiting dissonance arousal.

This line of thought can be specifically applied to the case of necessary and unnecessary noise if we assume that necessity does indeed act like justification. Given this assumption, we hypothesize that dissonance will be greatest where the subject voluntarily agrees to expose himself to unnecessary noise, and least where he is required to experience necessary noise. We may thus expect that reevaluation of the noise and consequent reduction of negative aftereffects will be greatest in the former condition and least in the latter condition. This prediction contrasts with the hypothesis, stated above, that perceived necessity of noise directly reduces its aversive effects. In these terms, voluntary agreement to experience necessary noise should produce less deleterious aftereffects than nonvoluntary exposure to unnecessary, and even necessary, noise. In order to test the validity of the hypotheses just described, Ilene Staff conducted the following experiment at Stony Brook.

Experimental Procedure

Forty-eight[2] subjects, 24 female and 24 male, participated in the study. They were individually scheduled and randomly assigned to one of four conditions: Necessary Noise–Choice, Necessary Noise–No Choice, Unnecessary Noise–Choice, and Unnecessary Noise–No Choice. Upon arrival at the laboratory, the student heard instructions appropriate to his condition. The instructions designed to create each treatment are given below.

Necessary noise. "The experiment you will be participating in today is designed to study galvanic skin response, that is, GSR. Have you learned about it in a psychology class? It is one of the most common physiological measures

---

[2] Fifty subjects were recruited for the study, but 2 were dropped from consideration: 1 because of apparatus failure, and the other because he was unable to comply with instructions.

used. It measures changes in the electrical conductivity of the skin. It's done by placing two electrodes on your skin, for example, on your hand and wrist. Don't worry about it; it's not at all painful. In fact, you don't even feel that it's on.

"[GSR] is usually used to measure reactions to stimuli; for example, a light or a sound is quite common, but you can measure the reaction to most anything. I'm interested in studying a person's GSR response while he is thinking through and solving a problem. I'll be presenting you with what we call box problems (I'll explain them in a minute) and will be measuring your GSR at the same time.

"Now that is the procedure used in a number of our studies. In this [particular] study, we are also interested in the effect of noise on GSR and problem solving. The procedure will thus be changed slightly. You will be seated in this chair and I'll attach electrodes to your wrist and hand and start measuring your reactions. I'll then start the machinery so that the box problems will appear one slide at a time [on that screen] and the noise will start coming on intermittently. O.K. I'll explain the box problems to you . . .."

In order to induce *perceived choice* in half of the subjects in this condition, the experimenter proceeded to say: "Now we're not having all of our subjects exposed to the noise. We've decided to ask subjects if they would be willing to listen to it. I'm going to let you hear a burst of noise to help you decide whether you will agree to listen to it, but first I'd like to explain that unfortunately not enough subjects have agreed to listen to the noise, so it really would help me a lot if you would. Of course it is your choice to make. You'll receive the same money (or credit) regardless of your choice."

After the sample noise burst and the subject's decision, the experimenter said: "If you don't have any questions, I'll attach the electrodes and we can begin." The other half of the Necessary subjects, those who were not given a choice, were told, "We have assigned some of our subjects to the noise exposure condition; you have been randomly chosen as one of these subjects. I'll let you hear a sample of the noise so you will know what to expect."

Unnecessary noise. Subjects assigned to this treatment received essentially the same instructions as those assigned to the Necessary Noise condition. However, the study was not presented as being concerned with noise effects. Instead, subjects were told, "There's one more thing I'd like to explain before we start. Changes in GSR are, as you might expect, quite small and it is very difficult to read data from the [recording] machine . . .. In order to help calibrate the machine, so that we can have an extreme reaction to use as a contrast, we're asking some of our subjects if they would mind being exposed to bursts of noise . . .. That way we can use the reactions between bursts of noise as our data and the reactions to the noise as guidelines to break up the data.

"I'm going to let you hear a burst of noise to help you decide whether you will agree to listen to it, but first I'd like to explain that unfortunately not enough subjects have agreed to listen to the noise, so it really would help me a lot if you would. Of course it is your choice to make. You'll receive the same money (or credit) regardless of your choice."

The latter instructions, designed to induce feelings of choice, were given to half of the subjects in the Unnecessary Noise condition. The remaining half of the subjects were given No Choice instructions as follows: "We're having some of our subjects exposed to bursts of noise . . .. That way we can use the reactions between bursts as our data and the reactions to the noise as guidelines to break up the data. You've been randomly chosen as one of the subjects that will be given the noise. I'll let you hear a sample of the noise so you will know what to expect."

GSR measures were not actually taken during the experiment. Electrodes were attached to the subject to lend credence to the experimental rationale. The subject was exposed to the 24-burst random noise tape played at 105 dBA, during which time the spatial relations problems were presented for solution. Following noise exposure, electrodes were removed and the subject was given the proofreading task and the paper-and-pencil version of the Stroop Color Word Test. The experimenter then gave each subject a postexperimental questionnaire and asked for "volunteer time" on the same basis as described earlier in the expectancy study.

Results and Discussion

The two manipulations—Necessity and Choice—had their intended effect as measured by questions in the postexperimental questionnaire. In response to a 7-point scale asking how much choice they had in undergoing the noise, subjects

TABLE 6.7

Effectiveness of the Necessity Manipulation[a,b]

Experimental condition	Questionnaire items	
	To test effects of noise	To help with machine calibration
Necessary noise	21	0
Unnecessary noise	6	15

[a]Since six subjects were given a different form of the questionnaire, their results are not comparable, and therefore are not included in the tabulation.

[b]Chi square = 22.5, $p < .001$.

in the Choice conditions reported a mean of 4.10, those in the No Choice conditions a mean of 1.35. The difference is significant at less than the .001 level. The Necessity manipulation was also effective. As shown in Table 6.7, when subjects were asked to check the reason for the noise during the study, those in the Unnecessary conditions were more likely to attribute it to an extraneous cause than subjects in the Necessary conditions, all of whom regarded it as central to the study.

Subjects in all four conditions showed a decrease in errors over time on the spatial relations problems. There were no between-condition differences nor condition-by-time interactions. The results were essentially the same as those reported for the other studies in this chapter.

The four experimental treatments did not, however, show a consistent pattern of behavioral aftereffects (see Table 6.8) They did not differ at all on proofreading; on the Stroop task, the Necessary-Choice condition was marginally ($p < .10$) different from the other three conditions on both the first page and the four-page total. But the volunteering measure did show some effects. These results are also presented in Table 6.8. There is a main effect attributable to Choice, as well as an interaction effect between Choice and Necessity. Subjects in the Choice conditions volunteered more time than did those in the No Choice conditions ($p < .05$). As would be expected by a dissonance interpretation, this effect was greatest in the Unnecessary Noise condition; that is, it is more dissonant to freely choose to undergo unnecessary noise than necessary noise. For the dissonance produced by choosing to experience necessary noise can be reduced by the consonance of added cognitions about the importance and justification of the sudy.

Overall, the Necessity manipulation had little or no effect, whereas the Choice variable had ramifications not only on volunteering but throughout the study. Compared to No Choice subjects, those allowed a choice reported the noise as less annoying ($p < .005$) and less disruptive of their performance

TABLE 6.8

Performance on Aftereffect Tasks

Experimental condition	Proofreading: Percent errors missed	Stroop task: Number of items completed		Volunteer request: minutes offered
		1st page	Total	
Necessary noise-Choice	43.1	92.6	358.4	62.5
Necessary noise-No choice	39.0	104.3	416.6	73.8
Unnecessary noise-Choice	43.5	106.6	418.3	95.5
Unnecessary noise-No choice	39.0	108.5	421.4	43.5

($p < .05$), and were more interested in tasks such as proofreading ($p < .025$). These findings are consistent with similar studies of the effects of choice (cf. Zimbardo, 1969), but are neither as powerful as those reported in other dissonance studies nor as compelling as those brought about by the closely related perceived control manipulation.

The failure of the Necessity induction to change the magnitude of adverse aftereffects is equivocal. It may simply be a contextual variable of no import. Or, given the opposing nature of our original speculations, it may have produced counteracting tendencies that canceled each other out. Our own hunch is that neither of these represents the main difficulty. Whereas in the world outside the laboratory, noise as intense as 105 dBA is occasionally both possible and unnecessary—the street outside your first floor window may be under repair by a jackhammer crew, or your neighbor's teenagers may be rehearsing their rock music group—experimenter credibility is diminished when these conditions are attempted in the laboratory. With a loudspeaker volume of 105 dBA, subjects simply refuse to believe that it is either accidental or not part of the experimenter's plans. At the very least, they feel that if the cover story of nonnecessity were true, a competent experimenter would cancel the session rather than have his results contaminated by the effects of random blasts of noise. Under these restraints, the present rationale was derived: the noise was presented as tangential to the main thrust of the study, but needed in order to calibrate the equipment. Thus necessity in the two conditions differed only in a mild degree, not in quality. We are still awaiting an adequate test of whether it matters if the noise has a utilitarian purpose or is merely gratuitous.

Conclusions

In this chapter, we have examined the impact of cognitive factors other than predictability and controllability upon noise effects and aftereffects. Relative deprivation was seen to be an effective moderating or amplifying agent, expectations of intensity were not. The arousal of dissonance yielded results that paralleled, in weakened fashion, dissonance effects upon other aversive stimuli and their consequences; finally, necessity was declared "No contest." In this way, we have proceeded with one sort of extension of our original investigation. We have examined the stress of noise in a variety of cognitive contexts. In the next two chapters we explore a different set of extensions. We examine whether the aftereffects produced by noise are also produced by other stressors, some physical and some social.

Behavioral Aftereffects of Unpredictable and Uncontrollable Electric Shock

All of the research presented thus far has been concerned with the effects of exposure to noise. However, we were careful in the second chapter, when we discussed the general background of behavioral aftereffects of stress, to delineate the issues in such a way that they would be applicable to any stressor. Noise was selected as our first exemplar for several reasons. It was easy to control and vary in the laboratory, it conveniently interacted with the cognitive factors of interest, and it provided a clear conceptual way to separate stressor effects from stressor aftereffects. Not least important was the fact that laboratory-produced noise was a reasonable analogue to sounds occurring in the natural environment. The possibility of contributing to the understanding of a contemporary social problem was and is an appealing one. But, so far, our exposition has completely confounded general aftereffect phenomena with specific noise-bound research. The generalizability of the findings and implications is an open issue.

Few people encounter electric shock in the course of their lives, yet this stimulus has been one of the more frequently used stressors in behavioral research. This emphasis on shock may have misrepresented the role of aversive stimulation in everyday life, but it has produced a sizable amount of information about the effects of stress on human behavior in the laboratory. And such behavior is not necessarily artificial or removed from the real world simply because it emerges in a laboratory setting. The use of shock as a stressor also has a number of experimental advantages, including the ability to control its intensity, frequency, time of onset, and termination. It is, therefore, a likely candidate for testing notions about the effects of unpredictability and perceived control on the aftereffects of stress exposure. Aside from permitting the development of generalizations about these variables, the application of shock in place of noise also allows us to make comparisons with classical escape and avoidance studies where shock has been the principal stressor. So, for these reasons, we conducted an experiment using electric shock as the stressor.

In Chapter 5, we saw that when noise is perceived as seemingly contingent on instrumental responses, this operates like the perception of escape; that is, the individual experiences feelings of having controlled the noise and deleterious aftereffects are reduced. The noise was aperiodic in that particular study, and we would have expected similar results with any unsignaled noise. Similarly, we anticipate that unsignaled electric shocks will produce impaired postshock performance, and furthermore, that these effects will be reduced if the subject perceives a contingency between his responses and the possibility of avoiding shock. A test of these hypotheses requires joint manipulation of the unpredictability and uncontrollability of shock, along with the usual measures of adaptation and poststressor effects. The following study by Bruce Reim at New York University satisfied these requirements.

Experimental Procedure

There were two shock conditions in the experiment—unpredictable and predictable. Unpredictable shock entailed 18 electric shocks randomly spaced over a 19-minute period. The random schedule was almost identical to the one used in the unavoidable noise experiment (see Chapter 5). Shocks were of approximately constant intensity at 3 milliamperes (mA), and each lasted for one-half second.[1] The shock supply was used in the direct current mode (Scientific Prototype AC-DC Isolated Shock Source, Model SS13), its activation being regulated by a locally constructed tape programmer. Shocks were delivered over two .625-inch-diameter silver electrodes attached to the middle of the inner surface of the subject's nonpreferred forearm. Along with regulating intershock intervals, the tape programmer controlled delivery of 18 one-half-second tones (30 dB, 500 Hz) from an audio oscillator. In the Unpredictable conditions, these tones were randomly interspersed throughout the shock sequence. Predictable shock involved precisely the same procedures described for Unpredictable shock, except the tones always appeared 3 seconds before each shock.

Within each of the two shock conditions, half of the subjects were exposed to the perceived avoidance manipulations used in the unavoidable-noise experiment, whereas the other half received the no perceived avoidance manipulations (see Chapter 5). Procedures and instructions were identical to those employed in the noise study, including the use of the soluble and insoluble graphic puzzles. The only exception was a slightly different soluble puzzle for the second position in the sequence of puzzles presented to subjects in the Perceived Avoidance and Soluble Control conditions.

Introductory remarks in this experiment differed somewhat from those used in the past and are therefore presented verbatim. After a subject was seated in the laboratory, the experimenter said the following.

"The purpose of this study is to investigate the effects of stressful stimuli on learning and performance. This problem has obvious implications for educators, management consultants, clinical and industrial psychologists, and others. As you well know, we are living in an increasingly complex environment, and urban dwellers in particular are continually confronted with physical stressors such as noise, overcrowding, air and water pollution, and so forth. The evidence we have so far suggests that learning and performance are severely impaired by such stress. Unfortunately, much of this evidence is based on anecdotal reports and casual observation. There is a clear need for more systematic and carefully controlled research on these problems.

"However, a major difficulty in doing such research is devising means of bringing urban stressors into the laboratory. For example, we cannot very well

[1] Each time a shock was delivered to the subject it was recorded on a Dynograph recorder. Previous calibration allowed the experimenter to determine at a glance the actual magnitude of shock. Since the range of intensities for the first shock varied from about 2.0 mA to 3.5 mA in each condition, it was often necessary to make adjustments on the impedance dial of the shock source immediately after the first shock. In this way, the experimenter was assured of delivering 3-mA shocks for the remaining 17 trials. Inspection of GSR responses to the first shock indicated that retention of these data would not have appreciably affected the adaptation results. We therefore analyzed the full set of 18 shocks.

pollute the air in this room or saturate it with urban noise—at least we cannot do it without losing the very scientific control we are aiming at. Fortunately, there are alternatives. One, in particular, has long been used by psychologists to study the effects of stress on learning and performance. I'm referring to electric shock. In the lab, the number and frequency of shocks can be easily controlled. This gives us a reliable experimental procedure for investigating stress. In today's study, we will be administering electric shocks as you work on a series of perceptual puzzles. Let me emphasize that the shocks you will be receiving are in no way dangerous. . . ." The remaining instructions were essentially the same as those used in the noise studies, including the rationale for physiological measurement and attachment of electrodes. Adaptation was measured by phasic skin conductance, and the poststressor measures were proofreading and the oral response version of the Stroop Color Word Test (see Chapter 5). Consequences of helplessness were measured by time taken to solve the soluble puzzle coming at the end of the sequence of puzzles.

No Shock Conditions

Along with the basic 2 X 2 design, two no-shock groups were included in the experiment to control for the effects of the different sequences of puzzles subjects worked on in Perceived Avoidance and No Perceived Avoidance conditions. The latter condition involved exclusively insoluble puzzles (except for the final one), whereas the former relied on predominantly soluble puzzles (four of the six, including the final puzzle). One of the control groups was therefore administered the soluble sequence, and the other, the insoluble sequence. By showing that these groups were similar on the dependent measures, we could attribute differences between experimental conditions to the manipulations and not to artifacts introduced by the fact that subjects worked on different sets of puzzles. These No Shock control groups, it will be remembered, were used to evaluate differences between experimental conditions in the unavoidable-noise study.

The No Shock subjects were told that the study was designed to investigate "differential effects of living in urban and rural environments on human performance and physiology," and that the stress of urban life has adverse effects requiring more systematic examination. They were then told that they constituted the urban sample and their "performance would be compared with a group of students now living in rural environments." The use of shock or noise was not mentioned, nor did the experimenter say anything about their use in other experimental conditions. Subjects were simply told to do their best on the assigned puzzles.

To maintain continuity of experimental designations, we hereafter refer to the no shock control groups as Soluble Control and Insoluble Control. The experimental conditions are labeled: Predictable Shock–Perceived Avoidance; Predictable Shock–No Perceived Avoidance; Unpredictable Shock–Perceived Avoidance; and Unpredictable Shock–No Perceived Avoidance.

Subjects

Subjects were 66 undergraduate males from the New York University subject pool. Sixty-eight cases were actually tested, but two had to be eliminated from the study, one because he misunderstood the instructions and the other because of equipment failure.

Results

Effectiveness of the Experimental Manipulations

Postexperimental ratings provided unequivocal evidence that subjects receiving signaled shocks felt they could predict the occurrence of each shock, whereas subjects receiving unsignaled shocks reported they were unable to make these predictions. On a 9-point scale ranging from "completely unable to predict" (1) to "completely able to predict" (9), the combined mean for Predictable Shock conditions was 7.72, and for Unpredictable Shock conditions, 2.77. Analysis of variance of ratings from all four conditions yielded a significant main effect for the predictability variable ($F = 143.48$, $1/40\ df$, $p < .001$). Subjects in the Predictable Shock conditions felt they were able to predict the shocks to a greater extent than subjects in the Unpredictable conditions.

As in the unavoidable-noise study, we used three items to check on whether the Perceived Avoidance manipulations were effective: (a) "To what extent did you feel that your performance on the puzzles enabled you to prevent the occurrence of some of the electric shocks?" where 9 = "Completely enabled me to prevent some of the shocks" and 1 = "Did not at all enable me to prevent some of the shocks"; (b) "How many shocks did you receive?" where 9 = "Very many" and 1 = "Very few"; (c) "To what extent did you feel that you could have controlled the occurrence of the electric shocks in today's session?" where 9 = "Definitely could have controlled the shocks" and 1 = "Definitely could not have controlled the shocks." Table 7.1 presents the mean ratings, and it is immediately evident that the expected controllability effects occur on two of the items. Also, the main effect for the predictability variable on the first item is not entirely unexpected, for it indicates that subjects believed they could avoid predictable shocks to a greater extent than unpredictable shocks. This is, after all, a veridical perception, since even No Perceived Avoidance subjects should experience a modicum of control where shock

TABLE 7.1

Mean Ratings on Scales Checking on the Effectiveness of the
Perceived Avoidance Manipulations

Experimental condition	Rating scale		
	Prevented shocks	Number of shocks received	Perceived control of the shocks
Predictable shock-Perceived avoidance[a]	7.55[b]	5.09[c]	6.27[d]
Predictable shock-No perceived avoidance	3.00	4.45	3.91
Unpredictable shock-Perceived avoidance	6.36	4.91	4.25
Unpredictable shock-No perceived avoidance	2.00	4.64	3.36

[a]There are 11 cases in each condition.
[b]F (Perceived Avoidance) = 129.77, 1/40 df, $p < .001$; F (Predictability) = 7.78, 1/40 df, $p < .05$; F (Interaction) < 1.
[c]$F_s < 1$.
[d]F (Perceived Avoidance) = 6.69, 1/40 df, $p < .05$; F (Predictability) = 2.15, 1/40 df, ns; F (Interaction) = 1.10, 1/40 df, ns.

occurrences are anticipated. Just why a similar effect did not appear on the item specifically designed to measure perceived controllability is unclear. It is also puzzling why Avoidance subjects did not report receiving fewer shocks than No Avoidance subjects. This was precisely the effect obtained with this item in the unavoidable-noise experiment. Despite these deviations from expectations, the results generally support the conclusion that the Perceived Avoidance manipulations had their intended effects.

Adaptation

Just as the predictability and controllability manipulations seem to replicate with electric shock, so do the GSR measures of adaptation. Analysis of these data followed procedures used in the noise research, including the grouping of the 18 shocks into three blocks of six trials each. Table 7.2 presents these change in log conductance scores for all six conditions. The results are quite simple: There is a significant decline in GSR scores over the course of the shock sequence ($F = 25.53$, 2/80 df, $p < .001$), while the two control conditions show a nonsignificant increment in reactivity ($F = 1.50$, 2/40 df). There are no differences between experimental conditions for either the first block or third

TABLE 7.2

Mean Changes in Log Conductance Responses to the Shocks

Experimental condition	Blocks of electric shocks		
	1 6 scores	2 6 scores	3 6 scores
Predictable shock-Per- ceived avoidance	.046	.036	.032
Predictable shock-No perceived avoidance	.059	.047	.039
Unpredictable shock-Per- ceived avoidance	.048	.037	.031
Unpredictable shock-No perceived avoidance	.072	.046	.043
Soluble control	.015	.014	.021
Insoluble control	.007	.009	.011

block of scores. An exception occurs in Block 1, where Unpredictable Shock–No Perceived Avoidance differs from Predictable Shock–Perceived Avoidance ($t = 2.00$, 40 df, $p < .06$). We are inclined to treat this difference as a chance effect, for both Perceived Avoidance and No Perceived Avoidance subjects expected, at least initially, to avoid some of the shocks. It is not likely that the latter group became aware of their inability to prevent shock until after the first block of trials. We made essentially the same point in Chapter 5 when discussing the GSR results for the unavoidable-noise study.[2]

The GSR results, then, indicate adaptation to shock. Note, however, that the magnitude of the monotonic decline was somewhat less dramatic than in the noise experiments (e.g., see Table 3.8). It should also be mentioned that skin conductance responses to the signal tones showed a conditioning effect in Predictable Shock conditions. Analysis of these scores (grouped into three blocks of 6 trials each) revealed significant effects of predictability ($F = 4.56$, 1/40 df, $p < .05$), increases in magnitude of GSR over trials ($F = 6.10$, 2/80 df, $p < .01$), and an interaction between the two ($F = 5.80$, 2/80 df, $p < .01$). Examination of relevant means showed that subjects in the Predictable conditions became more responsive to the tones as the session progressed, whereas Unpredictable Shock subjects barely made any changes in their reactions. This finding duplicates effects obtained in the signaled-noise study reported in Chapters 3 and 4.

[2] The difference in magnitude of GSRs in the two Control conditions is also significant at the .06 level ($F = 4.09$, 1/20 df), but it probably reflects nothing more than sampling fluctuations.

TABLE 7.3

Mean Corrected Reading Times on the Stroop Color Word Test[a]

PS-PA	PS-NPA	US-PA	US-NPA	SC	IC
59.00	80.73	65.36	102.18	67.73	72.82

[a]Time is given in seconds.

Postshock Effects

The principal measures of poststress consequences are the Stroop and the proofreading tasks. Table 7.3 presents mean corrected reading times on the Stroop Color Word Test. Analysis of variance revealed an avoidance effect ($F = 21.71$, 1/40 df, $p < .001$) and a predictability effect ($F = 4.90$, 1/40 df, $p < .05$). A Duncan Multiple Range Test showed that the two control groups did not differ from each other ($p > .10$), and that Perceived Avoidance groups were similar to the Soluble Control. Comparison of Unpredictable Shock–No Perceived Avoidance with Insoluble Control produced a significant difference ($p < .05$), but Predictable Shock–No Perceived Avoidance was not reliably greater than its appropriate control.

The proofreading scores parallel the results obtained with the Stroop (see Table 7.4). Analysis revealed a reliable effect of Perceived Avoidance ($F = 43.44$, 1/40 df, $p < .001$) and a marginally significant predictability effect ($F = 2.89$, 1/40 df, $p < .10$). A Duncan Multiple Range Test showed that Perceived Avoidance groups did not differ from the Soluble Control condition, whereas the two No Avoidance groups were statistically greater than Insoluble Control ($ps < .01$). However, the two controls were reliably different from each other ($p < .05$). We commented on this finding in our previous use of these data (see Chapter 5), and concluded that while there was no apparent reason for the difference, it was, in any event, opposite to an obvious artifactual interpretation of the perceived avoidance effect.

The marginally significant predictability term in the analysis of proofreading scores is not completely surprising. In the signaled-noise experiment, this variable also failed to produce any effect on proofreading performance. That it does so with signaled shock may attest to the greater importance of receiving warnings about shock than about noise. The former may be perceived as a more aversive kind of stress in this culture or, more likely, it may simply reflect procedural differences in the experiments. Subjects in the signaled-noise study worked on a experimenter-paced visual task during noise, which was signaled by a visual cue—a light. Subjects in the signaled-shock study worked on a self-paced

TABLE 7.4

Mean Percentage of Errors Missed in the Proofreading Task

PS-PA	PS-NPA	US-PA	US-NPA	SC	IC
29.45	45.64	33.73	49.64	37.18	29.64

visual task during shock, which was signaled by an aural cue—a tone. In all probability, noise subjects were distracted by the forced pacing of the task and the visual competition of task and signal stemming from the need to monitor the signal-stressor contingency. This distraction may have resulted in less reactivity to the signal.

Consequences of Helplessness

We have seen that active problem solving declines following exposure to seemingly unavoidable noise. The same effect occurs in this study, as can be seen in Table 7.5. The difference between Avoidance conditions is statistically significant at the .01 level ($F = 9.43$, $1/40\ df$), but signaling the onset of shock does not appreciably reduce the time taken to solve the puzzle ($F = 1.14$). The difference between Control groups, though sizable, does not even approach significance, and, as in the unavoidable-noise experiment, the No Perceived Avoidance conditions are not reliably greater than the Insoluble Control condition. There is substantial variability in these data, particularly in the Control conditions, yet expected effects are generally confirmed. Assuming time to solution reflects helplessness with respect to shock avoidance, we have not only replicated the noise experiment, but have provided additional support for a helplessness interpretation of the effects of perceived lack of control.

Still further support for this conclusion comes from a postexperimental rating scale anchored at one end by the word "helpless" (1) and at the other by the word "confident" (7). The combined mean rating for the two Avoidance

TABLE 7.5

Mean Time Spent Solving the Final Puzzle[a]

PS-PA	PS-NPA	US-PA	US-NPA	SC	IC
69.09	197.09[b]	140.64	181.91[b]	185.82[b]	124.55[b]

[a]Time is given in seconds.

[b]One subject took more than 400 seconds to solve the puzzle and, accordingly, he was assigned the maximum score of 400 on the test.

conditions was 5.50 and for the two No Avoidance conditions, 4.50. Analysis of the entire set of data revealed a significant Avoidance effect ($F = 8.26$, $1/40\,df$, $p < .05$). whereas the mean difference between Soluble Control (5.22) and Insoluble Control (4.45) was not statistically reliable. Of the other five adjective pairs in the questionnaire, two ("competence–incompetence" and "strong–weak") corroborated these results, and three ("intelligent–unintelligent," "friendly–hostile," and "relaxed–tense") did not show effects of perceived avoidance. Taken together, these data provide some phenomenological evidence for the notion that helplessness mediates the impact of perceived uncontrollability on the aftereffects of exposure to electric shock.

Discussion and Conclusions

The electric-shock experiment was undertaken as a replication of the noise research—at least major aspects of that research. Expectations have been generally confirmed. Subjects were able to adapt to the stress of unpredictable electric shocks, as shown by decrements in phasic skin conductance. However, when compared to nonshocked controls on two poststressor measures, subjects who received unpredictable as compared to predictable shocks showed greater deficits in proofreading efficiency and performance on the Stroop task. As in the noise studies, these aftereffects were substantially reduced among subjects who believed that shock avoidance had been contingent on their task performance. Even though these Perceived Avoidance subjects received the same amount and intensity of shock as those in No Perceived Avoidance conditions, the belief that they had avoided some of the shocks substantially reduced postshock deficits. In order to show a complete correspondence between noise and shock, it would be necessary to replicate each noise experiment with shock (e.g., aperiodic versus periodic, button versus no button, indirect control versus no indirect control). We have obviously not done this, and to that extent our comparison is incomplete. What we have done is to demonstrate that the basic phenomenon replicates with at least two physical stressors, and even with only one experimental overlap, this is a powerful kind of replication.

There is, however, a particularly compelling alternative explanation for the electric-shock effects, an explanation that, incidentally, is also applicable to the unavoidable-noise experiment. It may be argued that subjects in No Perceived Avoidance conditions became increasingly frustrated in their attempts to prevent shock, and this frustration led directly to negative aftereffects. Perception of lack of control was at best magnified by the frustration; at worst it was irrelevant. In order to separate a "frustration" explanation from the perceived-control explanation, we conducted another experimental treatment (the

Unpredictable Shock–No Perceived Avoidance II group). In this new condition 11 male subjects (from the N.Y.U. subject pool) received exactly the same instructions as did the first Unpredictable Shock–No Perceived Avoidance group. The only difference between the two occurred in the instructions for inducing initial perceptions of shock avoidance. The original instructions stated "the number of shocks you receive is determined only by you. That is, if you succeed in correctly tracing a figure, the next scheduled shock will not occur. In fact, after you solve a particular puzzle, you will notice a period of time during which there is no shock. Your successful performance . . . has prevented the next set of scheduled shocks . . . ." Subjects in No Perceived Avoidance conditions were then negatively reinforced in their attempts to solve the puzzles and prevent shock. In the new nonavoidance condition, the instructions were modified to "the number of shocks you receive is determined by a prearranged and mechanically controlled schedule. Your performance on the puzzles will in no way affect the occurrence of the shocks. Your success or failure at the task has nothing to do with the amount of shock you will be receiving . . . ." Subjects in this condition worked on the identical set of puzzles as subjects in the first nonavoidable condition and, of course, they received the same number of unpredictable shocks. The perceived control hypothesis predicts that negative aftereffects in this condition will be no greater than was observed in the first nonavoidable condition. The "frustration" explanation leads to the counterposed hypothesis that subjects in the first condition will experience greater frustration and, therefore, manifest greater postshock performance deficits.

The two nonavoidance-shock conditions received the same schedule of unpredictable shocks, and as expected, the GSR adaptation results did not differ. There was, however, a reliable difference between average GSR scores for the first block of shock trials ($t = 4.32$, 20 df, $p < .01$), with the new nonavoidable condition showing the lower log conductance score (.044 versus .072). Having been prepared for the inevitable shocks about which they could do nothing, subjects in the second No Perceived Avoidance treatment were less aroused by initial stimulation. Subsequently, the two conditions converged, and by the last shock, GSRs had waned to about the same magnitude in each group.

Both sets of subjects were asked about the unpredictability of shock and both gave similar responses (mean ratings = 2.45 and 2.09). Similarly, there were no differences in ratings on two of the scales checking on the Perceived Avoidance manipulations (see Table 7.1). Each group felt they were unable to prevent the shocks (mean ratings = 2.00 and 1.36), and each reported having received the same number of shocks (mean ratings = 4.64 and 4.46). There was, however, a difference on the item asking about whether they controlled the occurrence of the shocks. The original group gave a mean rating of 3.36, while the second gave a somewhat lower rating of 1.91 ($t = 2.01$, 20 df, $p < .10$). This result is surprising in view of the other two ratings. On the other hand, it is consistent with manipulations used in the second condition. Since subjects were explicitly told there was nothing they could do to avoid shock, we might expect somewhat exaggerated feelings of uncontrollability. In any event, the difference was marginal and had no real effect on either postshock measure. The corrected reading time on the Stroop was 102.18 in the first unavoidable treatment; the comparable mean for the second unavoidable group was 95.27. Average proofreading scores were also the same: 49.64 for the first group and 52.18 for the second group. The mean time taken to solve the final puzzle was 181.91 and 177.46 in the first and second groups, respectively. There were no differences between the two groups on self-ratings of helplessness and related adjectival descriptions.

Clearly, these results support a perceived control explanation. The perception of no control over shock leads to impaired postshock performance. The repeated frustration of being unable to avoid shock does not appear to be a major factor in the production of poststressor task degradations. The electric shock experiment, then, has allowed us to generalize the effects of perceived uncontrollability on behavioral consequences of exposure to aversive events. The limits of this generalizability are still an open issue, but one thing is clear: whether the stressor is aversive sound or aversive shock, the negative aftereffects in each case vary as a function of unpredictability and perceived lack of control over stimulation.

Behavioral Aftereffects of
Social Stressors

The theme of the preceding four chapters has been the immediate aftereffects of unpredictable and uncontrollable aversive events. Two physical stressors were used in the research: high-intensity noise and electric shock. While these stressors were easily manipulated in the laboratory, they do not represent analogues of basic social problems characteristic of complex urban life. Even noise and its control, an increasingly serious problem in cities, does not carry the same sense of urgency permeating discussions of educational deterioration, crime, inadequate health services, municipal bureaucracy, and racial discrimination. These so-called social stressors demand immediate attention (cf. Korten, Cook, & Lacey, 1970), and we may well ask what contributions our own research can make to understanding their impact on behavior. How can we extend our notions about the aftereffects of physical stressors to the domain of social and interpersonal stress? Answers to this question are extremely complex, for the effects obtained in our noise studies were intimately linked to the cognitive variables of predictability and perceived control. It would be difficult, at best, to operationalize these factors where the stressor stimulus was, say, racial discrimination, rather than noise or shock. On the other hand, the demonstration of behavioral aftereffects of social stressors would enable us to generalize our theoretic notions to a class of aversive events that have natural-world analogues of pressing importance. Accordingly, we decided to examine two socially relevant, nonnoise stressors: bureaucratic red tape and arbitrary discrimination. The logic underlying each study is discussed below, followed by a presentation of the experiment and its results.

Bureaucracy

It is inevitable that as cities become larger, they also become more formalized and structured. The effects of these changes are twofold. On the one hand, they mark a dissolution of extended familial bonds and the dissipation of intimate face-to-face relations characteristic of less urban societies. Zorbaugh's (1929) description of the furnished room dweller in Chicago portrays the ultimate in lack of affective interaction. Yet, even the socially isolated urban resident does have contacts with other people; the complicated, interdependent social system could hardly function otherwise. The nature of the interaction, however, is often bureaucratic, bounded by specific sets of rules, and administered by people with neither inclination nor authority to modify seemingly inappropriate or meaningless regulations.

The effects of working in or with a bureaucracy have not been intensively examined, although there have been many studies of selected aspects of bureaucracy. However, these have been usually focused upon the structure and function of the organization itself, rarely upon the person interacting with it. In 1952, the concluding paragraph of an essay by Robert Merton entitled "Bureaucratic Structure and Personality" issued an elegant call for "studies of ... bureaucracies dealing with the interdependence of social organization and personality formation [which] should constitute an avenue for fruitful research" (Merton, 1952). In the ensuing two decades, little experimental work has been done on this problem. A study by Evan and Zelditch (1961) stands as almost a lone exception, and even that experiment was more concerned with leadership than with bureaucratic interaction. Yet, just as with noise or shock, it seems clear that people adapt to the stresses and strains of a bureaucracy and function smoothly within its constraints. Once again, the question can be posed: are there deleterious consequences for interacting with a frustrating bureaucracy? For clearly, the smoothest running of bureaus is frustrating and stressful insofar as it places formalized and complex barriers between an individual and his goals.

Consider, for example, someone who works in the city and wishes to transact personal business, perhaps the registration of his car, during his lunch hour. He goes to the proper government office and fills in a series of complicated forms. He then waits on a long, slow-moving line, and when he finally gets to the clerk, he finds that he has made a trivial error on one of his forms and must start the process over again. Although time is short, the clerk is not willing to accept the incorrect or amended document. Irrespective of the outcome at noon, our subject must interact later in the day with his co-workers and his family. He must also perform his daily routine of cognitive and intellectual tasks. Has his noontime experience affected the quality of his subsequent performance or interaction, and if so, what aspects of the frustrating bureaucratic experience were operative in modifying his behavior?

There are at least two possible outcomes of bureaucratic involvement. After a period of bureaucratic obstinancy, a subject may either become surly and hostile, responding negatively to subsequent environmental contacts, or he may become passive and compliant, generalizing from his experience with a recalcitrant organization to subsequent, unrelated environmental demands. It is our belief that the two kinds of aftereffect are triggered by two kinds of systems, both equally bureaucratic. In one, the system is rigid and inflexible, with the organization's personnel being, at best, an irrelevant factor in its rigidity; in the other, it is the functionaries staffing the bureaucracy's posts that are the major source of harassment. In the former situation, the individual is confronted with an environment over which he has no expectation of control: it will yield to neither rationality nor interpersonal adroitness. The net outcome of such an encounter is likely to be a helplessness manifesting itself as compliance, triggered by an inability or unwillingness to frame any other behavioral strategy in future bureaucratic involvements. In the latter situation with hostile personnel, the semblance of control, through persuasion and interaction, is seemingly possible. When the bureaucrat fails to respond, not only is there the unpleasantness and frustration over loss of control, but the loss may be viewed as a threat to the individual's freedom and produce "reactance" (Brehm, 1966). That is, the individual adopts opposition to any demands placed upon him in order to show, by his freedom of action, that he is his own man.

An experiment was conducted by Janet Shaban and Gail Welling at Stony Brook to explore the comparative effects of these two kinds of bureaucratic harassment. One group of subjects, the Personally Responsible condition, engaged in a bureaucratic interaction involving an officious clerk who interpreted the system's requirements in rigid and petty fashion. Subjects in another group, the Regulations Responsible condition, confronted a clerk who, while personally pleasant, administered the inflexible rules of the organization that employed her. As a control, a third group of subjects, the No Harassment condition, was not subjected to bureaucratic harassment.

Procedure

A total of 72 male subjects participated in the experiment, 24 in each condition. One subject in the Personally Responsible condition filled out the dependent measure forms incorrectly and his results were not used in the analysis.

All subjects for the experiment were recruited from the introductory psychology course at Stony Brook; they were asked to volunteer for an experimental study of bargaining. When a subject arrived at the laboratory, the experimenter greeted him and explained that the study was concerned with exploring the relationship between cognitive skills and bargaining, and that the subject would first take a series of cognitive tests and then play against another person in a bargaining game. Before the "experiment" began, however, the subject was shown a memo from the Psychology Department to all experimenters requesting that they send all subjects to the Administrative Assistant of the department to complete some forms before they participated in experiments.

Each subject then went to the Assistant's office in an adjoining building. There the Assistant informed the subject that the Psychology Department had become concerned about the selective nature of their sample of experimental subjects—they all seemed to be urban, middle class, college students, teenage, white, and so forth. Therefore, each subject was required to fill out a questionnaire, which would enable the Department to characterize its subject pool. In the No Harassment condition, subjects were given a questionnaire in which all but the top questions, asking for name, address, age, and other simple facts, had been crossed out. In both the Personally Responsible and Regulations Responsible conditions, subjects were given the lengthier form, asking for names and addresses of relatives, high schools, and a host of other background details. Many of the questions were repetitious and the allotted space was often insufficient for the required answers. In the Personally Responsible condition, the Assistant examined the completed form and announced that since it had not been filled in to her satisfaction (e.g., ditto marks had been used or the subject had written in the margins), it would have to be done over before she could accept it. Just as the subject completed the second copy of the form, the Assistant received a phone call,[1] and spent several minutes discussing her

[1] The phone calls were not fortuitous. The Assistant had a special phone on her desk which she made ring via a hidden foot switch; the phone itself was not connected to a telephone line.

personal affairs while the subject waited to turn in the completed form. In the Regulations Responsible condition, after the subject had first completed the form, the Assistant also requested that he redo it. In this condition, however, she made it clear that although the form was readable, regulations of the department—she showed the subject a sheaf of memoranda—required that it be completed precisely. Again, just as the subject completed the second copy of the form, the phone rang and he had to wait for several minutes before he could turn in his form. This time, the Assistant, although trying to terminate the conversation so as to attend to the subject, was kept involved in a business conversation with someone who was obviously her superior.

After the form was finally accepted, the subject went back to the laboratory where the aftereffect measures were administered. Three measures were used, as described below.

1. The proofreading task utilized in the noise experiments.

2. A variation of Orne's (1962) "demand-characteristics task." The experimenter put two large piles of paper face down on the subject's desk. One pile contained simple arithmetic problems, the other pile instruction sheets. The subject was told to complete the first page of problems, then to read the first page of instructions and follow them, then go on to the next page of instructions, and so on. The experimenter excused herself saying that she had to attend to another subject, ostensibly the one with whom the protagonist would be bargaining. She pointed to a button on the side of the desk and told the subject that it was an intercom buzzer; if he wanted her for any reason he merely had to press the button. The experimenter left the room and observed the subject through a one-way vision screen. Each of the instruction sheets contained the same message. It told the subject to take the completed arithmetic problem sheet and rip it into no fewer than 32 pieces, then to proceed to the next problem sheet. The experimenter coded the subject's behavior on a standard form, noting whether the instructions were followed, circumvented, or disobeyed, and either at the end of 20 minutes or in response to a call from the subject over the intercom, whichever came first, she entered the subject's room and terminated the task.

3. The subject was then given a bargaining task. He was presented with a buyer's cost and price sheet from a simulated bilateral monopoly trading situation modified from Siegel and Fouraker (1960). This is a bargaining game in which buyer and seller negotiate the price at which a quantity of goods is to be sold. The higher the price, the more profit to the seller; the lower, the more profit to the buyer. The subject was asked to plan his strategy by listing what his first seven offers to the seller would be. He was then given a second strategy sheet, in which he was asked to outline his first seven offers, and also to predict what he thought the seller's response to each one would be.

At this point, the experiment was ended and each subject was given a four-page series of questions accompanied by graphic rating scales designed to check on the subject's perceptions of the tasks, his reactions to the independent variables, and his suspicions. A debriefing concluded the session.

Results

The postexperimental questionnaire contained two questions testing whether subjects perceived the situation in ways the manipulations were designed to produce. The responses to a query on how irritated they were and a second question on whether the irritation was attributable to regulations or to the Assistant are presented in Table 8.1. Both of the groups were significantly more irritated than the control ($ps < .001$); they did not differ from each other. The Personally Responsible subjects attributed significantly more ($p < .01$) irritation to the Assistant than did Regulations Responsible subjects. The No Harassment group is appropriately in between. The number of subjects is 22 in the Personally Responsible condition and 22 for the second question in the Regulations Responsible condition. In both cases, subject attrition was due to errors in completing the forms. Nine subjects in the No Harassment condition did not answer the second question. Their reasons can be inferred from one of their marginal comments. Reasonably enough, they said that since they were not irritated, they could not attribute irritation.

Nine other questions in the postexperimental form, combined into three 3-item scales, were also analyzed. All three conditions were equal in their moderately positive responses regarding their interest in the experiment. All three conditions had nondiffering high evaluations of the experimenter (mean

TABLE 8.1

Checks on Manipulations

Experimental condition	Rating scale	
	Irritation[a]	Attribution of irritation[b]
Personally responsible	10.6 (N=22)	9.1 (N=22)
No harassment	2.4 (N=23)	6.6 (N=15)
Regulations responsible	10.3 (N=24)	5.3 (N=23)

[a]On a 15-point scale, 1 = "none" and 15 = "most."

[b]On a 15-point scale, 1 = "regulations" and 15 = "assistant."

response = 2.1 on a scale ranging from −3 to +3). However, they differed significantly in their appraisal of the Assistant. The mean (on a 7-point scale ranging from −3 to +3) for the Personally Responsible condition was −.4; in the No Harassment condition it was 1.3; and in the Regulations Responsible condition it was .5. Overall, the difference was significant at the .001 level, and for each pair of means the reliability of the difference was at least of the magnitude p less than .01.

The proofreading task was used, as in the noise studies, as a measure of the adverse consequences of exposure to a stressor, in this case bureaucratic harassment. The results, presented in Table 8.2, show that after a bureaucratic encounter, subjects do not proofread as well as the controls, although comparison with the parametric results of the noise studies (e.g., see Table 5.5) reveals that the effect was not as severe as it was for subjects who had just experienced unpredictable and uncontrollable noise. There is, however, an alternative explanation for the results that must be considered. Subjects in the two harassment conditions had just spent 20 minutes or so filling in two copies of a long form; those in the No Harassment condition did not. The differences on proofreading may be attributable to clerical fatigue, not to the aftereffects of stress exposure. There is no evidence to refute this possibility, but some post-experimental pilot work ($N = 3$) indicated that it was not an overriding possibility. Similarly, subjects in appropriate conditions in the noise experiments were able to achieve equivalent proofreading scores after 24 minutes of clerical work.

The remaining two dependent measures, the Orne task and the bargaining planning sheet, were analyzed so as to detect differences in negativism and compliance. The Orne task responses were divided into three categories. Since all subjects were left with a meaningless task, there were several options as to how they could cope with the assignment. Those subjects who correctly carried out the assignment by doing the arithmetic and tearing up the sheets were considered to have exhibited compliance; those who cheated by not doing the

TABLE 8.2

Mean Percentage of Errors Missed
on the Proofreading Task[a]

Personally responsible	32.3
	($N=23$)
No harassment	25.0
	($N=23$)
Regulations responsible	29.3
	($N=24$)

[a]$F = 3.48$, 2/67 df, $p < .05$; Harassment (PR + RR) versus No Harassment, $p < .01$; Personally Responsible versus Regulations Responsible, $p < .20$.

assignment (e.g., fudging answers or tearing up blank sheets of paper) were considered to have been negativistic. The use of the buzzer to summon the experimenter was considered neither negative nor compliant, and were it not for the value judgment implied, we would label it rational.

The distribution of these types of response across conditions is presented in Table 8.3. The results can be viewed in a number of ways. Looking at the row for the Personally Responsible condition, the use of cheating was the prevalent strategy; for the No Harassment condition, the use of the buzzer was the dominant strategy; for the Regulations Responsible condition, correct procedure was the modal response. A similar analysis can be made for the columns. Actually, the precise prediction generated by our hypothesis is that there is a monotonic relationship between experimental conditions, as ordered in the table, and modes of response also as ordered in the table. That is, as one proceeds down the conditions, the responses should shift across modes. The appropriate statistic for analyzing whether such a shift occurs is Kendall's S statistic, derived from *tau* (Kendall, 1948). S/σ_s is distributed as the normal deviate, and for Table 8.3, it has a value of 2.23, significant at better than the .03 level. Thus, as subjects move (conceptually) from a Personally Responsible condition through a No Harassment condition to a Regulations Responsible condition, they became less negativistic and more compliant.

The bargaining strategy sheet, upon which subjects reported both how they intended to bargain as well as how they expected their opponents to bargain, was based upon a zero-sum game. Subjects in all conditions planned to arrive at close to a break-even point for a final outcome. All predicted a small profit for themselves and although there was some marginal indication that the Personally Responsible group would demand a higher profit than the other conditions, there were no real differences in outcome. But there were differences in how the bargaining was expected to progress. Subjects could plan to make an offer, which if accepted, would result in a loss for themselves, or they could

TABLE 8.3

Orne Task

Experimental condition	Number of subjects using each mode of response		
	Cheat and cheat/buzzer (negativistic)	Buzzer	Correct (compliant)
Personally responsible	13	7	3
No harassment	6	12	6
Regulations responsible	8	6	10

TABLE 8.4

Loss Bids in Bargaining:
Number of Subjects in Each Category

Experimental condition	Opponent's loss bids compared to own		
	More losses for opponent than self (negativistic)	Equal	Fewer losses for opponent than self (compliant)
Personally responsible	13	8	2
No harassment	7	13	4
Regulations responsible	3	12	9

make a profitable offer. Being a zero-sum game, their losses were the opponent's profits and vice versa. Subjects also estimated how their opponents would bargain. We considered that a subject was negativistic if he believed his opponent would make more loss bids than he would. Conversely, a subject who planned to make more loss bids than he expected of his opponent was considered to be compliant. A subject who felt he and his opponent would make an equal number of loss bids was neither. Table 8.4 shows the distribution of responses across conditions. The array has the same characteristics as the one displayed in Table 8.3, and Kendall's S statistic confirms this. The table is monotonic, in the sense discussed above, at better than the .001 level.

Even more to the point is the fact that subjects were consistent in their responses. Those who were negativistic on the Orne task, for the most part, were negativistic on the bargaining task; similarly, for those who were compliant. The extent to which this occurred can be seen in Table 8.5. The first column, labeled Negativistic, shows only those subjects who behaved in that fashion on both tasks. The third column, labeled Compliant, contains only those subjects who

TABLE 8.5

Combined Responses:
Orne Task and Bargaining Strategy

Experimental condition	Number of subjects in each category		
	Negativistic	Mixed	Compliant
Personally responsible	11	10	2
No harassment	5	15	4
Regulations responsible	2	13	9

were compliant on both tasks. The middle column, labeled Mixed, contains the remaining subjects—those who were neither negativistic nor compliant, or who differed in their mode of responding to the two tasks. The implications of the tabulated data are clear: subjects in the Personally Responsible condition became negativistic; those in the Regulations Responsible condition became compliant; those in the No Harassment condition became neither. Kendall's S statistic ratifies that judgment, for $S/\sigma_s = 3.47$ ($p < .001$).

In summary, when subjects were subjected to a bureaucratic stressor, there were adverse aftereffects both general and specific. The general aftereffect was a drop in efficiency of cognitive functioning as measured by proofreading. The specific effects were that subjects who attributed their bureaucratic troubles to an immutable system over which they felt little control became docile and compliant; subjects who attributed their bureaucratic troubles to the people involved (presumably over whom control was more likely) became reactive and negative.

Implicit in our interpretation of these findings is the concept of perceived control, which played a central role in the noise studies. We can now be more precise in detailing how the present results relate to controllability. Although subjects who were exposed to the stress of bureaucratic harassment showed adverse aftereffects, they demonstrated them in different ways as a function of what they learned about the controllability of their environment. Those subjects who were harassed by the Administrative Assistant learned of their potential control of the system, had it rendered ineffectual, and then attempted to regain control and to exercise it over those with whom they subsequently interacted— the experimenter and their bargaining opponent. Those subjects who were harassed by departmental regulations learned that they were in a system in which they could not exercise control—there was no point of leverage—and in subsequent exchanges they quickly acceded to the other's control rather than expend useless effort in a chimerical quest to establish their own control.

Discrimination

This section attempts to extend our findings to another social-environmental stressor, namely, arbitrary discrimination resulting in socioeconomic deprivations. We selected this variable for analysis because it, too, is intimately involved in contemporary urban life, and because discrimination is itself a form of perceived uncontrollability (cf. Caplan & Paige, 1968). An individual, after all, has no control over his skin color, sex, or physical stature, each of which may be the basis for one or more social and economic discriminations. We define discrimination as the exercise of unfair, arbitrary, and irrelevant criteria to deprive a person of his status, rights, power, and possessions. A good deal of scholarly material has been written about discrimination, but the concept, to paraphrase Ebbinghaus' appraisal of psychology, "has a long past, but only a short history" (cited in Boring, 1950). The literature on discrimination is inextricably linked to that of prejudice and race relations. It is beyond the scope of this chapter to review the extensive psychological research on these topics, let alone sociological, literary, and journalistic materials. It is instructive to note, however, that two recent social-psychological reviews, one by Ashmore (1970), and the other by Harding, Proshansky, Kutner, and Chein (1969) have over 300 bibliographic entries each. The fact that some of these entries are duplicates is offset by other entries which themselves are reviews of a number of earlier studies.

A key concept in much of the research on discrimination is "relative deprivation," which we discussed earlier in connection with some of the noise studies (see Chapters 5 and 6). The source of relative deprivation may be either an arbitrary discrimination or a chance event (cf. Rotter, 1966; Lefcourt, 1966). It probably makes a difference in degree of felt discrimination if the individual believes chance has deprived him rather than some discrimination on the part of powerful others. One can adapt to unwanted chance events by using a variety of defense and coping mechanisms (Haan, 1963; Janis, 1959). Discrimination, by contrast, is less easily defended against, since it is usually based on a trait or state over which the deprived individual has no control. For these reasons, we include both sources of relative deprivation—chance and discrimination—in the experimental design presented below.

There are three major problems in attempting to treat previous discrimination research as an instance of the aftereffects of stress. The first is the separation of the effects of discrimination from its aftereffects; we discuss this issue in the concluding part of this chapter. The second problem is one of untangling the effects of discrimination from the disadvantages it produces. For example, the assignment of a black child to a vocational, rather than an academic, course in school on the basis of race is discrimination. The progressive decrement in academic knowledge is a result not only of discriminatory stress and its aftereffects, but also of the consequences that ensue from the special treatment entailed by the discrimination. A third problem in our interpretation of previous experimental results concerning discrimination is that of subject selection—in particular, lack of randomization. When blacks and whites are compared on an experimental task, more than just discrimination is being varied. Life style, personality traits, life histories, and a host of other factors that cannot be expected to disappear with large samples also separate the two groups.

For purposes of extending our notions about the aftereffects of aversive stimulation, it would be advantageous to have a study in which subjects were randomly assigned to either a discriminatory or nondiscriminatory experience, in which the experience entailed no cumulative disadvantage, and in which a test of postdiscrimination consequences was possible. Usually, the advantageous study is difficult to obtain, but the next experiment, conducted by T. Edward Hannah for his doctoral dissertation at Stony Brook, is addressed precisely to the points at issue.

Overview of the Experiment

Seventy-one subjects were randomly assigned, 10 to each of the cells in a 3×2 factorial design, and 11 to an independent control group. Subjects were exposed to either a discriminatory experience arbitrarily based on their sex, a discriminatory experience based on chance, or no discrimination. In each of these conditions, half the subjects were given a choice of their experimental tasks, whereas the other half were not given the option. Each subject was then tested on a complex task (an aftereffect measure), administered a questionnaire, and asked to volunteer additional experimental assistance.

Procedure

Subjects were recruited by sign-up sheets prominently posted on the Stony Brook campus. These sheets described an experiment of less than an hour's duration, involving paper-and-pencil measures, and promised $3.00 for participation. Subjects were scheduled individually. When each subject arrived, he was treated in a manner appropriate to the experimental condition to which he had been preassigned. In the No Discrimination condition, the subject was paid his $3.00 and signed a receipt, and was told that two kinds of tasks were being studied: easy ones, and difficult, complex ones. In the Arbitrary Discrimination condition, the experimenter told each subject that both males and females were being used in this study but that since he was a male, he would only receive $1.00, not the advertised $3.00. The reasons given were that males did not make good subjects and that too many had signed up.[2] The subject was given $1.00, signed a receipt, and the experimenter proceeded by describing the two types of tasks. In the Chance Discrimination condition the subject was told that because so many people had volunteered, the experimenter had insufficient money to pay all subjects $3.00 and, by necessity, was paying some only $1.00. The decision to pay $1.00 or $3.00 to a given subject was made by a flip of a coin. The coin was flipped, the subject lost, was given his $1.00, signed a receipt, and

___

[2] Both male and female subjects were used in the experiment, in equal numbers in each condition (except for the Control group, which included 7 males and 4 females). The discrimination instructions were appropriately modified to give parallel discrimination to females. Since there were neither main effects nor interactions attributable to sex, the variable will not be discussed further.

the experimenter then proceeded by telling the subject about the two types of tasks. Within each of these conditions, half the subjects were told that they could choose which task to work upon, while the other half did not receive a choice. The procedure was derived, in part, from the perceived controllability manipulations used in the noise experiments, and was designed to assign subjects to the complex task while giving them the perception of control and free choice (cf. Stotland & Blumenthal, 1964). The Control group was paid $3.00, in the same fashion as the No Discrimination condition, but they were not told that there were two kinds of tasks so that they experienced neither control nor arbitrary assignment.

Each subject was then administered the paper-and-pencil version of the Stroop Color Word Test (see Chapter 6). The testing itself was conducted by an undergraduate assistant of the experimenter who was unaware of the subject's experimental condition. At the completion of the Stroop test, each subject was given a questionnaire that contained checks on the manipulations and measures of attitudinal dependent variables. The undergraduate assistant then made a personal appeal to each subject, explaining that he needed subjects for his experimental course project. Since, unlike the experimenter, he was unable to pay subjects, he gave the subject a sign-up form and asked him to volunteer for as much time as he could spare.

The experimenter then debriefed each subject. Subjects in the discrimination conditions were given an additional $2.00, so that they ultimately received the $3.00 originally promised in the recruitment advertisement.

Results

The postexperimental questionnaire contained two items that served to check on the effectiveness of the discrimination manipulations. On a 25-point scale, in response to "How satisfied are you with the amount of money you received?," the mean score for the Control group was 23.3; the No Discrimination condition mean was 22.7. The two means did not differ from each other, but both differed, at better than the .01 level of significance, from the means of Arbitrary Discrimination and Chance Discrimination, 7.1 and 10.2, respectively. The latter two means did not differ from each other. When asked whether they thought the method of determining payment was fair, the Control mean of 20.2, the No Discrimination mean of 17.6, and the Chance Discrimination mean of 16.7 all differed (at better than the .01 level) from the Arbitrary Discrimination mean, but not from each other. In summary, subjects in both the Chance Discrimination and Arbitrary Discrimination conditions felt they were underpaid, but only Arbitrary Discrimination subjects felt it was for an arbitrary reason.

The 30 subjects who were ostensibly offered a choice of tasks, although all were maneuvered into selecting the complex one, when asked whether they thought they had a choice, responded with a mean of 16.3 on a 25-point scale. The 30 subjects who were assigned to the complex task with no choice had a mean scale score of 1.1, different from the Choice subjects' mean at better than the .001 level of significance.

The Stroop task was used as a measure of the aftereffects of discrimination. Subjects were given 2 minutes to work on each of four critical pages of the test, and the total completed entries per page was used as the dependent measure. Subjects were told to self-correct errors, hence mistakes were infrequent and did not differ among conditions. Table 8.6 reports the four-page totals for the task. The No Discrimination subjects did significantly better than either of the Discrimination groups. The Chance Discrimination mean was not different from the Arbitrary Discrimination mean; both differed from the Control group at better than the .05 level. The mean scores for all the Choice subjects did not differ from the mean of the subjects in the No Choice conditions. However, when page-by-page comparisons were made, of the 12 comparable pages (4 each in three conditions), Choice subjects had higher scores in 10 of them, a finding significant at the .025 level by a sign test. The net results of the Stroop indicate that after a discriminatory experience, whether as a result of chance or arbitrary action, subjects do worse than similar subjects unexposed to discrimination. Choice of outcome, in terms of opportunity for task selection, had some effect on the discriminatory results.

The postexperimental questionnaire contained four questions concerning the subject's satisfaction with the experimental experience. The results of these questions show parallel outcomes and have therefore been combined to yield a single index of attitude toward the experiment following discrimination. The means for the various conditions are reported in Table 8.7. There is a significant effect attributable to discrimination. The Arbitrary Discrimination mean was lower than those of Chance Discrimination, No Discrimination, and Control ($ps < .05$). The effects of the Choice manipulation are also apparent and account for much of the discrimination results. The mean of the Arbitrary Discrimination–Choice group (85.7) does not differ from the Control group or either of the two Chance Discrimination or two No Discrimination groups. The mean of the Arbitrary Discrimination–No Choice group (69.4) was different from all of the other six groups ($ps < .05$).

TABLE 8.6

Stroop Color Word Test
Total Number of Words Completed

	No discrimination	Chance discrimination	Arbitrary discrimination	Control
Choice of tasks	452.4	415.7	393.0	449.6
No choice of tasks	449.3	387.1	386.7	

TABLE 8.7

Questionnaire Index of Satisfaction

	No discrimination	Chance discrimination	Arbitrary discrimination	Control
Choice of tasks	95.0	88.9	85.7	90.2
No choice of tasks	85.1	90.2	69.4	

A similar pattern is evident in the results of the volunteering measure. Each subject was asked to contribute up to 90 minutes to assist a student helper; the results of these requests are presented in Table 8.8. The top half of the table shows the mean number of minutes volunteered. The only significant finding is that the Arbitrary Discrimination group was lower than either the Chance Discrimination, the No Discrimination, or the Control groups. Since these data are somewhat skewed, the bottom half of Table 8.8 displays the number of subjects who offered any volunteer time. As before, the Arbitrary Discrimination group is discernibly less likely to volunteer ($\chi^2 = 9.09$, 2 *df*, $p < .025$).

Overall, an interesting pattern emerges from the effects of discrimination. Subjects who were treated in an arbitrary discriminatory fashion, when compared to those not subject to discrimination, show a decrement on both performance measures (Stroop task) and attitudinal measures (Questionnaire and Volunteering). Those subjected to a Chance discrimination also evince a performance decrement, but do not show attitudinal differences from nondiscriminated subjects.

TABLE 8.8

Willingness of Subjects to Volunteer Experimental Time

	Mean number of minutes volunteered			
	No discrimination	Chance discrimination	Arbitrary discrimination	Control
Choice of tasks	43.0	49.0	14.0	35.5
No choice of tasks	34.0	34.0	20.0	

	Number of subjects volunteering time		
	No discrimination	Chance discrimination	Arbitrary discrimination
Offered some time	19	16	11
Did not offer time	1	4	9

Discussion and Conclusions

The two experiments reported here go a long way toward demonstrating that adverse aftereffects can result from exposure to social stressors. We recognize that a liberal interpretation is required in order to assume that the bureaucracy and discrimination studies manipulated perceived control, and it is certainly not reasonable to argue that they varied predictability of stressful stimulation. However, broadness of application is perhaps more important in new areas of research than point-by-point comparability between two or more similar types of stimuli. The strategy of testing for aftereffects over a number of stressors was part of the rationale for the studies reported in this chapter. A strong case can now be made for the conclusion that exposure to a variety of aversive events, both physical and social, produces negative behavioral aftereffects.

The electric-shock experiment reported in Chapter 7 provided a direct parallel to the studies of noise. Since shock, like noise, is primarily a physical stimulus, it was easily controlled, timed, and meted out to the subjects. And the results for shock were very close to those of the unpredictable and uncontrollable noise studies discussed in Chapters 4, 5, and 6. The two social-stressor studies, while less easily linked to the noise paradigm, demonstrate effects generally consistent with the noise research. Adaptation to a stressor is more difficult to define when the stressor is bureaucracy rather than noise. But subjects in the bureaucracy study can be said to have adapted; in all three conditions they performed a task while under procedural harassment, that is, they filled out the forms requested by the Administrative Assistant. The experimental tasks were measures of postexperimental consequences, and here, the hypothesis was clearly confirmed. The two heavily harassed groups showed the expected deleterious aftereffects, namely, a decrement in proofreading, and less rational (definable as counterproductive for future behavior) responses to the Orne task and the bargaining strategy task.

The discrimination study is harder to compare with the noise experiments. Subjects were not performing a standardized task at the time of the principal manipulation, so it is not possible to show even suggestive evidence of task adaptation. And given the design of the study, it was neither feasible nor plausible to attach electrodes and report psychophysiological data indicative of adaptation. But at some point, a little introspective common sense is in order. People work and function without doing standard laboratory tasks and without the attachment of recording electrodes. They walk, talk, think, and go about their daily life. Subjects in the discrimination study were behaving normally while being told about their payment. We submit that this maintenance of normal routine was indicative of adaptation. Now, since Arbitrary and Chance

Discrimination conditions were more aversive than No Discrimination and Control conditions, we would expect the former groups of subjects to show greater postdiscrimination deficits. This is, of course, precisely what occurred. Subjects in the Discrimination conditions did less well on the aftereffects test (the Stroop) than did No Discrimination subjects. Even more convincing is the way in which the crosscutting variable of choice affected the results. For choice was manipulated in a way similar to that used by other investigators as a means of varying perceived control over the environment (e.g., Stotland & Blumenthal, 1964). That Choice subjects (i.e., those with more perceived control) showed better performance on the Stroop than their No Choice counterparts, and that Choice ameliorated the effects of Arbitrary Discrimination on the volunteering measure, is almost a reechoing of the controllability effects documented in Chapter 5.

We have drawn few general implications from the social-stressor studies. We have refrained from discussing obvious theoretical and practical questions about formal organization, social consequences of increased bureaucratization, prejudice and discrimination. But as we noted earlier in this chapter, we are neither insensitive to nor unaware of the relationship of work on bureaucracy and discrimination to a general framework of social structure. Such questions are not, however, germane to the points at issue; namely, social and personal factors can be stressors, people can adapt to the stresses so produced, and they result in adverse aftereffects detectable in behavior. The overall conclusion is important: it matters not whether the sound is coming from a steam turbine or the Radio City Music Hall organ, the piper will be paid.

Psychic Costs of Stress:
Exposure or Adaptation

We have presented the results of almost two dozen experiments, all of which indicated that behavioral impairments are an immediate consequence of unpredictable and uncontrollable aversive events. We interpreted these effects in terms of a general helplessness hypothesis, but we are still left with the theoretical question posed at the outset of this book: Granting the existence of differential aftereffects, do they occur because of stress adaptation or in spite of it? Do behavioral impairments appear only after an accumulation of stressful experiences and following their termination? Or do the impairments reflect the effort entailed in achieving adaptation to the stressor? We cannot be sure from the designs and findings of our research that negative aftereffects reflect a price paid for the individual's adaptation, rather than a residual effect of mere exposure to noxious stimulation. Let us begin by considering the alternative that assumes adaptation itself is costly to the organism.

An adaptive-cost hypothesis implies little or no behavioral change during noise exposure because of adaptation, but that changes can be measured if one probes tasks that are sensitive to changes in the subject as a result of this adaptation process. The hypothesis also implies that the individual has a finite amount of psychic energy for coping with his environment, and that adaptation to an aversive event depletes the energy reserve needed for coping with subsequent demands and frustrations. To test whether postnoise task deficits are in fact a result of the effort entailed in adapting to noise, we need to make the following two assumptions: (a) unpredictable (and uncontrollable) noise, in contrast to predictable (and controllable) noise, entails greater adaptive effort; (b) decrements in GSR response to noise are valid indices of the cognitive effort involved in adaptation.

Given these assumptions, we proceeded to conduct an internal analysis of one of the aftereffect measures—proofreading. Subjects from the various unpredictable and uncontrollable noise conditions were ranked according to the magnitude of the difference between their first- and last-block GSR scores. Larger differences presumably reflected a greater degree of adaptation and, by inference, a greater amount of adaptive effort. The distribution of 53 cases[1] was divided into fourths and the upper and lower quartiles used in an analysis of covariance of the proofreading scores, where the covariate was the first-block GSR scores. The adaptive-cost hypothesis would predict that poorer proofreading varies directly with degree of adaptation, but the results did not confirm this expectation. The adjusted mean proofreading score was 43.57 for the quartile showing greatest adaptation and 45.59 for the quartile showing least adaptation ($F < 1$). A correlation between the entire distribution of GSR difference-scores and proofreading revealed a nonsignificant coefficient of $-.20$. These results suggest that adaptive effort may not be responsible for postnoise performance deficits. A similar conclusion can be drawn from the magnitude of GSR decrements in the electric-shock experiment reported in Chapter 7. Table 7.2 shows that the size of these decrements is generally less than in the noise studies (see Tables 3.1, 3.2, and 3.3), yet parametric values of the proofreading scores were essentially the same (see Tables 5.5 and 7.4). If differences in the extent of adaptation were responsible for impaired proofreading, we would have expected better *postshock* performance than comparable *postnoise* performance. We have,

---

[1] Failure to include identification numbers in tabulating some of the results made it impossible to match GSR and proofreading scores for 18 subjects. We did not include 10 additional cases from the unavoidable-noise condition (Chapter 5) because this study differed in other ways from the other unpredictable/uncontrollable noise studies.

then, still another piece of evidence inconsistent with an adaptive-cost interpretation.

The direct manipulation of effective adaptation is, of course, a more efficient test of the relationship between this variable and negative aftereffects. Consider two groups of individuals who are exposed to equally loud unpredictable noise. One group attempts to adapt and succeeds, but the other is somehow inhibited from even trying to adapt. The adaptive-cost hypothesis would predict more adverse aftereffects among the former than the latter, for with noise termination, the nonadapted individual is prepared to cope with a new set of stressors. The aversive impact of noise ceases with its offset and leaves the individual with sufficient resources for dealing with a new set of environmental demands. By contrast, the adapted subject uses up a good deal of energy in habituating to the sound and is therefore less prepared to cope with new task requirements. An important point to bear in mind is that the hypothesized depletion of energy stems not from adaptation itself but from the effort expended in trying to achieve this state. Similarly, it is not enough to constrain adaptation in one group and allow it to occur in the other, since the results produced in such a study might not provide a valid test of the adaptive-cost hypothesis. The nonadapt group could exert just as much effort in failing to adapt—perhaps even more—than the group that sucessfully achieves noise adaptation. However, in the absence of a technique for effectively preventing subjects from trying to adapt, two experiments were conducted aimed at differentially inhibiting the adaptive process. The first was designed and carried out by Lucy N. Friedman at New York University.

Differential Adaptation I

Procedure

Three types of noise stimuli were employed in the experiment: (a) fixed intermittent, in which twenty-five 92-dBA noise bursts of approximately 9 seconds duration were presented at the same place about every minute over a 25-minute period (Predictable Adapt condition); (b) random intermittent, in which twenty-five 92-dBA noise bursts of variable length were randomly spaced over the 25-minute period (Unpredictable Adapt condition); (c) random intermittent with variable intensity, in which the intensities of the 25 random bursts were also randomly varied from 70 dBA through 108 dBA in approximately 10-dBA steps, for an average of 92 dB (Unpredictable Nonadapt condition). The use of the intensity variation was designed to inhibit the usual course of adaptation as measured by changes in GSR amplitude (cf. Uno & Grings, 1965). It was assumed that decreased physiological adaptation would reflect reduced cognitive work in the adaptive process.

The ease with which adaptation occurs may vary with the complexity of the task on which the subject works during noise exposure. We have seen that performance of certain types of complex tasks is impaired by unpredictable noise, and it is not unreasonable to assume that the effort of adapting in these circumstances might also increase. Accordingly, the dimension of task difficulty was factorially added to the basic design of this study; that is, within each of the three noise treatments, half of the subjects worked on difficult arithmetic problems (Difficult condition), while the other half worked on easy problems (Easy condition).[2] It was expected that adaptive effort and consequent negative aftereffects would be greater in the Unpredictable Nonadapt–Difficult condition and least in the Predictable Adapt–Easy condition.

The Easy treatment consisted of 600 problems of the kind: 9–6+2. The subject worked on half of these problems during the first 13 minutes of the noise period and on the second half during the second 13 minutes. The Difficult condition consisted of 120 problems of the kind: 9–6+2; 4+3–5; 7+8–3. The instructions told subjects to solve the top line and remember the answer, and then solve the middle line and remember that answer. Next, they were told to solve the third line. If the sum of the two top solutions was larger, they subtracted the botton answer from it. If the sum of the two top lines was smaller, they added the bottom solution to the sum of the two top answers. Again, subjects worked on half of the problems during each part of the noise session.

The general instructions and experimental procedures were virtually identical to those used in the other noise experiments. Recording and analysis of GSR was also the same as before. The dependent variables were the first insoluble puzzle depicted in Figure 4.1, and an 8-minute version of the proofreading task. Three additional proofreading passages were administered over a subsequent 25-minute period. Since only partial counterbalancing of the four passages was possible with 60 subjects in a 3 × 2 design, analysis required a transformation of proofreading error scores into standard equivalents. Such a transformation eliminated the repeated-measures term (i.e., the trend of proofreading errors over time), and we therefore report only the means of the transformed scores for the passages administered in the first position of the sequence of four passages.[3]

[2] Subjects were 60 paid female volunteers of college age. They were randomly assigned, 10 to each of the 6 experimental conditions.

[3] Along with the 8-minute version of the proofreading passage from Jane Jacobs' book, the other three excerpts were taken from: *Modern Artists on Art* edited by Robert Herbert (1965); *The Children of Sanchez* by Oscar Lewis (1961); and *Soul On Ice* by Eldridge Cleaver (1968). All four passages were about equal in length and contained the same number of errors.

Results and Discussion

In order to determine whether or not the experiment was successful in varying perceived difficulty of the arithmetic tasks, all subjects were asked to respond to the following rating scale administered at the end of the experiment: (1) "The arithmetic tasks I completed during the noise were:" where 1 = "Not at all difficult" and 9 = "Extremely difficult." The means for Unpredictable Adapt, Unpredictable Nonadapt, and Predictable Adapt were 6.10, 4.95, and 5.45 under the Difficult treatment. The corresponding means for the Easy treatment were 4.25, 2.45, and 2.25. Analysis of these data revealed the expected effect due to the Easy–Difficult variation ($F = 35.58$, $1/54\ df$, $p < .02$).

Additional support for the effectiveness of the Easy–Difficult manipulation comes from the actual percentage of errors made by subjects in the two types of task treatments. Percent-error scores were computed separately for each half of the two arithmetic tasks, and the means of these scores are reported in Table 9.1. Analysis of variance of these data revealed the expected Easy–Difficult effect ($F = 46.11$, $1/54\ df$, $p < .001$). It is clear, then, that the arithmetic problems successfully varied task difficulty—both in actual fact and as perceived by the subjects.

The other experimental manipulation requiring assessment is whether subjects in the Nonadapt conditions showed less noise adaptation than subjects in the Adapt conditions. Confirmation of this hypothesis would require a reliable Conditions X Blocks interaction for the change in log conductance scores. Analysis of the scores shown in Table 9.2 yielded this interaction. There is the usual monotonic decline in reactivity in all conditions ($F = 23.00$, $4/216\ df$, $p < .005$), but the magnitude of the decrement is least in the two Nonadapt treatments (Interaction $F = 2.40$, $8/216\ df$, $p < .025$). Analysis of the scores in Block 5 revealed that Nonadapt groups were significantly different

TABLE 9.1

Average Percentage of Errors on First and Second
Parts of the Arithmetic Tasks

| Type of arithmetic task | Experimental noise condition | | | | | |
| | Unpredictable nonadapt | | Unpredictable adapt | | Predictable adapt | |
	Part 1	Part 2	Part 1	Part 2	Part 1	Part 2
Easy	2.22	2.31	5.39	3.23	8.02	3.40
Difficult	36.10	38.20	28.30	20.40	39.50	28.70

TABLE 9.2

Mean Changes in Log Conductance Responses to the Noise Bursts

Experimental condition	First 5 scores	Second 5 scores	Third 5 scores	Fourth 5 scores	Fifth 5 scores
Unpredictable nonadapt-Easy	.057	.042	.035	.047	.027
Unpredictable nonadapt-Difficult	.041	.048	.036	.038	.028
Unpredictable adapt-Easy	.059	.035	.031	.013	.018
Unpredictable adapt-Difficult	.045	.034	.018	.024	.014
Predictable adapt-Easy	.057	.026	.023	.015	.008
Predictable adapt-Difficult	.065	.035	.026	.021	.016

from each of the other four conditions $(ps < .05)$, and the only reliable differences in the first block were between Predictable Adapt–Difficult and the two Unpredictable–Difficult treatments $(ps < .05)$. We are unable to explain these latter differences at this time.

Further evidence of differential noise adaptation might be inferred from the decrements in errors on the arithmetic tasks. Table 9.1 presents the relevant results. There is a significant decline in errors from first to second parts of the tasks $(F = 21.93, 1/54 \, df, p < .001)$, and the expected interaction between this decline and the adaptation manipulation is also significant $(F = 9.88, 2/54 \, df, p < .01)$. On the basis of these and the GSR results, we conclude that subjects showed differential noise adaptation and, by inference, that greater adaptive effort probably occurred in Adapt than Nonadapt conditions.

Behavioral aftereffects of these differences in adaptation can be seen in Tables 9.3 and 9.4. Analysis of variance of each set of data revealed a significant interaction between experimental variables $(F = 8.71, 2/54 \, df, p < .01; F = 9.13, 2/54 \, df, p < .01)$. Postnoise frustration tolerance and proofreading errors were lower in the Nonadapt condition than the Adapt condition for subjects who worked on simple arithmetic addition. Just the reverse effect occurred for subjects who performed difficult additions; that is, the Nonadapt condition showed more adverse aftereffects than the Adapt conditions. Taken together, these data certainly do not support an adaptive-cost hypothesis. A further complication in the results has to do with the Predictable Adapt treatment, which was included in the design primarily for purposes of control. Tables 9.3 and 9.4 show that for subjects working on difficult problems, higher frustration tolerance and better proofreading occurred in the Unpredictable Adapt condition than in the Predictable Adapt condition. This was the first and only time in our research that such a clear reversal has occurred.

TABLE 9.3

Average Number of Trials on the Insoluble Puzzle

Type of arithmetic task	Unpredictable nonadapt	Unpredictable adapt	Predictable adapt
Easy	10.90 (optimal)	6.00 (low)	10.60 (low)
Difficult	3.50 (high)	13.30 (optimal)	7.90 (low)

TABLE 9.4

Mean Percentage of Errors Missed in the Proofreading Task[a]

Type of arithmetic task	Unpredictable nonadapt	Unpredictable adapt	Predictable adapt
Easy	-.61 (optimal)	+.68 (low)	-.61 (low)
Difficult	+.17 (high)	-.28 (optimal)	+.71 (low)

[a]Scores are given in standard-score units. A positive score means that a higher percentage of errors was missed than does a negative score.

A seemingly plausible explanation for the results of this study derives from the general notion of an inverted-U relationship between performance, level of arousal, and task complexity (e.g., Fiske & Maddi, 1961; Janis, 1967). This theory assumes that for any task, there is a level of arousal necessary for maximum performance efficiency. At low arousal levels, the individual may be inattentive and easily distracted; at somewhat higher levels, he is alert and therefore performs to be best of his ability; at still higher levels of arousal, however, anxiety and other strong emotional states appear that interfere with task efficiency. If we assume that arousal varied with degree of unpredictability and task difficulty, the least aroused subjects in our study were those working on simple arithmetic problems in the Predictable Adapt treatment. Conversely, the most aroused group were those working on difficult problems in the Unpredictable Nonadapt treatment. In this condition, noise bursts were randomly varied as to length, spacing, and intensity, whereas only two of these parameters were involved in the Unpredictable Adapt treatment and none were operative in the Predictable conditions.

Given the assumption about differential arousal, we might expect greater postnoise task degradations in Unpredictable Nonadapt than in Unpredictable Adapt under the Difficult treatment. We would also expect impairments to occur among Predictable Adapt subjects, for arousal level in that group was likely to be too low for optimal performance. The theory makes somewhat different predictions for the Easy treatment. Minimal task degradations would be anticipated in the Unpredictable Nonadapt group, where arousal level was presumably optimal. By contrast, maximal impairments should appear in the Predictable Adapt and Unpredictable Adapt groups, for arousal in these conditions was likely to be below that necessary for optimal performance. The predictions of differential arousal are presented in parentheses in Tables 9.3 and 9.4. The corresponding behavioral results for the Difficult treatment conform very nicely to these expectations. However, comparable data for the Easy treatment are less consistent; specifically, performance was relatively unimpaired in the Predictable Adapt condition. This discrepancy might be explained as an instance of self-stimulation. Subjects in this condition were "underaroused" because they worked on a boringly simple task under relatively innocuous noise. This state may have produced a need for stimulation (Berlyne, 1960) that, in turn, increased level of arousal to a point where it approached that of the Unpredictable Nonadapt group. While this explanation is gratuitously self-serving, a field study by Schachter, Willerman, Festinger, and Hyman (1961) and a laboratory replication by Latané and Arrowood (1963) document the point that when a task is highly stereotyped and easy, extra-task considerations play a substantial role in modifying both task performance and arousal-like emotional states.

It would appear, then, that differential arousal, and not adaptive effort, may be the mechanism accounting for such postnoise deficits as lowered frustration tolerance and impaired proofreading. However, we have no direct evidence for the hypothesized differences in arousal. It is difficult to achieve agreement on the psychological interpretation of any basal measure of autonomic activity, but tonic skin conductance has sometimes been used as an index of arousal (e.g., Lykken, 1968). Examination of the 25 basal points immediately before each noise burst (in log conductance units) did not reveal between-conditions differences ($ps > .20$), although there was a reliable increment in these scores over the course of the noise session in each condition ($F = 35.34$, $4/216\ df$, $p < .001$). Tonic increments of this same kind were noted in each experiment reported thus far in the book, but only one of them (i.e., the indirect control study in Chapter 5) showed a tendency for the increments to vary with experimental treatment. The fact that one autonomic measure fails to reveal expected differences does not necessarily rule out the existence of arousal differences as assumed by an inverted-U hypothesis. Individual response stereotypy in autonomic functioning and stimulus–response specificity are both well established phenomena that often interfere with the assessment of arousal by means of a single autonomic channel (Sternbach, 1966; Lacey, 1967). We may conclude, therefore, that differential arousal is a possible mechanism responsible for poststressor effects. That the consequences of unpredictable and uncontrollable noise operate through an arousal mechanism is fully consistent with the notion that mere exposure to stress causes adverse aftereffects in spite of adaptation. Indeed, the arousal concept suggests a specific mechanism by which negative aftereffects are produced. However, these conclusions must be treated as only tentative, for a single experiment does no more than suggest an explanation. We are really left with two theoretical interpretations for all of the experimental results reported in this book. The adaptive-cost hypothesis, as initially stated, is satisfactory with the exception of the internal analyses reported earlier and the last study described above. The stress-exposure/inverted-U explanation is equally satisfactory, with the exception of a recalcitrant cell in the last experiment. In addition, the arousal hypothesis is formulated in a way that makes it remarkably resistant to disconfirmation. It is therefore difficult to choose between two partially adequate explanations. Data from the next experiment provides a solution to this problem—or at least a tentative adjudication of the exposure and adaptive-cost explanations of stress aftereffect phenomena.

Differential Adaptation II

The previous experiment produced differential noise adaptation by randomly varying the intensity, spacing, and length of a series of noise bursts. Aside from the complexity of experimental results, partly attributable to the additional variation of task complexity, interpretation of the last study was made more difficult by the fact that intensity variations can also be viewed as increasing unpredictability of the noise. A simpler and less equivocal way of inhibiting physiological adaptation is suggested by previous studies showing that GSRs to simple stimuli habituate more rapidly with decreased interstimulus intervals (Coombs, 1938; Geer, 1966). The experiment by Geer, for example, demonstrated that longer interstimulus intervals between 65-dB sounds were associated with greater resistance of GSR amplitude measures to habituation. We therefore decided to follow this procedure as a way of producing differential adaptation to complex sounds. We reasoned that if such a difference could be effected, it was then a simple matter to examine aftereffects as a function of the extent of physiological adaptation to noise. We could not rule out the possibility that the Nonadapt group was in fact exerting considerable effort in trying to adapt, but at least we could say that adapted subjects probably expended more effort than nonadapted subjects. Given this assumption, the adaptive-cost hypothesis predicts greater proofreading errors among the former, the Adapted group, than the latter, Nonadapted group, whereas the stress exposure interpretation predicts equal impairment in the two experimental groups. The following study was conducted by Bruce Reim to test these counterposed predictions.

Experimental Design and Procedure

The experiment was a 2 × 2 factorial with two types of noise scheduling and two types of interstimulus intervals. Forty male undergraduates from the N.Y.U. subject pool were randomly assigned, 10 to each of the four cells.[4] Twenty of these subjects were exposed to 16 bursts of noise at 108 dBA, where intervals and burst-lengths were randomly varied in our customary fashion (Unpredictable). The remaining 20 cases listened to sixteen 9-second bursts of noise with fixed interburst intervals (Predictable). The total amount of noise was 2 minutes, 24 seconds in each condition. For half of the cases in each treatment, the interburst interval averaged to 96 seconds (Long Interstimulus Interval). In the Predictable condition, all intervals were 96 seconds, while they varied in the Unpredictable condition from 60 to 140 seconds with a mean of 96 seconds. The other half of the cases in each noise treatment were exposed to interburst intervals that were either 51 seconds or varied from 10 to 94 seconds with a mean of 51 seconds (Short Interstimulus Interval). The design, then, consisted of the following conditions: Unpredictable–Long Interstimulus Interval; Unpredictable–Short Interstimulus Interval; Predictable–Long Interstimulus Interval; Predictable–Short Interstimulus Interval.[5] The two Predictable treatments were included in the design for purposes of experimental and statistical control; previous research would lead us to expect no aftereffect differences between Predictable-Noise conditions, irrespective of variations in the length of interburst intervals.

The actual experimental procedure was almost identical to that used in previous noise experiments. Instructions to subjects were essentially same; decreased amplitude of phasic skin conductance responses was the measure of

---

[4] Forty-two subjects were actually used in the study, but 2 refused to continue after the first few noise bursts.

[5] The total amount of time spent working on tasks during the noise session was 22.5 minutes for subjects in Short ISI conditions and 28.5 minutes for subjects in Long ISI conditions. The difference in time was inevitable, given the required variation of interburst intervals. Six of the 22.5 minutes in the Short ISI occurred after the last noise burst. In order to equate total task time in the two conditions, it would actually have been necessary to add 12 and not 6 minutes to the Short condition. This amount of terminal no-noise time might have created special problems in the interpretation of the proofreading results, although even 6 additional minutes present some difficulties in this connection. Fortunately, as we will see, proofreading scores did not differ between Long and Short Interval conditions.

adaptation; slightly longer versions of verbal and numerical tasks used in the first of our noise studies were used here as the tasks during noise exposure; and the aftereffects of noise were measured by the 15-minute proofreading passage.

Results

Phasic skin conductance results were unequivocal in demonstrating that variations in Interstimulus Intervals (ISI) were sucessful in inducing differential physiological adaptation to noise. Table 9.5 presents the relevant change in log conductance scores. Analysis of variance of these data revealed a significant ISI effect ($F = 12.03$, $1/36$ df, $p < .001$), the usual blocks effect ($F = 16.18$, $3/108$ df, $p < .001$), and an interaction between blocks and ISI ($F = 18.59$, $3/108$ df, $p < .001$). The schedule of noise bursts within the two ISI conditions had no effect on GSR reactivity ($F = 1.46$, $1/36$ df, $p > .20$). In other words, the magnitude of GSR decreased over sucessive noise trials in Short ISI conditions and increased in Long ISI conditions—or at least showed an increase during the third or fourth block of trials following an initial decrement. Analysis of the fourth block of scores revealed a significant ISI effect ($F = 31.54$, $1/36$ df, $p < .001$), whereas a similar analysis of the first block was nonsignificant ($F = 2.09$, $1/36$ df, $p > .10$), despite seemingly greater GSR scores in Short than Long ISI conditions (see column 1 of Table 9.5). Resting-level skin conductance measured during the last 3 minutes of the hydration period at the beginning of the experiment also failed to show between-conditions differences ($F = 1.34$, $1/36$ df, $p > .20$). The results, then, indicate that initial GSR reactivity was about equivalent in the four experimental conditions, adapted in the Short ISI treatment, but was inhibited from so doing in the Long ISI treatment.

Two curious features of these autonomic data should be noted here. The first is that we did not expect longer ISIs to lead to increments in GSR amplitude during the final set of noise trials. Previous research (e.g., Geer, 1966), it will be recalled, simply showed that resistance to adaptation increased with longer intervals; it did not indicate greater reactivity during final trials, as data

TABLE 9.5

Mean Changes in Log Conductance Responses to the Noise Bursts

Experimental condition	First 4 scores	Second 4 scores	Third 4 scores	Fourth 4 scores
Unpredictable-Long ISI	.090	.079	.093	.105
Unpredictable-Short ISI	.129	.037	.025	.023
Predictable-Long ISI	.114	.107	.103	.131
Predictable-Short ISI	.145	.058	.027	.025

from our experiment seem to show. We are at loss to explain the discrepancy, other than to note that prior research used simple low-intensity stimuli, whereas our noise bursts were both complex and loud.

The other feature of the GSR scores requiring comment has to do with generally higher levels of reactivity in this experiment compared to some of the other studies reported in this book. This fact is particularly evident in the first-block scores shown in Table 9.5 in contrast to comparable scores in, say, Table 9.2 or 3.1. Again, we are unable to account for this discrepancy.

Despite unexpected and not fully understood patterns in the GSR results, we may still summarize our findings by stating that longer ISIs were associated with inhibited physiological adaptation to noise, whereas shorter intervals produced usual adaptation effects. This conclusion is applicable whether the noise bursts were presented on random (Unpredictable) or fixed (Predictable) schedules.

Evidence of differential adaptation in performance data is less clear-cut. For one thing, the total amount of time spent working on the cognitive tasks was different for the Long and Short ISI conditions. Subjects in the Long treatment had 6 additional minutes to work on these tasks (see Footnote 5), hence it is difficult to compare performance levels between conditions. For example, some subjects in the Short ISI treatment did not reach Part II of the Addition test (the second test in the sequence of three tests) until after noise presentation had ceased, whereas all subjects in the Long treatment completed this part of the test during the actual noise session. However, since all subjects completed Parts I and II of the Number Comparison test during noise exposure, we were at least able to examine the decrement in errors on this particular test as a function of experimental treatment. Table 9.6 presents the mean Number Comparison errors during the first and second parts of the noise session. There were no experimental differences on either part of the test ($Fs < 1$). However, analysis of the decline in errors from Part I to Part II revealed that the magni-

TABLE 9.6

Average Number of Errors on First and Second Parts of the Number Comparison Test

| | Noise condition | | | |
| | Predictable | | Unpredictable | |
Interstimulus interval	Part I	Part II	Part I	Part II
Long	4.2	3.1	2.9	1.6
Short	3.6	1.7	3.6	1.7

TABLE 9.7

Mean Percentage of Errors Missed in the Proofreading Task

	Noise condition	
Interstimulus interval	Predictable	Unpredictable
Long	29.80	48.70
Short	31.60	47.50

tudes of decline were significantly different from zero ($ps < .05$) in the two Short ISI conditions and in the Unpredictable–Long ISI condition. The decrement in errors was not reliable in Predictable–Long ISI ($t < 1$). These results suggest a tendency toward greater improvement of task performance in adapt (i.e., Short Interval) conditions than in nonadapt (i.e., Long Interval) conditions. We cannot assert that inhibition of physiological adaptation was unequivocally associated with reduced improvement of performance, but the trend of results was certainly in that direction.

On the basis of both physiological and Number Comparison data, we conclude that subjects adapted to the noise where intervals between bursts were short (51 seconds on the average) and failed to adapt where intervals were longer (96 seconds on the average).

The aftereffects of differential noise adaptation can be seen in the proofreading error scores presented in Table 9.7. It is obvious that predictability/unpredictability of the noise bursts is the only variable exerting an effect on the error scores ($F = 44.48$, $1/36\ df$, $p < .001$). Since length of the interstimulus interval did not influence proofreading performance ($F < 1$), we conclude that differences in degree of adaptation (and adaptive effort) are unrelated to the magnitude of postnoise performance degradations. We can no longer assert that noise aftereffects are postadaptation phenomena; rather, they appear to be postnoise residues occurring in spite of adaptation to noise.

The magnitude of the predictability effect in Table 9.7 is about as great as we have ever obtained in our research (see, for example, Table 4.3). It is therefore interesting to note that, for the first time, we also found highly significant differences in the perception of the unpredictability of the noise bursts. Table 9.8 presents mean ratings to the postexperimental question: "The noise bursts seemed to occur at:" where 1 = "Completely irregular intervals" and 9 = "Completely regular intervals." It is immediately apparent that subjects in the Predictable conditions correctly perceived the noise bursts as occurring at more regular intervals than subjects in the Unpredictable conditions ($F = 74.38$, $1/36\ df$, $p < .001$). Similar empirical efforts to assess perceived unpredictability were made in other studies reported in this book, but these earlier data were

TABLE 9.8

Mean Ratings of the Regularity or Irregularity of the Noise Bursts

	Noise condition	
Interstimulus interval	Predictable	Unpredictable
Long	7.10[a]	2.80
Short	6.70	3.10

[a] A high score means the noise bursts were perceived as occuring at regular intervals.

uniformly unsuccessful in showing differential perceptions (see Footnote 8 in Chapter 4). The significant effect reported here may be due to the clear phrasing of the present item, although it may also reflect the particular scheduling of noise-to-silence in this experiment. The fact that proofreading performance was so strongly affected by the predictability variable in this study argues for the latter interpretation. Subjects not only experienced the noise as unpredictable, but were also so explicitly aware of it as to be able to give a veridical report of the experience.

Discussion

The principal results of this study demonstrate that shorter interstimulus intervals are associated with physiological adaptation to high-intensity noise, whereas longer intervals lead to inhibition of adaptation. The findings show, moreover, that variations in GSR adaptation are accompanied by a parallel tendency toward differences in amount of decline of task errors during the period of noise exposure. However, we found that differential adaptation was unrelated to the magnitude of deleterious postnoise consequences. Proofreading performance was equally impaired in both of the Unpredictable conditions and, as expected, was significantly poorer than in the two Predictable conditions. It would appear, by inference, that differential adaptation exerts minimal impact on noise aftereffects. We conclude, therefore, that postnoise task degradations do not represent a price paid for adaptation to noise. More generally, we may state that negative aftereffects of stress exposure are not the result of adaptation; rather, they appear to be a residual consequence of cumulative noxious stimulation in spite of adaptation.

We cannot be sure, from the findings of our research, which mechanisms are vital to the production of behavioral residues. It may be something like differential arousal, which, it will be recalled, was assumed to vary with the experimental noise conditions and the nature of the task being performed during noise exposure. It is conceivable that adverse aftereffects occur only where heightened arousal is produced by an overload of the organism's information-processing capacity, as where he is required to perform tasks during disruptive noise intrusions (cf. Wohlwill, 1972, in press). If the individual has no task to perform, negative aftereffects might not appear. We did, after all, discover an overload effect in the subsidiary task study reported in Chapter 3. Admittedly, those results represented performance impairments during noise, but a similar logic may apply to aftereffect phenomena. These and related interpretations are, of course, clearly speculative; only future research can establish the precise factors responsible for the negative consequences of unpredictable and uncontrollable aversive events. One thing is clear, however. It is not the adaptive process that causes adverse aftereffects, but the fact of mere exposure in spite of adaptation.

Let us conclude with a broad perspective. People expend energy and commit resources to coping with physical and social stress and, most often, they successfully adapt. In many cases, the successful adaptation permits nonstress levels of performance to be maintained during stress exposure. Irrespective of whether adaptation was successful, the greater the commitment to coping with the stressor, the greater the adverse aftereffects; the size of commitment to coping is a function not only of the intensity of the stressor, but of a person's appraisal of it. This appraisal will be influenced by contextual variables with which the stressor is associated, such as controllability, predictability, relative deprivation, and choice. The present chapter has added one more element to our conclusions: because adaptation is a common occurrence, it is apt to overshadow adverse effects, and when finally noticed, it is apt to be blamed for them. Neither of these views is tenable. Adaptation is merely a process that may or may not occur as people assess a stressful event, cope with it, and suffer its aftereffects.

Summary and Implications

Having investigated the behavioral aftereffects of exposure to unpredictable and uncontrollable aversive events, let us attempt to summarize our major findings and fit them into a more general formulation of stress and the adaptive process. It is generally agreed that high-intensity noise *per se* has little effect on human performance on a wide variety of tasks. Previous research, as well as data in Chapter 3, indicates that noise does not affect man's ability to do mental and psychomotor tasks ranging from the boringly simple to the oftentimes interesting. People who listen to a sequence of 108-dBA sounds spaced over approximately 25 to 30 minutes perform no worse than people who are not exposed to noise. This result is true both for older-aged and college-aged men and women. Perhaps, as some have suggested (cf. Kryter, 1970), noise exposure over prolonged periods of time will produce task degradations, but acute noise for brief

155

periods of time does not have these effects. On the other hand, the evidence is also clear that noise will produce performance impairments depending on the complexity of the task and the cognitive context in which noise occurs. Interference with the information-processing demands placed on the individual, as where he works on two tasks simultaneously or must maintain continual vigilance on a tracking task, is associated with deterioration of performance. This effect is most likely to occur where the noise is experienced as unpredictable and/or uncontrollable. These findings underscore the importance of cognitive factors in mediating the effects of noise on behavior, for unpredictability and uncontrollability are extrastimulus variables, and task complexity is an instance of cognitive overload.

It would appear, then, that the effects of noise on task performance are related to the extent to which it interferes with some ongoing activity, the extent of interference varying with the information-processing demands placed upon the subject. It is conceivable, as we noted earlier, that even unpredictable noise will have minimally aversive effects on individuals who are not performing a job; it might even provide relief from boredom inherent in a monotonous work situation. This possibility has great significance for those concerned, more generally, with the effects of the physical environment on behavior, since stressor stimuli of any kind may result in adverse effects only where they produce cognitive overload that disrupts an individual's organized activity.

The absence of noise-induced impairments of simple task performance has often been attributed to adaptation of physiological stress reactions. Autonomic responses to noise appear during initial exposure, but they wane with repeated stimulation. Assuming stress reactions interfere with efficiency, we would expect some initial task errors which then decline over the course of noise exposure. The results reported in Chapter 3 demonstrate quite clearly that physiological adaptation is a pervasive phenomenon, and that the occurence of task errors tend to conform to expectations based on the assumed effects of noise adaptation. It ought to be noted, moreover, that adaptation of autonomic responses occurred on several different channels, thereby lending support to the notion of a generalized stress response to noise which declines with repeated stimulation. It should also be noted that this adaptive process occurred irrespective of the unpredictability and uncontrollability of the noise; hence, we can be certain of the noise-adaptation phenomenon and its associated effects on task performance.

What about behavioral aftereffects of noise? Tolerance for frustration, quality of proofreading performance, and ability to resolve cognitive conflict (i.e., response competition) were all impaired following exposure to high-intensity noise, providing the schedule of stimulation was aperiodic or unsignaled. Just as unpredictable noise had a greater impact on certain types of complex tasks during actual exposure, postnoise behavior also showed greater impairment if the noise had been unpredictable rather than predictable. Even though adaptation to noise occurred to an equivalent degree under both conditions, the magnitude of adverse aftereffects was far greater in the unpredictable condition. The obvious next step in our research was to explain why unpredictability had these effects. We reasoned that unpredictable aversive events, including noise, achieve their stress-arousing effects because the individual believes he cannot control the onset and/or offset of the stressor. Previous research has demonstrated the stress-reducing attributes of perceived control over environmental demands. These ameliorative effects (e.g., reduced autonomic reactions) were shown to occur where the individual could in fact escape or avoid aversive stimulation, and also where he simply believed that escape or avoidance behaviors were possible. The perception of potential control over noise termination was deliberately manipulated in our own research, with the result that adverse aftereffects of unpredictable noise were appreciably reduced. This effect was true under a number of experimental variations, and with several different procedures for inducing perceived control. Data were also collected in various studies that indicated a tendency toward reduced physiological stress reactions where subjects believed they could terminate noise. Taken together, these results strongly suggest that perception of control reduces the aversive impact of unpredictable noise, hence the deleterious aftereffects of such noxious stimulation. In other words, noise stressors occur in a context of cognition and social circumstance, and consideration of these variables is essential for accurate prediction of residual effects of noise. Psychological factors, not simply physical parameters of the noise stressor, are the important elements in the production of noise aftereffects.

But what specific stress-reducing mechanisms are aroused by the manipulation of perceived control? In answering this question, we reasoned that inescapable and unpredictable noise confronts the individual with a situation in which he is at the mercy of his environment; that is, he is powerless to affect the occurrence of the stressor and he cannot even anticipate its occurrence. In these circumstances, we may describe his psychological state as one of helplessness. It follows from this line of thought that the perception of control over unpredictable noise would reduce the individual's sense of helplessness and thus the magnitude of his stress response. If feelings of helplessness are minimized by belief in potential control, adverse aftereffects should also be minimized. This is, of course, precisely the result obtained in our controllability studies. Since we also obtained data suggesting greater helplessness under No Perceived Control conditions than Perceived Control conditions,[1] we tentatively conclude that unpredictable noise produces deleterious aftereffects because it is more aversive

[1] See the unavoidable-noise study in Chapter 5.

than predictable noise, its greater aversiveness being a function of the sense of helplessness induced in an individual who is unable to control and/or predict the onset and offset of noise. The need for further experimental evidence of this interpretation is self-evident.

The results and interpretations presented in this book were concerned primarily with the consequences of noise stimulation. We believe, however, that the influence of unpredictability and uncontrollability is applicable to any stressor. In an effort to generalize our findings, we conducted experiments with several other aversive events. Data from the electric-shock experiment demonstrated that adverse consequences of shock are reduced if stimulation is predictable and/or is perceived as controllable—an effect that closely replicates our findings with noise. Still other research indicated that these cognitive variables produce similar effects with social stressors, thereby permitting the general conclusion that deleterious aftereffects of stress are a function of the unpredictability of aversive stimulation and the belief that one has little control over stimulus occurrence and nonoccurrence.

This conclusion does not, however, allow us to characterize negative aftereffects as the psychic price paid by the individual for his adaptation to noxious stimulation. It is true that all subjects adapted to noise or shock, and that the aftereffects were as much postadaptation phenomena as poststressor phenomena. Yet, our initial research did not indicate whether aftereffects occurred in spite of adaptation or because of it. Further analysis and experimentation enabled us to adjudicate this rather nice theoretical issue. We assumed that adaptation was a cognitive process involving one or another mechanism designed to filter out of awareness certain aspects of the aversive event, or in some other way reappraise it as benign. We assumed, further, that physiological adaptation was an index of this process, and that the effort entailed in achieving adaptation is reflected in the magnitude of decline of physiological responses to the stressor. Given these assumptions, we were able to demonstrate that greater adaptation was not associated with greater poststressor task impairments. We concluded, therefore, that deleterious aftereffects represent behavioral residues of noxious stimulation, despite the fact that individuals almost invariably adapt to such stimulation.

We are still left with the problem of what mechanisms may be responsible for behavioral residues. The arousal concept might provide at least a partial answer, but we were unable to demonstrate consistent associations between arousal, as measured by tonic skin conductance, and differential noise aftereffects. This does not mean such a correlation is implausible; data from a single autonomic channel are hardly conclusive. What is obviously needed to test the hypotheses in question are multiple measurements of autonomic and electrocortical activity. There are, undoubtedly, other explanations for aftereffect phenomena. A particularly compelling alternative is that postnoise impairments may be due to an overloading of the individual's information-processing capacity, brought on by the accumulated stress of unpredictable noise interfering with task performance. An obvious test of this hypothesis would be to expose subjects to unpredictable noise under conditions where they had or did not have a task to perform. Since both groups would likely adapt to the noise, we could test for the presence of aftereffects as a function of the task–no-task variable. Failure to find aftereffects in the no-task group would be presumptive evidence of the cognitive overload interpretation. The preceding two explanations of aftereffect phenomena certainly do not constitute an exhaustive list of possible hypotheses. Though we are unable to suggest additional mechanisms at this time, we feel sure they exist. An important goal of future research in this area ought to be the enumeration and testing of these alternatives.

Additional gaps in our research are also evident. The dependent measures were a limited sample of the effects we might expect following exposure to aversive events. Human task performance, tolerance for frustration, and ability to resolve response conflict represent individual behaviors that are sensitive to stress arousal, but interpersonal activities are also influenced by aversive events. Unpredictable and uncontrollable noise should affect aggressiveness, exploitative behavior, liking for others, and general irritability in interpersonal relations. Anecdotal reports cited in the second chapter document these expectations, yet, with the possible exception of the "volunteering" results reported in Chapter 6, we have little systematic data either from our own or others' research that demonstrates adverse interpersonal consequences of noise exposure. The need for future research on this problem is clear.

A related limitation of our findings concerns the persistence of negative effects of environmental stressors. The aftereffect measures were invariably administered between 10 and 40 minutes after final stimulus presentation. Perhaps immediate aftereffects of noise disappear with elapsed time. Or, they may remain evident even several hours after noise termination. If they do not, we may ask whether aftereffects decline differentially for various measures. These and related questions are especially significant, not only for a fuller understanding of what we mean by adverse aftereffects, but also for a specification of the mechanisms that determine behavioral residues of stressful stimulation.

The question of persistence of aftereffects is related to the issue of long-term consequences of environmental stress. Those looking for the psychic costs of stress and adaptation (e.g., Dubos, 1965) are vitally concerned with the effects of these variables over many years. Indeed, the ultimate criterion of stress effects and aftereffects is probably genetic; that is, the subtle and sometimes massive changes produced in the gene pool of man as a result of continued

exposure and adaptation to environmental conditions. We have obviously ignored such problems in the research reported in this book. Relevant data would,
of necessity, come from longitudinal studies, which were beyond our scope and
resources. But these studies must certainly be carried out if we are ever to
understand the adaptive process, as well as the effects of noise and other
stressors on man. It is true that field studies and surveys of reactions to noise
have been conducted during the last few years (see Kryter, 1970, for a review of
some of this work), but almost none of these have definitive data on long-term
effects. More long-term, nonlaboratory study of possible behavioral changes
consequent to noise exposure is needed. Processes of adaptation also require
evaluation in such long-term research. The nature and course of noise-induced
stress, adaptation, and resultant aftereffects need to be described for individuals
who experience months and even years in noisy environments (cf. Cohen, 1969).

There is still another theme for future research that should be emphasized—one that appears in many of our studies on both physical and social
stressors. We refer to the general lack of correspondence between annoyance or
discomfort, on the one hand, and behavioral effects on the other. For example,
the first study described in Chapter 4 dealt with effects of high- and low-intensity noise and with predictable and unpredictable noise. In simplest terms, the
intensity of noise did not affect task performance: that was a function of the
predictability variable. But, conversely, predictability did not affect annoyance
levels: they were a function of noise intensity. An analogous result was found in
the discrimination study in Chapter 8. Discrimination, whether by chance or
arbitrary action, adversely influenced task performance. Annoyance was only
reported by those who were the victims of arbitrary discrimination.

Although the focus of much of this book has been upon behavioral and
psychophysiological effects, the importance of annoyance should not be minimized. It is undoubtedly a more potent force in individual motivation than are
behavioral aftereffects. Because of the nature of our interests, we did not
explore its effects systematically, but casual observation and anecdote document
its ability to shape behavior. Witness the subjects who refused to continue in
some of the noise studies after the first few bursts. The total duration of noise to
which they were exposed was less than 30 seconds, an amount unlikely to
produce any behavioral deficit. Yet, it generated enough unpleasantness and
annoyance to overcome the subject's commitment to participate in the study
and the demand characteristics keeping him in it; that is, the special trip to the
lab, the potential forfeit of the rewards to be earned, and the inconvenience to
the experimenter. We surely would have discovered behavioral consequences of
the annoyance produced by noise if we had specifically chosen to study such
indirect effects. Indeed, in the discrimination study mentioned above and the
relative deprivation study described in Chapter 6, subjects' annoyance was re-

flected in how much time they were willing to give to the undergraduate experimental assistant. The more annoyed they were, the less they volunteered to assist the undergraduate. The discrimination study is a particularly cogent example. Two groups were equally discriminated against and both showed performance decrements. The arbitrary group, which was annoyed, did not volunteer, but the chance group, for whom discrimination and its consequences were not accompanied by annoyance, volunteered as frequently as did nondiscriminated subjects.

The implications of the annoyance–performance distinction can be examined from two points of view. Those who wish to minimize deleterious effects of noise may disregard the importance of annoyance in those cases where there is no behavioral deficit. For just as there may be behavioral effects without physiological damage, so may there be irritation and unpleasantness without behavioral damage. On the other hand, those who wish to magnify the adverse effects of noise may point to annoyance effects in those cases where there are no behavioral consequences. Depending upon the perspective, the behavior–annoyance distinction can be adduced as evidence for the view that noise is a greater threat than popularly supposed or that noise is actually a lesser threat.

The annoyance issue can be applied to a wider range of phenomena than noise. For whenever a stress irritates or annoys people, it becomes a social problem by definition. If the irritation is coupled with behavioral or physiological deficit, consensus can easily be gained as to its deleterious qualities. However, when a stress seemingly produces only the subjective state, it is apt to be passed off as harmless. We wish to emphasize that such a position has no foundation in our research; we have not shown effects attributable to annoyance only because we sought none. We do not wish our findings to be regarded as supporting the null hypothesis.

Alternatively, stressors that are not annoying may be overlooked as damaging, even by those suffering the effects. Again, the discrimination study supplies an illustration. Subjects in the Chance Discrimination condition were not annoyed—they felt they had lost a fair gamble and had no hard feelings. They were even willing to do a favor—volunteering time for the undergraduate experimental assistant. Despite their good feelings, the discrimination took its toll; the subjects did worse on the Stroop task than those who suffered no discrimination. Note that the same effect would have occurred had the subjects lost a fair coin toss: the actual loss was rigged from the experimenter's point of view, not the subject's. Because the victims did not feel aggrieved, behavioral consequences of discrimination were not noted by them, and perhaps were also overlooked by an outside observer.

This chapter has been concerned up to this point with some of the theoretical implications of our research findings. We have also tried to specify questions for future research, and, in so doing, suggest what we believe to be rigorous tests of alternative explanations of stress effects and aftereffects. We now turn to a very different set of issues, namely, social and public policy implications of the noise studies. We confine ourselves to some of the more important of these, rather than attempting a general discussion of the social relevance of our work.

Social Implications of the Noise Research

One of the teachings of our research is that noise can be a stressor with demonstrable effects on task performance and physiology. Man adapts to acoustic stimulation, but there are aftereffects inimical to his subsequent functioning. It is true that these consequences largely depend on the cognitive context in which noise occurs, and it is also true that physical parameters of the stimulus (e.g., intensity) are less important than psychological factors (e.g., unpredictability) in producing stress-related effects. Yet, it is these very factors which characterize the noisy environments to which most of us are exposed. Jets, air compressors, sirens, rock-and-roll music, automobile traffic are generally unpredictable and often uncontrollable sources of stimulation that contribute to making the sound of our environment almost unbearable and, indeed, dangerous for behavioral efficiency and mental well-being. We are immediately reminded, in this connection, of the sounds in a typical middle-class urban or suburban home. The washing machine provides a steady hum, but the clothes dryer suddenly begins to vibrate; then the telephone jangles while the delivery boy rings the doorbell; a jet aircraft rumbles overhead and automobile horns are heard, from time to time, in the background; amidst this confusion, the children begin to fight, cry, and scream. The overall noise level is not very high by damage-risk criteria, but the mother and housewife will attest to her frustration, irritability, and even anger. Over the years, she does manage to adapt to this noise routine; at least millions of women seem to do so. However, we would not be at all surprised to find these same women making errors in the balancing of their checkbooks, screaming at their children for minor transgressions, greeting their husbands with irritability when they return home in the evening, and generally showing signs of fatigue and exhaustion by the end of the day. The occurrence of these effects may seem self-evident, but they are no less serious for all that. Unpredictable and uncontrollable noise is a hazard of contemporary life that can and must be controlled—by personal measures, appropriate laws, and community action.

It has, of course, been argued that even if noise is more than a nuisance, it cannot be ranked high among the multitude of social problems confronting society. Noise abatement does not warrant classification with major issues such as the Viet Nam war, racial injustice, economic recession, student unrest, crime, and even the pollution of air and water. But this argument should not be used as an excuse to avoid taking action, for the financial and manpower resources needed to cope with the noise problem do not in any way preclude efforts to solve the other problems as well. Noise control and abatement will be achieved only if society values nonnoisy environments. If, on the other hand, it places greater importance on the automobile, rapid air travel, and innumerable pieces of equipment for efficiency and convenience, we cannot expect an immediate reduction in the din surrounding us. Antinoise legislation follows from community pressure on legislators and manufacturers (cf. Baron, 1970). Home and commercial equipment must be made quieter; noisy factories should be placed far from residential areas; construction techniques must make walls effective barriers against noise; and supersonic transports are not essential to the majority of citizens who wish to travel. In the final analysis, it is public action that produces abatement of noise.

What specific recommendations for noise control emerge from our research? What can we say to the concerned citizen and legislator? There are several general findings of the noise studies that have direct practical implications. The first is that the effects of noise depend, in part, on stimulus conditions that overload the individual's information-processing capacity. In other words, noise effects and aftereffects are maximized in situations where the individual is performing a complex task requiring vigilance and concentration. This finding suggests that work environments (e.g., offices, schools, and certain sections of factories) should not be subject to unpredictable noise intrusions. Proper construction of walls can be effective in this regard, as can the careful routing of automobiles, highways, and jet overflights. Business machines and equipment necessary for job efficiency must be constructed so as to minimize the irregular noise often associated with such equipment. And the summated sounds of the activity of large numbers of people should be carefully controlled by judicious allocation of manpower to physical work space.

The question of annoyance must also be dealt with here. It would be tempting to conclude that behavioral deficits are a function of such contextual variables as unpredictability and uncontrollability, whereas annoyance is a function of the noise's intensity. While such a conclusion is consistent with our research, it is at variance with our experience. Anyone who has ever been kept awake all night by a leaky faucet can attest that annoyance does accompany low-intensity noise. Even if the dripping water has no direct adverse behavioral consequences, it is likely to have indirect ones produced by lack of sleep. Annoyance is probably a complex function of the intensity of discrete sounds in relation to ambient noise level. The possibility exists that if stringent legislation and concerted social action eliminated high-intensity noise from the environment, noise of lower intensity would become more annoying, and a general downward spiral would ensue, with formerly innocuous sound becoming noxious. This prediction may, justifiably, be regarded as hyperbole, but it highlights an important consideration. Legislative and communal action programs can only deal with some aspects of the noise problem, and even then the effectiveness of their solutions wane over time.

Whenever the question of minimizing annoyance is raised, the counter, "it's only a value" may be offered, as if the need for eliminating task disruptions were unequivocally agreed upon but the need for eliminating annoyance were a matter of taste. Of course the desire for combatting irritation is a value, but so is the desire to keep task performance undisturbed, or for that matter, to avoid physiological damage. A concern for quality of life must be as concerned with subjective state as with clerical skills or cognitive functioning. For if not, it will be self-defeating. We cannot conceive that, in the long run, a thoroughly disgruntled and annoyed society can function or operate productively.

It has often been said that as long as man seems able to get used to a wide variety of environmental conditions, there is no urgency to expend money and technological personnel in devising techniques to change the environment. But our research shows that we should not put up with noise simply because we can adapt to it. There is a psychic cost attached to noise exposure in spite of adaptation. The implication of this third general finding is clear: Adaptation notwithstanding, we must attempt actual alterations of our environment aimed at reducing noise, as well as other kinds of environmental stress. These alterations, as we noted above, may involve personal measures or legislative and community efforts designed to produce changes in our "sound" environment. Thus, we can move away from a noisy neighborhood or even create a new neighborhood, as they did in West Germany when an entire town was relocated away from a noisy airport (New York Times, March 14, 1971). Alternatively, we can legislate construction codes, manufacturing regulations, and ordinances against jet overflights, the SST, and truck traffic at certain times of day and in certain areas of the city.

Recommendations about ambient noise levels for different environments are beyond the purview of this monograph. Such proposals are discussed in an excellent book, *The Effects of Noise on Man*, by a leading psychoacoustician, Karl D. Kryter. Our own research has emphasized the importance of cognitive variables in noise-produced stress effects. The context in which noise occurs, not its physical parameters, was shown to be a determining factor in the production of deleterious aftereffects. This fourth general result suggests that attempts to reduce noise intensity should also be concerned with reducing its unpredictability and unexpectedness, as well as the individual's sense of lack of control over the noise source. This latter point, in particular, has immediate applicability. You will recall the "indirect-control" experiment in which subjects did or did not have access to another person who had control over noise termination. Having such access was perceived as having control over noise, and in consequence, adverse aftereffects were substantially reduced. It is not too great an extrapolation to relate this finding to the notion of an "ombudsman" who mediates between community needs and governmental authority. Perhaps institutionalization of such a role is precisely what is needed to effect legislative action to reduce noise and other environmental pollutants. The perception of control, with the possibility for effective control in at least some instances, is both feasible and necessary. There is, of course, a danger in mere perception of control. The unscrupulous could use it in Machiavellian ways to serve their own interests and/or to maintain the oftentimes unacceptable *status quo*. A deliberately induced illusion of control could become a modern opiate of the masses. Nonetheless, man wants and should have some measure of control over aspects of his physical and social environment. The ombudsman concept and recent efforts at developing community participation in governmental affairs are attempts to provide such control.

We offer these suggestions with appropriate skepticism, for we realize there are many aspects of control beyond the purview of a mediator. For example, as long as the stenographer in the outer office is typing our work, the noise of her machine is not intrusive. Should we learn that she is typing our colleague's work, the sound of her machine will doubtlessly become disruptive. Granted that our colleague has equal access to the ombudsman, there is no equitable solution. Even more confusing are the paradoxes that are engendered by some of the solutions to unwanted noise intrusions. Many people combat noise by masking it, that is, by covering it with an overlay of music from radio, phonograph, or tape deck, or, in purer form, with the sounds produced by white-noise generators manufactured and marketed specifically for the purpose of drowning out noise. These strategies work for many people, presumably by regularizing the noise and putting it under one's control. Stated in physical terms, however, the solution seems absurd. A person disturbed by energy impinging on his eardrums eliminates the disturbance by increasing the impinging energy. Aside from adding yet another *caveat* against oversimplified physical solutions to what are essentially cognitive problems, this phenomenon reminds us of the conclusion of the Grimm fairy tale in which the cat, after eating his former friends, the mice, is heard to remark, "And that's the way of the world."

We did not begin our noise research for the purpose of coming up with specific recommendations for social policy. We have commented on some of the general implications of our results, but those who seek more concrete recommendations for noise abatement might better look to legal and legislative studies. A chief goal in studying noise and related stressors was to demonstrate that adaptation is not necessarily beneficial to man. It is certainly one way of coping with environmental stress, but it is by no means an unequivocally effective strategy. For we have shown that stress exposure leaves adverse behavioral residues in spite of adaptation. It is also important to remember that these aftereffects are determined by the cognitive and social setting in which the stressor occurs; mere intensity and similar physical parameters of the stimulus are not sufficient to produce psychological deficits in humans. We have reached these conclusions without fully understanding the mechanisms responsible for stress effects and aftereffects. We suggested several possible explanations in the hope that this would lead us, and others, to more rigorous inquiry. But, in spite of unresolved issues, new information has been added to our knowledge of the effects of noise on man.

One further word on the implications of our research. In the opening pages of this volume, and indeed, in the title, we stated our intention of commenting upon urban stress. We were explicit in stating that these observations, for the most part, would be in the form of laboratory analogues and replicas of urban stressors. Having made the point, we have refrained from translating at every point and have saved our urban discussion until this final chapter. Like a pair of bookends, the urban conception frames our work, giving it a start and stop as well as support without either harping on the obvious or engaging in premature point-by-point comparisons. The overall parallels are patent and provide validation for our research strategy as an analytic approach to the understanding of mechanisms of complex urban stress.

We cannot think of a better way to end this book than to quote the late Edward C. Tolman: "Since all the sciences, and especially psychology, are still immersed in such tremendous realms of the uncertain and the unknown, the best that any individual scientist, especially any psychologist, can do seems to be to follow his own gleam and his own bent, however inadequate they may be. In fact, I suppose that actually this is what we all do. In the end, the only sure criterion is to have fun. And I have had fun" (Tolman, 1959, p. 152). We have had fun too.

References

Amsel, A. The role of frustrative nonreward in noncontinuous reward situations. *Psychological Bulletin*, 1958, *55*, 102-119.

Anastasi, Anne. *Fields of applied psychology*, New York: McGraw-Hill, 1964.

Anderson, N. H. *Toward a quieter city*. A Report of the Mayor's Task Force on Noise Control. New York City, January 1970.

Appley, M. H., & Trumbull, R. On the concept of psychological stress. In M. H. Appley and R. Trumbull (Eds.), *Psychological stress*. New York: Appleton, 1967.

Ashmore, R. D. Prejudice. In B. E. Collins (Ed.), *Introduction to social psychology*. Reading, Massachusetts: Addison-Wesley, 1970.

Azrin, N. H. Some effects of noise on human behavior. *Journal of Experimental Analysis of Behavior*, 1958, *1*, 183-200.

Bailey, A. Noise is a slow agent of death. *New York Times Magazine*, November 23, 1969, 46, 131-135.

Bandler, R. J., Jr., Madaras, G. R., & Bem, D. J. Self-observation as a source of pain perception. *Journal of Personality and Social Psychology*, 1966, *9*, 205-209.

Baron, R. A. *The tyranny of noise*. New York: St. Martin's, 1970.

Basowitz, H., Persky, H., Korchin, S. J., & Grinker, R. R. *Anxiety and stress*. New York: McGraw-Hill, 1955.

Berlyne, D. E. *Conflict, arousal, and curiosity*. New York: McGraw-Hill, 1960.

Berrien, F. K. The effects of noise. *Psychological Bulletin*, 1946, *43*, 141-161.

Bexton, W. H., Heron, W., & Scott, T. H. Effects of decreased variation in the sensory environment. *Canadian Journal of Psychology*, 1954, *8*, 70-76.

Blum, S. Noise: How much more can we take? *McCall's*, January, 1967, *49*, 113-116.

Boggs, D. H., & Simon, J. R. Differential effects of noise on tasks of varying complexity. *Journal of Applied Psychology*, 1968, *52*, 148-153.

Boring, E.G. *History of experimental psychology* (2nd ed.). New York: Appleton, 1950.

Brehm, J. W. Motivational effects of cognitive dissonance. In M. R. Jones (Ed.), *Nebraska symposium on motivation*. Lincoln, Nebraska: Univ. of Nebraska Press, 1962.

Brehm, J. W. *A theory of psychological reactance*. New York: Academic Press, 1966.

Brehm, J. W., & Cohen, A. R. *Explorations in cognitive dissonance*. New York: Wiley, 1962.

Broadbent, D. E. Some effects of noise on visual performance. *Quarterly Journal of Experimental Psychology*, 1954, *6*, 1-5.

Broadbent, D. E. Effects of noise on behavior. In C. M. Harris (Ed.), *Handbook of noise control*. New York: McGraw-Hill, 1957.

Broadbent, D. E. *Perception and communication*. London, England: Pergamon, 1958.

Burns, W. *Noise and man*. London, England: John Murray, 1968.

Caplan, N. S., & Paige, J. M. A study of ghetto rioters. *Scientific American*, 1968, *219*, 15-21.

Champion, R. A. Studies of experimentally induced disturbance. *Australian Journal of Psychology*, 1950, **2**, 90-99.

Cleaver, E. *Soul on ice.* New York: Dell Paperbacks, 1968.

Cofer, C. N., & Appley, M. H. *Motivation: Theory and research.* New York: Wiley, 1964.

Cohen, A. Effects of noise on psychological state. In W. D. Ward, and J. E. Frick (Eds.), *Noise as a public health hazard: Proceedings of the conference.* ASHA Reports 4. Washington, D. C.: The American Speech and Hearing Association, February, 1969, 74-88.

Coombs, C. H. Adaptation of the galvanic response to auditory stimuli. *Journal of Experimental Psychology*, 1938, **22**, 244-268.

Corah, N. L., & Boffa, J. Perceived control, self-observation, and response to aversive stimulation. *Journal of Personality and Social Psychology*, 1970, **16**, 1-14.

Corso, J. F. The effects of noise on human behavior. Rept. WADC-No. 53-81. Wright Air Development Center, Wright-Patterson Air Force Base, Ohio, 1952.

D'Amato, M. E., & Gumenik, W. E. Some effects of immediate versus randomly delayed shock on an instrumental response and cognitive processes. *Journal of Abnormal and Social Psychology*, 1960, **60**, 64-67.

Davis, J. A. A formal interpretation of the theory of relative deprivation. *Sociometry*, 1959, **22**, 280-296.

Davis, R. C., & Berry, T. Gastrointestinal reactions to response-contingent stimulation. *Psychological Reports*, 1964, **15**, 95-113.

Davis, R. C., Buchwald, A. M., & Frankmann, R. Autonomic and muscular responses and their relation to simple stimuli. *Psychological Monographs*, 1959, **69**, (20 Whole No. 405).

Denenberg, V. H. Stimulation in infancy, emotional reactivity, and exploratory behavior. In D. C. Glass (Ed.), *Biology and behavior: Neurophysiology and emotion.* New York: Rockefeller Univ. Press and Russell Sage Foundation, 1967.

Dey, F. L. Auditory fatigue and predicted permanent hearing defects from rock-and-roll music. *The New England Journal of Medicine*, 1970, **282**, 467-469.

Dubos, R. *Man adapting.* New Haven, Connecticut: Yale Univ. Press, 1965.

Dubos, R. Environmental determinants of human life. In D. C. Glass (Ed.), *Biology and behavior: Environmental influences.* New York: The Rockefeller Univ. Press and Russell Sage Foundation, 1968.

Evan, W. M., & Zelditch, M., Jr. A laboratory experiment on bureaucratic authority. *American Sociological Review*, 1961, **26**, 883-893.

Feather, N. T. The relationship of persistence at a task to expectation of success and achievement related motives. *Journal of Abnormal and Social Psychology*, 1961, **63**, 552-561.

Festinger, L. *A theory of cognitive dissonance.* New York: Harper, 1957.

Finkelman, J. M., & Glass, D. C. Reappraisal of the relationship between noise and human performance by means of a subsidiary task measure. *Journal of Applied Psychology*, 1970, **54**, 211-213.

Fiske, D. W., & Maddi, S. R. *Functions of varied experience.* Homewood, Illinois: Dorsey, 1961.

Freeman, J. J. *Principles of noise.* New York: Wiley, 1958.

French, J. W., Ekstrom, R. B., & Price, L. A. *Manual for kit of reference tests for cognitive factors.* Princeton, New Jersey: Educational Testing Service, 1963.

Furedy, J. J., & Doob, A. N. Signaling unmodifiable shocks: Limits on human informational cognitive control. Unpublished manuscript, Univ. of Toronto, 1971.

Geer, J. H. Effect of interstimulus intervals and rest-period length upon habituation of the orienting response. *Journal of Experimental Psychology*, 1966, **72**, 617-619.

Geer, J. H. A test of the classical conditioning model of emotion: The use of nonpainful aversive stimuli as unconditioned stimuli in a conditioning procedure. *Journal of Personality and Social Psychology*, 1968, **10**, 148-156.

Geer, J. H., Davison, G. C., & Gatchel, R. I. Reduction of stress in humans through nonveridical perceived control of aversive stimulation. *Journal of Personality and Social Psychology*, 1970, **16**, 731-738.

Glass, D. C., Reim, B., & Singer, J. E. Behavioral consequences of adaptation to controllable and uncontrollable noise. *Journal of Experimental Social Psychology*, 1971, **7**, 244-257.

Glass, D. C., Singer, J. E., & Friedman, Lucy N. Psychic cost of adaptation to an environmental stressor. *Journal of Personality and Social Psychology*, 1969, **12**, 200-210.

Glorig, A. *Noise and your ear.* New York: Grune & Stratton, 1958.

Grinker, R. R., & Spiegel, J. P. *Men under stress.* New York: McGraw-Hill, 1945.

Groves, P. M., & Thompson, R. F. Habituation: A dual-process theory. *Psychological Review*, 1970, **77**, 419-450.

Haan, Norma. Proposed model of ego functioning: Coping and defensive mechanisms in relationship to I. Q. change. *Psychological Monographs*, 1963, **77**, (Whole No. 571).

Haggard, E. A. Some conditions determining adjustment during and readjustment following experimentally induced stress. In S. S. Tomkins (Ed.), *Contemporary psychopathology.* Cambridge, Massachusetts: Harvard Univ. Press, 1946.

Harding, J., Proshansky, H., Kutner, B., & Chein, I. Prejudice and ethnic relations. In G. Lindzey & E. Aronson (Eds.), *Handbook of social psychology*, (2nd ed.), Vol. 5. Reading, Massachusetts: Addison-Wesley, 1969.

Harris, J. D. Habituatory response decrement in the intact organism. *Psychological Bulletin*, 1943, **40**, 385-422.

Herbert, R. *Modern artists on art.* New York: Prentice Hall, 1965.

Houston, B. K., & Jones, T. M. Distraction and Stroop color-word performance. *Journal of Experimental Psychology*, 1967, **74**, 54-56.

Irle, M., & Rohrmann, B. Gesamtbericht über die Hamburger Vor-Untersuchung zum DFG-projekt Fluglarmforschung. Unpublished manuscript. Mannheim und Hamburg, West Germany, April, 1968.

Jacobs, Jane. *The death and life of great American cities.* New York: Random House, 1961.

Janis, I. L. *Psychological stress.* New York: Wiley, 1958.

Janis, I. L. Motivational factors in the resolution of decisional conflicts. In M. R. Jones (Ed.), *Nebraska symposium on motivation.* Lincoln, Nebraska: Univ. of Nebraska Press, 1959.

Janis, I. L. Psychological effects of warnings. In G. W. Baker and D. W. Chapman (Eds.), *Man and society in disaster.* New York: Basic Books, 1962.

Janis, I. L. Effects of fear arousal on attitude change: Recent developments in theory and experimental research. In L. Berkowitz (Ed.), *Advances in experimental social psychology*, Vol. 3. New York: Academic Press, 1967.

Jansen, G. Adverse effects of noise on iron and steel workers. *Stahl. Eisen.*, 1961, **81**, 217-220. (As cited in Kryter, 1970.)

Jansen, G. Effects of noise on physiological state. In W. D. Ward and J. E. Frick (Eds.), *Noise as a public health hazard: Proceedings of the conference.* ASHA Reports 4. Washington, D. C.: The American Speech and Hearing Association, February, 1969, 89-98.

Jensen, A. R., & Rohwer, W. D., Jr. The Stroop color-word test: A review. *Acta psychologica*, 1966, **25**, 36-93.

Jerison H. J., & Wing, S. Effects of noise and fatigue on a complex vigilance task. Rept. WADC-TR-57-14. Wright Air Development Center, Wright-Patterson Air Force Base, Ohio, 1957.

Jonsson, E., Kajland, A., Paccaguella, B., & Sorensen, S. Annoyance reactions to traffic noise in Italy and Sweden. *Archives of Environmental Health*, 1969, **19**, 692-699.

Kendall, M. G. *Rank correlation methods.* London, England: Charles Griffin & Co., 1948.

Korten, F. F., Cook, S. W., & Lacey, J. I. (Eds.), *Psychology and the problems of society.* Washington, D. C.: American Psychological Association, 1970.

Kryter, K. D. Noise and behavior. *Journal of Speech and Hearing Disorders*, 1950, No. 1.

Kryter, K. D. An example of "engineering psychology": The aircraft noise problem. *American Psychologist*, 1968, **23**, 240-244.

Kryter, K. D. *The effects of noise on man.* New York: Academic Press, 1970.

Kryter, K. D., Ward, N. D., Miller, J. D., & Eldredge, D. H. Hazardous exposure to intermittent and steady-state noise. *Journal of the Acoustical Society of America*, 1966, **39**, 451-464.

Lacey, J. I. Somatic response patterning and stress: Some revisions of activation theory. In M. H. Appley and R. Trumbull (Eds.), *Psychological stress.* New York: Appleton, 1967.

Lader, M. H. The effect of cyclobarbitone on habituation of the psychogalvanic reflex. *Brain*, 1964, **87**, 321-340.

Lanzetta, J. T., & Driscoll, J. M. Preference for information about an uncertain but unavoidable outcome. *Journal of Personality and Social Psychology*, 1966, **3**, 96-102.

Latané, B., & Arrowood, A. J. Emotional arousal and task performance. *Journal of Applied Psychology*, 1963, **47**, 324-327.

Lazarus, R. S. *Psychological stress and the coping process.* New York: McGraw-Hill, 1966.

Lazarus, R. S. Emotions and adaptation: Conceptual and empirical relations. In W. J. Arnold (Ed.), *Nebraska symposium on motivation.* Lincoln, Nebraska: Univ. of Nebraska Press, 1968.

Lefcourt, H. M. Internal versus external control of reinforcement: A review. *Psychological Bulletin*, 1966, **65**, 206-220.

LePanto, R., Moroney, W., & Zenhausern, R. The contribution of anxiety to the laboratory investigation of pain. *Psychonomic Science*, 1965, **3**, 475.

Lewis, O. *Children of Sanchez.* New York: Random House Paperbacks, 1961.

Lindzey, G., Lykken, D. T., & Winston, H. D. Infantile trauma, genetic factors, and adult temperament. *Journal of Abnormal and Social Psychology*, 1960, **61**, 7-14.

Lippold, O. C. J. Electromyography. In P. H. Venables and Irene Martin (Eds.), *A manual of psychophysiological methods.* New York: Wiley, 1967

Lovibond, S. H. The aversiveness of uncertainty: An analysis in terms of activation and information theory. *Australian Journal of Psychology*, 1968, **20**, 85-91.

Lykken, D. T. Neuropsychology and psychophysiology in personality research. In E. F. Borgatta and W. W. Lambert (Eds.), *Handbook of personality theory and research.* Chicago, Illinois: Rand McNally, 1968.

Mackworth, Jane F. *Vigilance and habituation: A neuropsychological approach.* Middlesex, England: Penguin Books, 1969.

Mandler, G. The interruption of behavior. In D. Levine (Ed.), *Nebraska symposium on motivation.* Lincoln, Nebraska: Univ. of Nebraska Press, 1964.

Mandler, G., & Watson, D. L. Anxiety and the interruption of behavior. In C. D. Spielberger (Ed.), *Anxiety and behavior.* New York: Academic Press, 1966.

Martin, Irene. Adaptation. *Psychological Bulletin*, 1964, **61**, 35-44.

Mayhew, Patricia. Perceived control and behavioral aftereffects of predictable and unpredictable noise. Unpublished doctoral dissertation, Columbia University, in preparation.

McGrath, J. J., & Hatcher, J. F. Irrelevant stimulation and vigilance under fast and slow stimulus. *ASW Technical Report No. 7.* Human Factors Research, Los Angeles, California, 1961.

McKennell, A. C., & Hunt, E. A. *Noise annoyance in central London.* London, England: The Government Social Survey, SS/332, March, 1966.

Mecklin, J. M. It's time to turn down all that noise. *Fortune,* October, 1969, 130-133, 188, 190, 195.

Merton, R. K. Bureaucratic structure and personality. In R. K. Merton, *Social Theory and Social Structure,* Glencoe, Illinois: Free Press, 1952.

Milgram, S. The experience of living in cities. *Science,* 1970, **13,** 1461-1468.

Miller, G. A. Psychology as a means of promoting human welfare. *American Psychologist,* 1969, **24,** 1063-1075.

Montagu, J. D., & Coles, E. M. Mechanism and measurement of the galvanic skin response. *Psychological Bulletin,* 1966, **65,** 261-279.

Mowrer, O. H., & Viek, P. An experimental analogue of fear from a sense of helplessness. *Journal of Abnormal and Social Psychology,* 1948, **43,** 193-200.

Orne, M. T. On the social psychology of the psychological experiment: With particular reference to demand characteristics and their implications. *American Psychologist,* 1962, **17,** 776-783.

Parsons, H. M. STAVE: STress AVoidance/Escape. SP-2459, System Developmental Corporation, Santa Monica, California, August, 1966

Pervin, L. A. The need to predict and control under conditions of threat. *Journal of Personality,* 1963, **31,** 570-587.

Pettigrew, T. F. Social evaluation theory: Convergences and applications In D. Levine (Ed.), *Nebraska symposium on motivation.* Lincoln, Nebraska: Univ. of Nebraska Press, 1967.

Plutchik, R. The effects of high-intensity intermittent sound on performance, feeling and physiology. *Psychological Bulletin,* 1959, **56,** 133-151.

Reim, B., Glass, D. C., & Singer, J. E. Behavioral consequences of exposure to uncontrollable and unpredictable noise. *Journal of Applied Social Psychology,* 1971, **1,** 44-56.

Riesen, A. H. Sensory deprivation. In E. Stellar and J. M. Sprague (Eds.), *Progress in physiological psychology,* Vol. 1. New York: Academic Press, 1966.

Rodda, M. *Noise in society.* London, England: Oliver & Boyd, 1967.

Rosen, S. Noise, hearing and cardiovascular function. In *Physiological effects of noise.* New York: Plenum Press, 1970.

Rosenthal, R. *Experimenter effects in behavioral research.* New York: Appleton, 1966.

Rosenthal, R., & Rosnow, R. L. *Artifact in behavioral research.* New York: Academic Press, 1969.

Rotter, J. B. Generalized expectancies for internal versus external control of reinforcement. *Psychological Monographs,* 1966, **80,** (Whole No. 609).

Sanders, A. F. The influence of noise on two discrimination tasks. *Ergonomics,* 1961, **4,** 253-258.

Schachter, S., Willerman, B., Festinger, L., & Hyman, R. Emotional disruption and industrial productivity. *Journal of Applied Psychology,* 1961, **45,** 201-213.

Seligman, M. E. P. For helplessness: Can we immunize the weak? *Psychology Today,* 1969, **3,** 42-44.

Seligman, M. E. P., Maier, S. F., & Solomon, R. L. Unpredictable and uncontrollable aversive events. In F. R. Brush (Ed.), *Aversive conditioning and learning.* New York:

Academic Press, 1971.

Selye, H. *The stress of life.* New York: McGraw-Hill, 1956.

Siegel, S., & Fouraker, L. E. *Bargaining and group decision making.* New York: McGraw-Hill, 1960.

Smith, K. R. Intermittent loud noise and mental performance. *Science,* 1951, **114**, 132-133.

Sokolov, E. N. Vospriiate i uslovny refleks. Moscow: Univ. of Moscow Press, 1958. (As cited in Berlyne, 1960).

Sternbach, R. A. *Principles of psychophysiology.* New York: Academic Press, 1966.

Stewart, W. H. Keynote Address. In W. D. Ward & J. E. Frick (Eds.), *Noise as a public health hazard: Proceedings of the conference.* ASHA Reports 4. Washington, D. C.: The American Speech and Hearing Association, February, 1969, 7-11.

Stotland, E., & Blumenthal, A. The reduction of anxiety as a result of the expectation of making a choice. *Canadian Journal of Psychology,* 1964, **18**, 139-145.

Teichner, W. H., Arees, E., & Reilley, R. Noise and human performance, a psychophysiological approach. *Ergonomics,* 1963, **6**, 83-97.

Thompson, R. F., & Spencer, W. A. Habituation: A model phenomenon for the study of neuronal substrates of behavior. *Psychological Review,* 1966, **73**, 16-43.

Tolman, E. C. Principles of purposive behavior. In S. Koch (Ed.), *Psychology: A study of a science.* Vol. 2. New York: McGraw-Hill, 1959.

Uno, T., & Grings, W. W. Autonomic components of orienting behavior. *Psychophysiology,* 1965, **1**, 311-321.

Weiss, J. M. Somatic effects of predictable and unpredictable shock. *Psychosomatic Medicine,* 1970, **32**, 397-408.

Weitz, J. Psychological research needs on the problems of human stress. In J. E. McGrath (Ed.), *Social and psychological factors in stress,* New York: Holt, 1970.

Welch, B. L. Psychophysiological response to the mean level of environmental stimulation: A theory of environmental integration. Symposium on medical aspects of stress in the military climate. Sponsored by Walter Reed Army Institute of Research, Washington, D. C., April 22-24, 1964.

Weybrew, B. B. Patterns of psychophysiological response to military stress. In M. H. Appley and R. Trumbull (Eds.), *Psychological stress.* New York: Appleton, 1967.

White, R. W. Motivation reconsidered: The concept of competence. *Psychological Review,* 1959, **66**, 297-333.

Wilkinson, R. Some factors influencing the effect of environmental stressors upon performance. *Psychological Bulletin,* 1969, **72**, 260-272.

Winer, B. J. *Statistical principles in experimental design.* New York: McGraw-Hill, 1962.

Wohlwill, J. F. The physical environment: A problem for a psychology of stimulation. *Journal of Social Issues,* 1966, **XXII**, 29-38.

Wohlwill, J. F. The emerging discipline of environmental psychology. *American Psychologist,* 1970, **25**, 303-312.

Wohlwill, J. F. Behavioral response and adaptation to environmental stimulation. In A. Damon (Ed.), *Physiological anthropology.* Cambridge, Massachusetts: Harvard Univ. Press, 1972, in press.

Woodhead, M. M. Effect of brief loud noise on decision making. *Journal of the Acoustical Society of America,* 1959, **31**, 1329-1331.

Wynne-Edwards, V. C. Population control and social selection in animals. In D. C. Glass (Ed.), *Biology and behavior: Genetics.* New York: Rockefeller Univ. Press and Russell Sage Foundation, 1968.

Zeitlin, L. R., & Finkelman, J. M. A "random digit" generation subsidiary task measure of operator perceptual-motor loading. *American Psychological Association Experimental Publication System*, 1969, Issue No. 1, Manuscript No. 035B.

Zeitlin, L. R., & Finkelman, J. M. A new method for estimating operator loading under high level noise. *Journal of the Acoustical Society of America*, 1970. (Research letter).

Zimbardo, P. G. *The cognitive control of motivation*. Glenview, Illinois: Scott, Foresman, 1969.

Zorbaugh, H. W. *The gold coast and the slum*. Chicago, Illinois: Univ. of Chicago Press, 1929.

Author Index

Numbers in italics refer to the pages on which the complete references are listed.

A

Amsel, A., 58, *167*
Anastasi, Anne, 15, *167*
Anderson, N. H., 15, *167*
Appley, M. H., 6, 12, 14, *167*
Arees, E., 19, *172*
Arrowood, A. J., 146, *170*
Ashmore, R. D., 131, *167*
Azrin, N. H., 16, 63, 79, *167*

B

Bailey, A., 15, *167*
Bandler, R. J., Jr., 68, *167*
Baron, R. A., 163, *167*
Basowitz, H., 11, *167*
Bem, D. J., 68, *167*
Berlyne, D. E., 20, 146, *167*
Berrien, F. K., 15, *167*
Berry, T., 19, *168*
Bexton, W. H., 13, *167*
Blum, S., 15, 17, *167*
Blumenthal, A., 32, 62, 63, 133, 137, *172*
Boffa, J., 34, 35, 62, 63, *168*
Boggs, D. H., 16, 39, *167*
Boring, E. G., 131, *167*
Brehm, J. W., 64, 68, 102, 123, *167*
Broadbent, D. E., 15, 16, 17, 18, 20, 46, *167*
Buchwald, A. M., 18, 34, *168*
Burns, W., 15, 19, *167*

C

Caplan, N. S., 130, *167*
Champion, R. A., 34, 35, 62, 63, *167*
Chein, I., 131, *169*
Cleaver, E., 142, *168*
Cofer, C. N., 12, *168*

Cohen, A., 19, 160, *168*
Cohen, A. R., 64, 68, *167*
Coles, E. M., 27, *171*
Cook, S. W., 121, *170*
Coombs, C. H., 147, *168*
Corah, N. L., 34, 35, 62, 63, *168*
Corso, J. F., 16, *168*

D

D'Amato, M. E., 30, 45, *168*
Davis, J. A., 76, *168*
Davis, R. C., 18, 19, 34, *168*
Davison, G. C., 34, 63, 79, 80, 81, *169*
Denenberg, V. H., 13, *168*
Dey, F. L., 15, *168*
Doob, A. N., 58, 61, *168*
Driscoll, J. M., 45, *170*
Dubos, R., 10, 11, 12, 159, *168*

E

Ekstrom, R. B., 37, 94, *168*
Eldredge, D. H., 15, *170*
Evan, W. M., 122, *168*

F

Feather, N. T., 48, *168*
Festinger, L., 68, 146, *168, 171*
Finkelman, J. M., 39, *168, 173*
Fiske, D. W., 145, *168*
Fouraker, L. E., 125, *172*
Frankmann, R., 18, 34, *168*
Freeman, J. J., 15, *168*
French, J. W., 37, 94, *168*
Friedman, Lucy N., 46, 64, *169*
Furedy, J. J., 58, 61, *168*

175

G

Gatchel, R. I., 34, 63, 79, 80, 81, *169*
Geer, J. H., 30, 34, 63, 79, 80, 81, 147, 149, *169*
Glass, D. C., 39, 46, 50, 64, 69, *168, 169, 171*
Glorig, A., 15, *169*
Grings, W. W., 141, *172*
Grinker, R. R., 11, 87, *167, 169*
Groves, P. M., 8, *169*
Gumenik, W. E., 30, 45, *168*

H

Haan, Norma, 131, *169*
Haggard, E. A., 32, 34, 35, 62, 63, *169*
Harding, J., 131, *169*
Harris, J. D., 8, *169*
Hatcher, J. F., 15, *171*
Herbert, R., 142, *169*
Heron, W., 13, *167*
Houston, B. K., 83, *169*
Hunt, E. A., 17, *171*
Hyman, R., 146, *171*

I

Irle, M., 17, *169*

J

Jacobs, Jane, 6, 45, *169*
Janis, I. L., 6, 45, 87, 131, 145, *169*
Jansen, G., 17, 18, 19, *169*
Jensen, A. R., 82, 83, *170*
Jerison, H. J., 16, *170*
Jones, T. M., 83, *169*
Jonsson, E., 17, *170*

K

Kajland, A., 17, *170*
Kendall, M. G., 128, *170*
Korchin, S. J., 11, *167*
Korten, F. F., 121, *170*
Kryter, K. D., 15, 16, 17, 18, 19, 25, 27, 43, 46, 155, 160, *170*
Kutner, B., 131, *169*

L

Lacey, J. I., 121, 146, *170*
Lader, M. H., 27, *170*

Lanzetta, J. T., 45, *170*
Latané, B., 146, *170*
Lazarus, R. S., 6, 7, 8, 9, 87, *170*
Lefcourt, H. M., 131, *170*
Le Panto, R., 62, 63, *170*
Lewis, O., 142, *170*
Lindzey, G., 13, *170*
Lippold, O. C. J., 26, *170*
Lovibond, S. H., 30, *170*
Lykken, D. T., 13, 146, *170*

M

McGrath, J. J., 15, *171*
McKennell, A. C., 17, *171*
Mackworth, Jane F., 8, *170*
Madaras, G. R., 68, *167*
Maddi, S. R., 145, *168*
Maier, S. F., 30, 63, 79, 88, *171*
Mandler, G., 87, *170*
Martin, Irene, 7, 12, *170*
Mayhew, Patricia, 65, *171*
Mecklin, J. M., 15, 18, *171*
Merton, R. K., 122, *171*
Milgram, S., 11, 16, *171*
Miller, G. A., 14, *171*
Miller, J. D., 15, *170*
Montagu, J. D., 27, *171*
Moroney, W., 62, 63, *170*
Mowrer, O. H., 62, 63, *171*

O

Orne, M. T., 125, *171*

P

Paccaguella, B., 17, *170*
Paige, J. M., 130, *167*
Parsons, H. M., 14, *171*
Persky, H., 11, *167*
Pervin, L. A., 45, 62, 63, *171*
Pettigrew, T. F., 73, *171*
Plutchik, R., 18, *171*
Price, L. A., 37, 94, *168*
Proshansky, H., 131, *169*

R

Reilley, R., 19, *172*
Reim, B., 50, 69, *169, 171*
Riesen, A. H., 13, *171*

Rodda, M., 15, 18, *171*
Rohrmann, B., 17, *169*
Rohwer, W. D., Jr., 82, 83, *170*
Rosen, S., 18, 19, *171*
Rosenthal, R., 72, 92, *171*
Rosnow, R. L., 72, *171*
Rotter, J. B., 131, *171*

S

Sanders, A. F., 16, 46, *171*
Schachter, S., 146, *171*
Scott, T. H., 13, *167*
Seligman, M. E. P., 30, 63, 79, 87, 88, *171*
Selye, H., 11, *172*
Siegel, S., 125, *172*
Simon, J. R., 16, 39, *167*
Singer, J. E., 46, 50, 64, 69, *169, 171*
Smith, K. R., 16, 46, *172*
Sokolov, E. N., 8, *172*
Solomon, R. L., 30, 63, 79, 88, *171*
Sorensen, S., 17, *170*
Spencer, W. A., 8, 9, *172*
Spiegel, J. P., 87, *169*
Sternbach, R. A., 146, *172*
Stewart, W. H., 18, *172*
Stotland, E., 32, 62, 63, 133, 137, *172*

T

Teichner, W. H., 19, *172*
Thompson, R. F., 8, 9, *169, 172*
Tolman, E. C., 166, *172*
Trumbull, R., 6, 14, *167*

U

Uno, T., 141, *172*

V

Viek, P., 62, 63, *171*

W

Ward, N. D., 15, *170*
Watson, D. L., 87, *170*
Weiss, J. M., 45, *172*
Weitz, J., 20, *172*
Welch, B. L., 14, *172*
Weybrew, B. B., 18, *172*
White, R. W., 88, *172*
Wilkinson, R., 15, *172*
Willerman, B., 146, *171*
Winer, B. J., 51, *172*
Wing, S., 16, *170*
Winston, H. D., 13, *170*
Wohlwill, J. F., 11, 153, *172*
Woodhead, M. M., 16, *172*
Wynne-Edwards, V. C., 12, *173*

Z

Zeitlin, L. R., 39, *173*
Zelditch, M., Jr., 122, *168*
Zenhausern, R., 62, 63, *170*
Zimbardo, P. G., 6, 102, 107, *173*
Zorbaugh, H. W., 122, *173*

Subject Index

A

Adaptation, 165-166, *see also* Coping,
    Habituation
  aftereffects of, 10-12, 139-145,
      152-153, 158
    differential arousal and, 145-147
  to bureaucracy, 136
  definition of, 7-8
  differential, 141-152
  to discrimination, 136-137
  ease of, 142-147
  to electric shock, 112, 114-115
  inhibition of, 141, 147, 152
  to light, 58
  long-term effects of, 159-160
  mechanisms of, 24-25
  to noise, 19, 20, 24, 95, 157
    autonomic reactivity and, 24-25,
        27, 28, 31
    control and, 32-36, 41-44
    performance and, 36-43, 156
    unpredictability and, 31, 39-41
  process of, 8-9
  to urban stressors, 9, 156
Aftereffects, 10-14, 156-158
  of adaptation, 10-12, 158
    differential, 139-147, 149-153
  of bureaucracy, 122-130, 136-137
  of discrimination, 132-137
  expectations and, 98-101
  explanatory mechanisms for, 158-159
  necessity and, 103-107
  noise intensity and, 51-54, 92-98
  perceived avoidance and, 80-86, 89
  perceived control and, 61-69, 89
    indirect, 69-74
    relative deprivation and, 74-78

persistence of, 159
production of, 157
relative deprivation and, 92-98
  perceived control and, 74-78
unpredictability and, *see*
  Unpredictability
Age, noise aftereffects and, 55
Annoyance, 17, 19, 163-164
  factors affecting, 160
  motivation and, 160-161
  necessity and, 101-103
  unpredictability and, 46
Anxiety, perceived control and, 87
Arousal, stress aftereffects and, 145-147,
    152-153, 158
Attitude,
  discrimination and, 134-135
  perceived control and, 67-68
Autonomic reactivity,
  adaptation and, 156
  arousal and, 146-147, 158
  to electric shock, 112, 114-115
  to noise, 18-19, 20
    adaptation of, 24-25, 27, 28, 32,
    intensity and, 27-28
    measurement of, 26-30, 140,
        149-150
    perceived avoidance and, 79-81
    perceived control and, 31-36, 62
Avoidance, perceived, 63, 79-80, *see also*
  Control
  autonomic reactivity and, 79-81
  performance and, 80-86, 89-90,
      110-120

B

Bargaining, 125
  bureaucracy and, 128-129

Behavior, *see also* Performance
    affected by stress, 159
Bias, experimental, 92
Bureaucracy, aftereffects of, 122-130,
    136-137

C

Childhood, stress in, 13
Choice, 133-134, 137
    annoyance and aftereffects of noise and,
        101-107
Cognition(s), 6
    aftereffects and, 166
        of noise, 54, 98-101
    effects of noise and, 20, 24, 156,
        164-165
Cognitive dissonance,
    annoyance and, 102-103
    perceived control and, 68
Competence, perceived control and, 88
Competition, effect of perceived indirect
    control and, 73
Complexity, *see* Task complexity
Compliance, 127-128, 129-130
Control, *see also* Avoidance
    bureaucracy aftereffects and, 130, 136
    discrimination aftereffects and, 136,
        137
    effect of noise and, 24
        on autonomic reactivity, 31-36
    legislative, of noise, 163-165
    noise aftereffects and, 41-44, 61-67,
        156, 164-165
        explanatory mechanisms for,
            67-69, 86-90, 157-158
        indirect control and, 69-74
        relative deprivation and, 74-78
    noise annoyance and, 17
Coping, *see also* Adaptation, Habituation
    effect of expectations on, 98, 101
    factors affecting, 6-7
    relative deprivation and, 97
    strategy of, 6
    as stressor, 10-11, 153

D

Demand-characteristics task, 125
    bureaucracy aftereffects and, 127-128

Deprivation,
    relative,
        in discrimination, 131-137
        noise intensity and, 92-97
        perceived control and, 74-78
    sensory, 13-14
Difficulty, *see* Task complexity
Discrimination, 130-131
    aftereffects of, 132-137
    annoyance and, 160, 161
Dissonance,
    annoyance and, 102-103
    perceived control and, 68

E

Electric shock,
    choice as experimental stressor, 110
    perceived avoidance of, 110-120
    perceived control of, 62, 158
Errors, *see* Performance
Expectation, effect on performance,
    98-101
Experimental bias, 92
Experimenter, attitudes of subjects
    toward, 67-68
Exposure, aftereffects as result of,
    145-147, 152-153

F

Frustration tolerance,
    differential adaptation and, 144-145,
        146
    electric shock and, 118-120
    noise and, 48-49, 51-52, 54, 156
        perceived control and, 65-67, 86
        relative deprivation and, 93
        signaling and, 56, 57, 58

G

GSR, *see* Skin conductance

H

Habituation, 8, *see also* Adaptation,
    Coping
Handling, benefits of, 13
Harassment, *see* Bureaucracy
Hearing loss, 15

Helplessness, 112
  bureaucracy and, 123
  electric shock and, 118, 120
  uncontrollability and, 86-90, 157-158

I

Incentive, perceived control as, 88, 89-90
Informational control, *see* Unpredictability
Information processing,
  arousal and, 153
  noise and, 16-17, 20, 156, 159
  predictability of, 39-41
Interstimulus interval, adaptation and,
  147-152

L

Legislation, to control noise, 163-165
Light, adaptation to, 58

M

Mental disorder, noise and, 17-18
Motivation,
  annoyance and, 160-161
  perceived control as, 89-90
  stress in, 12-13
Muscle action potentials, as measure of
  autonomic reactivity, 26, 30

N

Necessity, of noise, 103-107
  annoyance and, 101-103
Negativism, 127-128, 129-130
Noise, 156-158
  adaptation to, *see* Adaptation
  annoyance by, 17, 19, 46, 101-102,
    163-164
  aperiodic-periodic, *see* Unpredictability,
    Noise, predictability of
  autonomic reactivity to, 18-19, 20,
    24-25, 140, 149-150
    intensity and, 27-28
    measurement of, 26-30
  choice as experimental stressor, 14,
    109-110
  cognitive factors in effects of, 20
  definition of, 15
  intermittent, 16

mental disorders and, 17-18
  necessity and, 101-107
  performance and, *see* Performance
  positive effects of, 15
  predictability of, 16, 20, *see also*
    Unpredictability
  as social problem, 162-165
  unsignaled-signaled, 55-59, *see also*
    Unpredictability
Noise intensity, 51-54
  annoyance and, 160
  expectations for, 98-101
  relative deprivation and, 92-97

O

Orienting response, adaptation of, 8

P

Pain, perceived control and, 61, 62, 68
Performance,
  annoyance and, 16-17, 20, 160-161
  bureaucracy aftereffects on, 125-130,
    136-137
  differential adaptation and, 143-145,
    150-153
    differential arousal and, 145-147
  discrimination aftereffects on, 134-136
  effect of electric shock on, perceived
    avoidance and, 110-120
  effect of expectations on, 98-101
  effect of noise on, 16-17, 20, 24,
    155-158
    adaptation and, 36-43
    perceived control and, 41-44
    predictability and, 39-41, 46
  noise aftereffects on, 46-59
    perceived avoidance and, 80-86,
    89-90
    perceived control and, 61-78
    relative deprivation and, 77-78,
    95-98
Physiological changes, *see* Autonomic
  reactivity
Predictability, *see* Unpredictability
Psychic costs, 3
  of adaptation, 11-12, 139-141, 158,
    see also Adaptation, differential
  long-term, 159-160

R

Race relations, 130-131, *see also*
    Discrimination
Repetition, adaptation and, 8
Responding, instrumental, as perceived
    control, 63, 79-86, 88
Response sensitivity, 8, 9
Response tendencies, aftereffects of noise
    and, 82-83

S

Sensory deprivation, 13-14
Shock, *see* Electric shock
Skin conductance,
    arousal and, 146-147, 158
    as measure of autonomic reactivity,
        to electric shock, 112, 114-115
        to noise, 26-28, 140, 149-150
    perceived control and, 32, 34-36, 62
        avoidance as, 79-81
Startle response, 18, 31
Stimulation, lack of, 13-14
Stress, 5-6
    absence of, 13-14
    adaptation to, *see* Adaptation
    behaviors affected by, 159
    beneficial effects of, 12-14
    coping strategies for, 6-7
    definition of, 14
    induction of, 6
    long-term effects of, 159-160
    perceived control and, 86-88
Stressor(s), *see also* specific stressors
    coping as, 10-11
    equivalence of, 14
    social, 121-122, 158

bureaucracy, 122-130, 136-137
    discrimination, 130-137
    urban, 9, 11
    control of, 162-165
Stroop Color Word Test, 94
    discrimination and, 133, 134, 135
    electric shock and, 112, 116, 118, 120
    expectations and, 99, 101
    perceived avoidance and, 82-83, 85-86
    relative deprivation and, 95-97

T

Task complexity,
    ease of adaptation and, 142-147
    effect of noise on performance and, 16,
        20, 42, 156
Threat,
    in adaptation, 8
    in production of stress, 6
    relative deprivation and, 97

U

Unpredictability, 24, 29-30, 31, 39-41,
    45-59, 156-158, *see also* Noise,
        predictability of
    adaptation and, 30
    perceived avoidance and,
        of noise, 80-86, 89-90,
        of shock, 110-120
    perceived control and, 61-79, 89,
        157-158
    perception of, 151-152

V

Vasoconstriction, as measure of autonomic
    reactivity, 26, 28-30